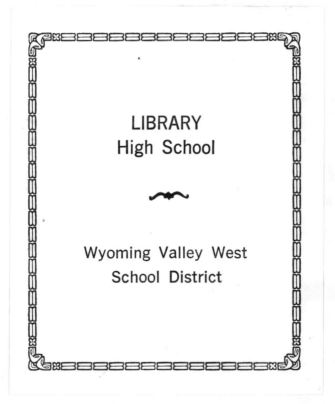

AIDS
in the Mind
of America

AIDS
in the Mind
of America

DENNIS ALTMAN

Anchor Press/Doubleday
GARDEN CITY, NEW YORK
1986

Library of Congress Cataloging-in-Publication Data
Altman, Dennis.
Aids in the mind of America
Includes index.
1. Acquired immune deficiency syndrome—Social
aspects—United States. 2. Acquired immune deficiency
syndrome—United States—Public opinion. 3. Public
opinion—United States. I. Title. [DNLM: 1. Acquired
Immunodeficiency Syndrome—occurrence—United States.
2. Politics—United States. WD 308 A468p]
RC607.A26A37 1986   362.1'969792   85-15055
ISBN: 0-385-19523-0

For Joshua Sippen,
who encouraged this project
from the beginning.

ACKNOWLEDGMENTS

The original suggestion for this book came from my agent, Peter Ginsberg, and Loretta Barrett at Doubleday. Loretta was joined by Paul Aron, and I am grateful to him for his constant support and editorial work. At Pluto Press, London, Paul Crane insisted that I make the book relevant to as international an audience as possible. My British agent, Anthea Morton-Saner, not only represented me but was also helpful in supplying me with British material. Special thanks to those people who read chapter drafts and offered advice—Peter Arno, John Boring, Michael Callen, Sandra Panem and, especially, Joshua Sippen.

I worked on this book in San Francisco, Santa Cruz and New York, and in all three places have particular debts to those who helped with both information and support. Above all I want to thank all the people at the Institute for Health Policy Studies, UCSF, especially Eunice Chee, Dennis Seely and the director, Philip Lee, who provided me with a base for the year during which this book was written. In San Francisco, I am indebted for the help and encouragement of Marcus Conant, Michael Helquist, Mark Ileman, Jeff Mandel, Andrew Moss, Helen Schietinger and Jim Wiley. In Santa Cruz, I owe particular thanks to Scott Brookie and John Kitsuse for their assistance with the word processor. In New York, Richard Berkowitz, Terry Fonville, Mathilde Krim, Pat Maher and Joseph Sonnabend were always helpful.

The various AIDS organizations have been particularly supportive; I owe particular thanks to Virginia Apuzzo and Jeff Levi at the NGTF, to Rodger McFarlane, Diego Lopez and Frederico Gonzalez at GMHC, to Garland Kyle and Judy Spiegel in Los Angeles, to Bill Kipp and Ginette Dreyfus in Miami and to numerous people at Shanti and the San Francisco AIDS Foundation. For help in writing related articles during the year, thanks to Jeff Escoffier of the *Socialist Review* and Richard Goldstein of *The Village Voice*. Thanks too to the gay press for the enormous amounts of information they have provided over the years, especially to *The New York Native*, in particular Larry Mass and James d'Eramo, to Nathan Fain at *The Advocate*, to Adam Carr at *Outrage* (Melbourne), to *Gay Community News* (Boston), to *Le Gai Pied* (Paris) and to Richard Turner for sending me copies of *The Star* (Sydney). And thanks to those conference organizers who invited me to participate, in particular the Institute for the Advancement of Health and Richard Burzynski at the Canadian National Conference on AIDS.

On my travels certain people were particularly generous with time and information: Richard Labonte in Los Angeles, Phil Nash in Denver, Glenn McGahee in Atlanta, Kevin Orr in Toronto, Susan Steinmetz and Tim Westmoreland in Washington. For help in visiting Europe, I am indebted to Erik Albaek (Aarhus), Rob Tielman (Utrecht) and, especially, Julian Meldrum and Simon Watney in England. Through phone conversations and letters I received help from Harold Daire (Dallas), David Ostrow (Chicago), Lex Watson (Sydney) and Michael Wilson (Houston).

CONTENTS

AIDS
in the Mind
of America

CHAPTER ONE

Living Through an Epidemic

The full implications of AIDS only hit me when a friend stopped me on Castro Street, in San Francisco, at the end of April 1984. "Paul just died," he said, speaking of someone I didn't know. "He's the fifth friend I've lost this year."

Michael, my friend, is in his early thirties; his own lover died from AIDS the previous fall. For those of us who have grown up in the Western world over the past half century, the experience of losing friends and lovers in large numbers has been confined to old age and war. With the onset of AIDS, familiar faces—the man in the bookshop, the mailman, casual acquaintances—began to disappear and funerals became an increasingly frequent part of our lives. That large numbers of able-bodied young men should die from disease in peacetime—by early 1985 the toll had reached 4,000, two-thirds of them under forty—despite the best efforts of modern medicine is something for which the only precedent is the epidemics—smallpox, cholera, the "Spanish" flu of 1919—of history.

Of the Vietnam War it was said that only the recognition of American casualties really fired the peace movement and gave it mass support. In the case of AIDS the high concentration of cases among certain groups and localities—namely, gay men, drug users, Haitians and hemophiliacs in a few urban areas—means that a few people have felt a disproportionate amount of personal loss. For most people it has been fear of contagion rather than experience of loss that has made the disease a reality. The ability of the media to create panic, not only in the United States but

virtually throughout the world, means that widespread awareness and fear of AIDS coexists with considerable ignorance of its
real impact.

Panic over AIDS is often based on false information and hysteria, as in the cases of people who avoided restaurants that employed gay waiters or bus drivers who feared AIDS could be
transmitted through paper transfers. From the very early days of
the epidemic it was clear that transmission could not occur
through mere casual contact, even if the routes of transmission
were not entirely clear. For those of us in high-risk groups, however, it is still not possible to escape the fear that we are next, that
something in our past—the incubation period for the disease is
believed to extend upwards to at least five years—puts us at
constant risk. Any gay man writing about AIDS, at a time when it
remains both unpreventable and incurable, will be constantly
brought face to face with questions of his own mortality and
fears.

It is my experience that homophobia adds a further dimension
of difficulty to writing about this topic. Although I have written at
length about the gay movement—my first book, *Homosexual:
Oppression and Liberation,* was published in 1971—I still find
myself almost apologetic when describing this current project,
and largely because it has tapped deep fears and insecurities
about sexual identity. There is little doubt that the social status of
working on the politics of cancer—a topic on which several fine
books exist—is very different from that of work on AIDS.

This book has been the most difficult piece of writing I have
ever undertaken. To deal with pain and suffering is never easy,
and those of us trained in the social sciences too often confront
death only as an interesting statistic. This has not been possible
with AIDS; I know too many people who have died. At the same
time, writing about AIDS has brought me into contact with quite
exceptional people—people with the disease, people involved in
caring for them in hospitals and at home, people dedicated to
developing services for the sick and education for the well. By no
means are all of these gay men; many of those most involved in
AIDS work, as well as some who have experienced considerable
loss, do not belong to groups normally thought of as at risk.

But the experience of writing has had its fascinations as well.

Few other topics have involved people from such a multitude of backgrounds, bringing together medical researchers, gay activists and welfare bureaucrats in a constant round of conferences and meetings. For someone well acculturated into the view of doctors as arcane specialists whose word is to be heeded unquestioningly, it has been a salutary experience to sit in on hospital conferences and argue public health policy with medical experts. For someone as protected from the experience of death as are most middle-class Westerners it is terrifying to know that many of the people I have met and talked with will in all probability be dead before these words are printed.

As the epidemic has unfolded I have seen people behave at both their best and their worst. Worst has been the cynicism of those in the media who have seized upon AIDS as the latest sensation and contrived to blame the victim in a way unknown for other diseases, egged on by numerous spokespersons claiming to stand for Christian morality. Best have been the very many people who have accepted the enormous stress and anxiety involved in providing care and services for the sick and, in the United States above all, have worked to fill in the enormous gaps left by the existing health care and welfare systems. The latter have understood that AIDS is as horrible and lethal a disease as any yet known, and should be dealt with as a disease. The former are too preoccupied with their agendas of moral control and hatred to see this reality.

It has taken me a long time to come to terms with AIDS on both a personal and a social level, and I feel an obligation to explain my own experiences before attempting to analyze the broader social and political picture. I left Australia to live in the United States in the fall of 1981, just at the time when awareness of AIDS was beginning to percolate through society. (The Centers for Disease Control had established their Task Force on AIDS that summer.) I must have known about AIDS—I am, after all, a diligent reader of the gay press, which for a long time was the only place where articles from the *New England Journal of Medicine* and *The Lancet* were interpreted for lay comprehension—but for a long time I thought of it only in very personal terms: was I at risk? I remember a lunch in the winter of 1982 with Larry Mass, the first doctor to write regularly in the gay press about AIDS, at which I asked him—very tentatively, not to appear too much the hypochondriac I am accused of being— about my own risks. In May of that year I went to a doctor after a chiropractor had thought he detected swollen lymph glands, the first of several (as yet) false alarms.

I lived in New York from October 1981 through January 1983. During this time, pushed and prodded by a few people, of whom author Larry Kramer was the most vocal, I became more and more conscious of AIDS. In April I went to the first major Gay Men's Health Crisis fund-raiser, a party at the Paradise Garage disco, but I was preoccupied with romance and my forthcoming book. During the summer I toured to promote that book *(The Homosexualization of America)* and I remember no question, whether on television/radio or in private, relating to AIDS.

In terms of popular awareness the turning point was not to occur until the spring of 1983, when stories about AIDS began to appear with great frequency following scares about possible transmission through blood transfusions and even "close contact." AIDS was now a cover story in both *Time* and *Newsweek*, yet in the course on lesbian/gay politics which I co-taught in the spring of 1983 at the University of California in Santa Cruz, I ignored it, despite some gentle prodding from my colleague David Thomas. This was to change in a major way in the summer when my agent suggested I should write about AIDS, but it would have changed anyway.

Many of the people who have become actively involved with the AIDS issue explain their commitment in very personal terms: their friends, their lovers, often they themselves are dying. As Cindy Patton wrote in *Gay Community News:*

> The final assault on my consciousness came in the form of a late night call from a friend in North Carolina. In May 1983 I learned that my best friend from high school had just died of AIDS. . . . I felt his death as a personal loss, and as an attack on the very fabric of the community we had both in our own ways struggled to build. Things came together quickly, though I felt very guilty for not having developed a perfect analysis of AIDS when I first read that clipping two and a half long years ago.[1]

By early 1983 few gay men in large American cities had not lost someone to AIDS, and some people, such as Larry Kramer, had seen their social networks decimated:

> I am angry and frustrated almost beyond the bounds my skin and bones and body and brain can encompass. My sleep is tormented by nightmares and visions of lost friends and my days are flooded by the tears of funerals and memorial services and seeing my sick friends. How many of us must die before all of we living fight back?[2]

In the Pines, an almost exclusively homosexual resort on New York's Fire Island, people pointed to a legendary house, almost all of whose occupants from the previous summer were dead. By mid-1984 testimony of bereaved friends and lovers was being heard not just in New York, San Francisco, Los Angeles and Miami but also in smaller cities and other countries; when I went back to Australia for a while over the (northern) winter of 1983–84, at least one acquaintance was reported to be in the hospital with AIDS-like symptoms; he died the following June.

By the spring of 1984 I was back in the States working on this book. Over the course of the following year I moved between California and New York, with side trips to Europe and several other North American cities, engrossed in the developing world of AIDS research and politics. For a while I prided myself on my ability to remain detached from the subject, modeling myself on doctors and nurses who, to be effective, must learn an apparent callousness. This pose was shattered in the fall when my lover's sister, then thirty-six, suddenly fell ill and died six weeks later of non-Hodgkin's lymphoma. As we waited in the hospital, hostages to the ever-growing machinery of modern medicine, it was hard not to think that both Joshua and I had a much greater statistical probability of joining her than we would have imagined a few years earlier. The similarity of her illness to AIDS—its sudden onset, its severity, the apparent inability of the doctors to save her—was an enormous shock in the context of struggling to finish this book.

How does one capture what an epidemic like AIDS really means in terms of human experience and suffering? I have learned a great deal from the testimony of those who are ill and dying, from the bereaved, from those who have lost too many to know how to grieve anymore. One learns, too, from the response of others, both the horror stories of abandonment by lovers, family and friends and the outpourings of love and support that others who have AIDS have experienced. I count myself privileged to have taken part in one such event, an evening entitled "a grove of connectedness" that was organized in San Francisco in the fall of 1984 to raise money for one person with AIDS and his family.

In articles, in speeches, in evidence presented at legislative hearings, people with AIDS try to capture the reality of an experience for which nothing had prepared them:

> At the age of 28 I wake up every morning to face the very real possibility of my own death.
>
> Whenever I am asked by members of the media or by curious healthy people what we talk about in our group I am struck by the intractable gulf that exists between the sick and the well: what we talk about is survival.
>
> Mostly we talk about what it feels like to be treated like lepers who are treated as if they are morally, if not literally contagious. We try to share what hope there is and to help each other live our lives one day at a time. What we talk about is survival.[3]

One month before his death Mark Feldman addressed a Candlelight March in San Francisco, and concluded with the words:

> On November 1, 1982, I was just a person, a human being. On November 23, my medical diagnosis and so much of the world labelled me a "victim"; then it proceeded to call me "a patient with AIDS." Well, as many of you know I'm in the process of defining myself. I am a person with AIDS, a human being, not a victim, and only a patient when I am in a hospital. If anyone ever doubts that I have one more thing to say: As far as AIDS goes, "Phooey, phooey, phooey on AIDS!"
>
> L'Chayim. To life.[4]

Within the gay world AIDS is becoming omnipresent; gay men stand in bars talking earnestly about T-cell counts and retroviruses; on the ferry between Fire Island and the Long Island shore I overhear a man, ten years younger than me though he looks older, describing the chemotherapy that made his hair drop out; in Honolulu, where I stopped on my return to the States in the spring of 1984, a man in an outdoor bar tells me he has left San Francisco because he cannot live any longer surrounded by dying friends. I go to dinner in Denver and soon we are talking about the number of cases in Colorado; I attend a gay/lesbian health conference in Atlanta and am taken around the city by someone who wears a pocket buzzer so he can be contacted immediately by anyone who calls the AIDS hot line. (Just before we go out he is called by a married man with some homosexual experience, living in a small Georgia town, whose doctor has told him, with no further examination, that his swollen glands "probably" indicate AIDS.)

While media attention has focused on changes in gay sexual behavior—never before has it been discussed and analyzed in such detail—the changes go far deeper, for they involve questions of both identity and ideology. To fundamentally alter sexual behavior is considerably more far-reaching than giving up smoking or even drinking, at least for most people. For many of us a certain sexual style was inextricably intertwined with being gay: "For gay men, sex, that most powerful implement of attachment and arousal, is also an agent of communion, replacing an often hostile family and even shaping politics. It represents an ecstatic break with years of glances and guises, the furtive past we left behind."[5]

Groups other than gay men have been affected by the disease; indeed, during the writing of this book there was increasing evidence of the spread of AIDS to other populations. It has been far more difficult for me to fully empathize with the experience of, say, drug users and Haitians, and this book reflects my own position in the world as a white, middle-class gay man. In particular I have felt difficulties in coming to terms with the experience of drug users, probably the least articulate and understood of the affected groups. This does not mean, however, that I see AIDS as only a gay issue, either on a personal or on a political level. In many situations the gay/straight divide becomes absolutely irrelevant; no one stops to ask in the AIDS ward of San Francisco General Hospital which staff are gay and which not.

I have never believed in "objective" analysis of politics. What we choose to write about, whom we choose to talk with, which sources we rely upon, are all reflections of underlying values and biases. In the course of writing this book I have experienced terror and grief and anger, and they will all be reflected in these pages. I have attended meetings and conferences as more than an observer, and I have taken positions on matters of controversy, some of which I shall discuss. To do otherwise I would regard as unconscionable on an issue where public policy may literally decide who lives and who dies.

Developments come fast in the world of AIDS research and politics. As I write this (in mid-1985) there are unresolved questions about the implications of widespread blood testing for the AIDS-related virus and new fears of AIDS spreading into the population at large. The cover of *Life* in July 1985 proclaimed, in large red letters: "Now No One Is Safe From AIDS." (The managing editor, in an introduction that made it clear she holds a limited view of who reads *Life,* wrote: "For a long time it seemed possible to exclude ourselves and our families from the threat, but now it is clear that as the numbers of victims grow, the problems of AIDS in American society will affect everyone."[6]) By the end of the year quite different issues may be dominant. To write about AIDS during the epidemic is enormously difficult; only the perspective of history will allow us to say conclusively what is and what is not important in the events we are now living through. But unless the disease spreads in unpredictable ways or quite unexpected advances are made in medical treatment and prevention, the experiences of the early eighties are likely to remain relevant to any ongoing discussion of the epidemic.

The one thing that seems certain about AIDS—I would be delighted if I were proven wrong—is that it will continue. In January 1985, Dr. Merle Sande, chief of the University of California's AIDS research task force, summed up the position: "We are clearly in the midst of a major medical catastrophe, the potential impact of which is now only beginning to be realized and the eventual magnitude of which could be absolutely enormous."[7] Against this somber warning AIDS can be seen as a major social and cultural event. Both the ways in which the state, the media, the medical profession and the affected communities respond, and the irrational fears and prejudices aroused by the disease, bring into question how far we have progressed since the great plagues of pre-modernity.

CHAPTER TWO

A Very Political Epidemic

The real plague is panic.
—*Guardian* editorial, February 19, 1985

We are not used to thinking of illness as political. Even when we recognize the political dimension to health care and research—for example, the fact that prevention of lead poisoning or curing sickle-cell anemia is less glamorous and less well financed than heart transplants—it is still difficult to conceive of disease itself as a political construct. As Lesley Doyal has pointed out, we see the determinants of health and illness as predominantly biological, and assume that medicine is a science, capable of producing "an unchallengeable and autonomous body of knowledge which is not tainted by wider social and economic considerations."[1]

We are most likely to think of disease as purely individual, something that hits us at random rather as does falling in love (also a phenomenon with considerable political overtones, as numerous feminists have argued). But we also know how much of health is due to social and political factors: malnutrition, bad water supplies, pollution, radiation, are all major causes of illness. Most of us fluctuate, in fact, between *three* models of disease, seeing it as the consequence of microorganisms that strike haphazardly, as the result of personal behavior—not enough exercise, smoking, the wrong diet, too much alcohol, drugs or stress, even the wrong character structure (type A versus type B personality in the terminology of heart disease)—or as a consequence of larger socioeconomic factors. In the popular mind cancer is attributed to all three; it is seen as hitting at random, as a direct result of "lifestyle" and "personality factors," and as the product of the wastes of industrial society.

Perhaps the clearest insight into the confusion between a public and a private analysis of disease comes in Samuel Butler's nineteenth-century novel *Erewhon*, in which in a mythical land criminality is regarded as bad luck and illness as something for which punishment is appropriate:

> In that country if a man falls into ill health or catches any disorder or fails bodily in any way before he is seventy years old, he is tried before a jury of his countrymen and if convicted is held up to public scorn and sentenced more or less severely as the case may be. But if a man forges a check, or sets his house on fire, or robs with violence from the person, or does any such things as are criminal in our own country, he is either taken to a hospital and most carefully tended at the public expense, or if he is in good circumstances he lets it be known to all his friends that he is suffering from a severe fit of immorality, just as we do when we are ill, and they come and visit him with great solicitude—for bad conduct, though considered no less deplorable than illness with ourselves, and as unquestionably indicating something seriously wrong with the individual who misbehaves, is nevertheless held to be the result of either pre-natal or post-natal misfortune.[2]

Butler is being satirical, but even today the line between illness and criminality is not as clear-cut as we might think. As Irving Zola has argued: "It is not clear that the issues of morality and individual responsibility have been fully banished from the etiological scene itself. The issue of 'personal responsibility' seems to be re-emerging within medicine itself."[3] Certainly the response to AIDS often seems closer to that described by Butler than to contemporary assumptions about disease.

But it is not only individual transgressions that are seen as leading to illness; there is a powerful tradition of seeing epidemics as the result of social collapse and degeneracy. It was widely believed that the Black Death was a sign of God's displeasure at the flouting of his commands, and in nineteenth-century America cholera was seen as a consequence of widespread sin. Both the Moral Majority, who are recycling medieval language to explain AIDS, and those ultra-leftists who attribute AIDS to some sort of conspiracy, have a clearly political analysis of the epidemic. But even if one attributes its cause to a microorganism rather than the wrath of God or the workings of the CIA, it is clear that the way in which AIDS has been perceived, conceptualized, imagined, researched and financed makes this the most political of diseases.

A number of circumstances set AIDS apart from other epidemics and help explain why it has been so politicized. The first is that it has occurred at a time when modern medicine was believed to be well on the way to abolishing epidemic diseases altogether, at least in the Western world. AIDS emerged at a time when there was a sufficiently sophisticated knowledge of the immune system to make it possible to conceptualize it—and to track down its agent. (Had large numbers of young men started dying in the 1950s of Kaposi's sarcoma, pneumocystis pneumonia and toxoplasmosis, it is unlikely that the connections between them could have been established nearly so quickly. It is, of course, conceivable that AIDS has been around longer than we know—there has been some speculation about its role in cases of Kaposi's sarcoma among young African men over the past several decades—but there is little doubt that its presence in the rest of the world is new.) The dysfunctions of the T-cell systems which open the body up to the ravages of opportunistic diseases, believed to be the basic nature of AIDS, could only be analyzed once immunologists had developed a theory of the cellular basis of the immune system, first proposed by Macfarlane Burnet in 1959.[4] The discovery of retroviruses able to infect human cells came only at the end of the 1970s, almost at the exact same time as the first cases of AIDS were being reported.

William McNeil, a pioneer in integrating disease into our understanding of history, wrote (ironically ignoring the AIDS stories which then filled the newspapers):

> One of the things that separates us from our ancestors and makes contemporary experience profoundly different from that of other ages is the disappearance of epidemic disease as a serious factor in human life. Nowadays if a few score of people die of an infection, officials declare an epidemic, the newspapers are full of it, and medical resources are quickly marshalled to find the course and check the further progress of the disease.[5]

The belief that modern medicine can control and cure any disease that comes along means that there is immediate pressure on governments to act once an outbreak of disease occurs. The onset of AIDS unleashed disputes over the mobilization of resources to research, monitor and care for the disease and its victims, as well as over scientific theories.

The second factor which explains the politicization of AIDS is that AIDS, at least in North America and most of the rest of the developed world, has been very specific in the groups it has affected, above all male homosexuals. Much of this book is concerned with working through the very real social and political consequences of a disease whose major targets are groups—intravenous drug users and Haitians, in addition to gay men—who already occupy stigmatized positions within society. Unlike other major epidemics, of which polio is the most recent (for both Legionnaires' disease and toxic shock syndrome, while seemingly debuting in the same dramatic manner as did AIDS, proved fairly rapidly susceptible to medical control), AIDS is not seen as threatening the entire population. Since the media began discussing the illness in late 1981 the public at large has fluctuated between short-lived panic about its spreading (in particular through blood transfusions) and regarding it as a curse of "the other," something that strikes only those groups already singled out for misfortune. (This attitude has begun to change, with growing evidence of heterosexual transmission.)

The epidemiology and the social response to AIDS are both bound up with major changes in the way in which homosexuality is socially constructed in the Western world, above all in the United States. We can think of these changes as amounting to the transition from a psychological truth to a sociological untruth, by which I mean the shift from seeing homosexuality as a form of behavior, a universal possibility within human sexuality, to a specific identity which sees homosexuals as forming a community similar to an ethnic group. Through the 1970s the gay movement had insisted with some success on the recognition of gay community; the *Newsweek* cover story of August 1983 stated that "gays and lesbians are routinely estimated to be a 1-in-10 minority in America."

This shift, which saw homosexuals emerge as a recognized

social, cultural and political minority during the 1970s, had several immediate consequences for the development of the epidemic. It meant there existed a basis for the sort of organized response that has allowed AIDS political and welfare organizations to come into being. The CDC Task Force on AIDS has been careful to maintain constant consultation with gay groups; that they saw this as necessary—and that the channels for such consultation existed—is a product of these changes. In other Western countries, particularly in the Netherlands, Scandinavia, Canada and Australasia, the gay movement was recognized officially in government dealings with AIDS. This was clearly impossible in states which deny the legitimacy of a gay identity, the situation in almost all authoritarian states, whether of the left (e.g., Cuba) or the right (e.g., Haiti).

As the spread of AIDS became linked in the public imagination to the very presence of homosexuals—including lesbians—the gay visibility and affirmation of the past decade allowed for some very nasty scapegoating. AIDS came along just when the old religious, moral and cultural arguments against homosexuality seemed to be collapsing. The 1970s saw a whole series of shifts in the dominant ideology concerning sexuality, making the status of homosexuality increasingly problematic; for a time the state of Wisconsin, like the Australian state of New South Wales, included homosexuals under the protection of its anti-discrimination laws, while retaining criminal sanctions against sodomy, which seemed to capture perfectly this ambivalence. Under siege from the rapid changes which were turning homosexuality into a "lifestyle" rather than a "deviance," right-wing moralists sought to shore up traditional condemnations of homosexuality; AIDS provided a godsend to them (quite literally, in the eyes of the religious right). In the words of an editorial in the *Southern Medical Journal:* "Might we be witnessing, in fact, in the form of a modern communicable disorder, a fulfillment of St. Paul's pronouncement: 'the due penalty of their error'?"[6]

In epidemiological terms the rapid spread of AIDS was certainly due in part to the increased opportunities for homosexual encounters existing in the large cities of North America, Europe, Australasia and parts of Latin America. It is important to recognize that during the 1970s opportunities for casual sex expanded greatly for everyone in the Western world; while Gay Talese rhapsodized about the new freedoms of massage parlors and encounter groups[7] (ignoring the economic realities that forced women into new forms of prostitution), gay men found similar freedom in the burgeoning bathhouses and back-room bars of the large cities.

We don't know, in real quantitative terms, what really changed in homosexual behavior in the 1970s, but it is possible to identify three major areas of change: the expansion of homosexual bathhouses and sex clubs, which facilitate numerous sexual contacts in one night (by 1984 one bathhouse chain included baths in forty-two North American cities, including Memphis and London, Ontario), the emergence of sexually transmitted parasites as a major homosexual health problem, especially in New York and California,[8] and a boom in "recreational drugs"—that is, the use of chemical stimulants such as MDA, angel dust, various nitrites, etc.—in conjunction with what came to be known as "fast-lane sex." These three elements would all be linked to various theories about AIDS during the 1980s.

The fact that AIDS was firmly linked with sex—although this is not the only way it can be transmitted—is the third factor in explaining the politicization of the disease. Susan Sontag, in her influential book *Illness as Metaphor*, pointed to the ways in which diseases such as tuberculosis and cancer take on a whole set of non-medical overtones and become markers of personality and character flaws, rather than problems of medicine. What Sontag calls "diseases of passion" share certain characteristics: they are ambiguous in origin, they are sufficiently lingering to seem an expression of the victim's personality, and they are not highly infectious, seeming to single out individuals for judgment and guilt.[9] But except for syphilis before the discovery of antibiotics, no life-threatening illness has had the potential of AIDS to be linked so clearly to sexuality and personal behavior. The comment of historian Allan Brandt on venereal disease is equally true of AIDS: ". . . it is seen as a revenge against the sexual revolution and the modern medical technology that helped to make it possible."[10]

Fourth, while AIDS seemed at first to be a disease primarily confined to male homosexuals, so, too, it seemed largely an

American disease, and even the increasing likelihood that its origins lay in central Africa did little to shake this image of it as somehow linked to modern America. In its first several years it seemed largely confined to large American cities with particularly prominent gay populations—New York, San Francisco, Los Angeles—or otherwise particular populations, such as Miami and Newark (Haitians and drug users). By 1983, however, figures started mounting in other cities, indeed other countries; in Europe cases were climbing into the hundreds in France and West Germany by late 1984, and there were estimates that suggested it was only a matter of time before the case load would be similar to that in the United States. At the international AIDS conference sponsored jointly by the CDC and the World Health Organization in April 1985 in Atlanta, researchers were present from thirty countries on all continents; even the Soviet Union acknowledged several AIDS cases. There were reports of substantial numbers in some South American countries, especially Brazil, although considerable underreporting seemed probable.[11] Only some parts of Asia seem so far to have escaped the disease, and evidence is mounting that by far the worst incidence is to be found in central Africa, where thousands of people appear to be affected. The problems of accurate diagnosis and reporting mean we may never know the full extent of the epidemic outside the Western world.

Despite this evidence, the perception of AIDS as an American import—"the curse which came from America," headlined the Parisian journal *Nouvel Observateur*[12]—has persisted. Just as modern homosexuality seemed to be an import from the United States—in Paris gay bars adopted names like Le Manhattan, Le Bronx, Le Village; in Manila, Melbourne and Munich gay discos played American music and men (and to a lesser extent women) aped American fashions—so, too, AIDS seemed to have spread from the new gay meccas of New York and San Francisco. Epidemiologists speculated about the role of air stewards as carriers of the disease, and there was considerable discussion of the travel patterns of gay men. In Britain there was a strong tendency to blame AIDS on "homosexuals who have been on 'sex holidays' to America,"[13] and a popular belief among gay men persisted for some time that one ran no risk if one confined one's sexual partners to those who had never been to North America. An American visitor to South Africa in 1985 reported being told by a health official there: ". . . what else could you expect from the United States except AIDS."[14]

It is true that the first diagnosed cases of AIDS in Western Europe and Australasia were either among gay men who had spent time in the United States or among people—not necessarily gay—who had had contact with Africa or, in several cases, Haiti, and in some countries it took several years before indigenous cases appeared. Equally, with the exception of France and Belgium where local researchers experienced some tension with their American counterparts, the United States was looked to as providing the necessary information and treatment, and the Centers for Disease Control in Atlanta sent experts across the world to brief physicians and health authorities. We needn't spend a great deal on AIDS research, one Australian official told me, we know everything the Americans are doing. But the central factor in promoting the American image of AIDS and creating a major hysteria around the disease in a number of countries was the media.

AIDS and the Media

How AIDS was perceived and reported was also due more to political than to medical factors. In its early days the media tended to shy away from AIDS, seeing it as a gay story they shouldn't touch. (As Robert Bazell said at a forum organized by the Scientists Institute for Public Information: "It would be dishonest not to say we couldn't sell the AIDS story early on because it was about gays."[15]) Once the illness appeared among infants and those who had received blood transfusions, this attitude changed dramatically, and from early 1983 on, AIDS has been a continuing preoccupation of the media, not only in the United States but in most of the non-Communist world as well, a rather striking example of the way in which the American media defines what is news for the rest of the world.

The early reports on AIDS tended to set the tone for future journalism, in particular the categorization of AIDS as intrinsically "gay," which was all the more newsworthy when it affected anyone else. Press headlines from the early days tell the story: "Gay Plague Baffling Medical Detectives" (Philadelphia *Daily News*, August 9, 1982), "Being Gay Is a Health Hazard" *(The Saturday Evening Post*, October 1982), "Gay Plague Has Arrived in Canada" (Toronto *Star*, November 26, 1982). The popular magazine *Us* managed to combine panic and morality by proclaiming: "Male homosexuals aren't so gay anymore," and relating the story of a dying young man who told his nurse that "if I pull through I promise I'll find a girlfriend."[16]

The homosexual character of the disease was firmly established by the media, and the discovery of other affected groups did little to change this perception. Almost a third of those with AIDS in New York are not homosexual, yet when *New York* magazine ran a cover story about AIDS in mid-1983, non-gays were only acknowledged in passing.[17] Although the first *Newsweek* cover story in April 1983 did devote some space to non-gay AIDS patients and included some of the few photographs of people with AIDS who were not white, male and homosexual, when it returned to the story four months later it was in terms of "gay America," with a cover picture of two homosexuals and virtually no mention of anyone else.[18]

The real spark for the media blitz in the spring and summer of 1983 was probably reports of AIDS in young children and, in particular, the suggestion, albeit tentative, by both Dr. James Oleske of the New Jersey School of Medicine and Dr. Anthony Fauci of the National Institutes of Health, that AIDS might be communicable through "routine close contact."[19] In April, *Newsweek* had already proclaimed on its cover: "The mysterious and deadly disease called AIDS may be the public health threat of the century. How did it start? Can it be stopped?" In July, *Time* made AIDS its cover story: "Disease Detectives Tracking the Killers. The AIDS Hysteria."[20]

Through much of the year AIDS was to be the major health story, not only in the United States but in countries as far away as Finland and Australia. In Finland, where there is a strong tradition of homophobia, it was reported:

By the time the first Finnish case of AIDS was announced in June 1983, already more than 50 scare articles had appeared in the press. Following the first case a wave of fear and panic swept the country in what people interviewed by me described as a "nightmare." The afternoon press created a national alarm by presenting the disease in extremely sensational and biased coverage, false information, or were simply irrational; some were intentionally (as my interviews with the editors and journalists revealed) designed to create panic and hatred against gay men by screaming headlines and fear-provoking pictures of dying people whose eyes had been damaged by cancer . . .[21]

In Australia a similar press panic was partly stemmed for the time being by the creation of a National Advisory Committee headed by the country's best-known woman journalist.

It would take a full-length study to do justice to the way in which the media dealt with AIDS. In the United States coverage ranged from newspapers which ran large and thoughtful special series on AIDS, such as the Philadelphia *Inquirer* (January 2–8, 1983) and the Charlotte *Observer* (June 5–8, 1983) to the sort of prejudice found in an editorial in the Wheeling *News Register* headlined "AIDS, Homos Stir Ugly Scene" (August 19, 1983). A further *Newsweek* cover story on August 8 ("Gay America: Sex, Politics, and the Impact of AIDS") included a poll which showed that 91 percent of the population had heard of AIDS, up 14 percent from June, and in its end-of-the-year roundup *Newsweek* listed AIDS as the year's most significant story in science and medicine. Television had been covering AIDS since late 1982 (the first national discussion came on the MacNeil-Lehrer report on August 26, and AIDS was featured on the Phil Donahue show of November 19), but in mid-1983 the coverage increased dramatically, with high-rating shows like ABC's *20/20*, on which the death of AIDS patient Kenneth Ramsauer was directly covered.[22] At the end of the year the series *St. Elsewhere* ran a story revolving around a young politician afflicted with AIDS, and several documentaries on AIDS went into production.

It is impossible to make any generalized judgments about the way in which the media has covered AIDS; it is my impression that the most extensive coverage has come in the San Francisco *Chronicle;*[23] that other papers with good coverage have included the Philadelphia *Inquirer* and the Los Angeles *Herald;* that it has been largely neglected in the "journals of opinion" such as *The Nation* or *The Public Interest;* and that the New York print media, which has a major impact on the rest of the country, has been uniformly disappointing in coming to terms with the epidemic. The gay movement was particularly bitter about the New York *Times,* which despite its status as a newspaper of record was seen as very slow to report on non-medical aspects of AIDS. (One estimate claimed that in the first eighteen months of the epidemic the *Times* ran only seven articles on AIDS, compared with fifty-four articles during the three-month scare about poisoned Tylenol in 1982, with its far lower death toll.[24]) The New York *Post*'s coverage was both sensational and superficial, and even *The Village Voice,* despite several openly gay writers, tended to favor sensationalism over careful reporting or analysis. A report for the Twentieth Century Fund spoke of the American press coverage as marked by "sensationalism" and "exaggeration,"[25] and the examples given are less horrendous than those one could quote from the popular press in Britain, Australia and West Germany. (At the end of 1984 the London *Sun* was still referring to "the gay plague," despite the fact that the National Union of Journalists Equality Council had publicly disavowed this term, and the *News of the World* referred to "the gay killer bug."[26]) One of the few transnational generalizations that could be made was that some of the most sensational and least responsible reporting came in papers belonging to the Murdoch chain, whether in London (the *Sun,* the *News of the World*), New York (the *Post)* or Sydney (the *Mirror).*

The central point is that from mid-1983 on AIDS had entered the popular consciousness and was widely discussed. Nor did press attention go away; at different times over the past several years AIDS has dominated headlines and the electronic media across the world. This is hardly surprising. Medical stories are particularly attractive to the media, and where they can be linked to both high fatalities and stigmatized sexuality we have all the ingredients for banner headlines.

On a purely medical level AIDS is very exciting; the more scientifically oriented stories about the disease tend to emphasize its implications for immunology, virology and oncology, three of the "hottest" areas of modern medicine. Moreover, AIDS was a crisis with deadly consequences; the increase in cases was very rapid, and the spread across the country—and around the world—even more so. While doctors could sometimes do something for the various opportunistic diseases—in general, Kaposi's sarcoma is less immediately life-threatening than pneumocystis pneumonia—the long-run prognosis for those with the disease has remained extremely poor (and "long run" means two to three years for patients whose average age is between thirty and forty).

In addition to its interesting medical aspects, AIDS was used by the media to appeal to both voyeurism and fear. While AIDS could be portrayed as a disease of gay men and other disreputable groups, it allowed for reportage of "lifestyles" that was both titillating and smug. When AIDS was seen as moving beyond these groups—whether due to blood transfusions (or plasmapheresis), intimate contacts or heterosexual intercourse—it signaled considerable panic (thus the banner headlines around the world when a drug-free white heterosexual grandmother on Long Island came down with AIDS—"Gay Bug Kills Gran," screamed the London *Sun*, apparently not realizing that the death threw into doubt its characterization of the disease). Even the San Francisco *Chronicle* could not escape such judgments, claiming that the death of a woman from AIDS in the fall of 1984 following a blood transfusion was "the worst nightmare of the AIDS crisis."[27] A good example of how easily panic could be aroused came in early 1985 when AIDS hot lines were flooded with calls after the San Jose *Mercury-News* carried a front-page headline proclaiming: "AIDS Victim's Housemates at Risk, Study Says." The study was of a small number of cases in Zaire which suggested on the basis of not very conclusive evidence that there could be household transmission in certain cases. (More probable means of transmission through sexual contacts and shared needles were not properly investigated.) The use of one small and not very well supported study to make a banner headline was a case study of the way in which the media can distort scientific news and create considerable anxiety.[28]

As media attention made discussion of AIDS commonplace, AIDS jokes surfaced in all sorts of places—the comedian Eddie

Murphy was boycotted by some gays as a result of remarks he claimed were meant humorously—graffiti referring to AIDS cropped up across the country and AIDS references began penetrating popular culture. (Was it just an accident that in the film *Dune* the homosexual villain had suppurating sores on his face?) As awareness of the epidemic spread, the groups most affected by AIDS, above all male homosexuals, found their lives fundamentally affected.

Coming to Terms with AIDS

Even though AIDS is in no intrinsic sense "a gay disease," the fact that, at least in the Western world, it has been primarily experienced by male homosexuals has shaped the entire discourse surrounding the disease. Partly because the other groups at risk are often too invisible to merit the attention of calumny, AIDS becomes seen as a "gay" rather than a "health" issue, thus reinforcing the perception of the disease as highly political: the more a disease is experienced collectively, particularly by an already stigmatized group, the clearer will be its political dimensions. Too often AIDS leaves the medical pages only when it can be invoked to underline the "otherness" of gays or other affected groups. (An early paper of mine on the epidemic was rejected by an allegedly progressive journal on the grounds that it was "something that could be read in the gay press," thus ignoring the fact that I had submitted it to them precisely to reach a nongay audience.)

Even among gay men, however, it took a long time for a real awareness of the full implications of AIDS to develop. Nothing in our past had prepared us for a major epidemic which would strike down thousands of young men and open us up to both personal and political attacks. AIDS has personal, communal and social dimensions; it involves us on every level of our lives and threatens to isolate us from the broader society and turn us into the twentieth-century equivalent of moral lepers. As one gay journalist wrote at the end of 1984, when AIDS stories dominated the front pages and television screens of Australia: "The AIDS epidemic is not going to go away. It is going to get worse.

We know what it is, we know how we are spreading it. We are doing nothing about it. Unless we do something to take control of our situation, and do it soon, we are going to find ourselves, personally and collectively, in the deepest crisis of our lives."[29]

Resistance to such analyses was the dominant reaction of most gay men when they first heard about AIDS. (The Health Crisis Network in Miami experimented with a poster proclaiming in bold letters: AIDS IS AN EPIDEMIC. When I asked the point—this was in January 1985—I was told it was because denial remained so high.) My own inability to grasp the significance of the epidemic was matched by a larger denial among many of us of what was happening. As one man told a gay journalist: "Until you made me think about it, I realized I didn't want to think about that fucking disease. It's killed a friend, and it's hurt other friends. Sure, I've changed things in my life because of that, but I don't read stories in the papers about AIDS and I don't go to give money at fund-raisers. I'm bored by it because there's nothing I can do about it. If you tell me there's a cure, that would matter—but until then I guess I don't want to hear about the whole thing."[30] Perhaps the disease was too horrifying for us to fully comprehend it; psychologists talked of a grief overload.

Grief, at least, is an emotion of some nobility; we exhibit photographs of people mourning as a way of empathizing with and honoring them. Grief, too, can strengthen bonds. As the poet Aaron Shurin wrote: "The more developed your sense of community, of a gay community, the deeper this terror is going to be for you because you experience it not just on a personal level, but on a community level. 'My sweet brothers'—this is something I started to feel—'my brothers who have been my tender ones for so many years, are falling down.' "[31] But grief was matched by fear and anxiety, as those who are at risk experience every ache or blemish as the onset of fatal symptoms, just as in the summers of the 1950s a sudden headache or stomach pain was feared as a warning of polio.[32] The most characteristic gay activity of the eighties, quipped one man, is examining one's skin for signs of Kaposi's.

As grief, fear and anger spread they began to be reflected in the writings of both those affected and those sensitive to the onset of the epidemic. The first mention I know of in literary works came in 1981, in a rather trashy novel, *Another Runner in the Night,* in which Robert Granit referred to reports of "a sexually transmitted cancer." This was followed by several non-gay works; in a little-known novel by Dorothy Bryant, called *A Day in San Francisco,* and in Robin Cook's *Godplayer,* both published in 1983, there is mention of AIDS, in both cases with some suggestion that the sick had brought it upon themselves. (In Bryant's novel a mother visiting her son, who is sick with hepatitis, deplores gay "excesses" in language that would become increasingly familiar.) Later that year Andrew Holleran, whose novel *Dancer from the Dance* is perhaps the best fictional account of "fast-lane" gay life during the seventies, wrote in *Nights of Aruba:* "Not only was erotomania something which had finally loosened its grip on me, but everyone was suspect now. Celebrities of our sexual demimonde were dying of bizarre cancers and an epidemic of intestinal parasites had subverted the pleasures of promiscuous sex as abruptly as OPEC had ended the era of cheap energy."[33] AIDS is an underlying motif in Armistead Maupin's *Babycakes,* the fourth in his "Tales of the City" series about life in San Francisco, and in Samuel Delaney's "The Tales of Plagues and Carnivals" in his science fiction work *Flight from Neveryon,* and in mid-1984 the first novel centered on AIDS appeared, Paul Reed's *Facing It,* [34] in which the AIDS crisis is described through the story of a gay couple, one of whom dies of AIDS.

While novels using AIDS as their central theme were fairly slow to appear, this was not true for plays, and there exists a growing collection of dramatic works seeking to come to terms with the epidemic. The first of these, Jeff Hagedorn's one-man show *One,* has been performed in such disparate cities as Milwaukee and Schenectady, and was soon followed by plays such as Bob Chesley's *Night Sweat,* Larry Kramer's *The Normal Heart,* a biting indictment of the response to the epidemic in New York City, and William Hoffman's *As Is,* which moved to Broadway after a very successful off-Broadway debut. A group known as Artists Involved with Death and Survival presented a collective presentation of theater pieces related to AIDS at Theater Rhinoceros in San Francisco in late 1984.[35] The traditional use of theater for catharsis has been of considerable value to gay men during the present epidemic.

It is not only gay men who have experienced the heavy impact of loss, of anxiety and of the fear of social opprobrium and persecution as well as of the disease itself. Stories began cropping up about hemophiliacs hiding their condition because of fear of stigma and avoiding others because of fear of being thought of as contagious, even though the disease was clearly transmitted via blood products and not social contact. It is very difficult to establish the full impact of AIDS among the Haitian community in the United States, many of whom are illegal immigrants and live in fear of deportation, but anecdotes of overt discrimination, above all of dismissal from jobs, are very common. Paranoia is what we call fear when it seems unreasonable; the line is never clear. When gays or Haitians talk of looming threats of quarantine, of sexuality being used as a criterion for exclusion from jobs and benefits, of police and governments using information gathered in AIDS research for other purposes, which side of the line are we broaching?

The most mysterious of the populations at seeming high risk are the intravenous drug users (a term I prefer to "drug abusers," which seems unnecessarily moralistic and implies there are good and bad IV users). For fairly self-evident reasons they do not form a community in any meaningful sense, and the impact of AIDS upon them is almost impossible to evaluate. It seems likely that their access to information about the disease is significantly less than that of the other groups, but this does not mean they are without fear; a report from Dr. DesJarlais, a New York City health official, spoke of street hawkers selling new needles with the words "Get the good needles. Don't get the bad AIDS."[36]

In both statistical and political terms the experience of gay men is clearly the most important. Of the others regarded as "high-risk groups" only hemophiliacs had sufficient communal organization and political clout to articulate demands concerning AIDS, and their organizations have chosen to approach AIDS in a very low-key way. Among gay men AIDS has become an omnipresent nightmare: "AIDS has infected my dreams," begins one article on the epidemic.[37] AIDS haunts us both asleep and awake, and it changes not just our behavior but our very conception of who we are and our belief in ourselves.

The equation of AIDS with gay men carried with it a strain of blaming gays for the introduction and spread of the disease, and the concomitant idea that others who fell sick were somehow "innocent victims." Such a view could draw on a powerful fundamentalist tradition which reinforced beliefs that in some ways AIDS is divine punishment, and hence deserved, a tradition that moral rightists sought to exploit. "What I see," said Ronald Godwin of the Moral Majority, "is a commitment to spend our tax dollars on research to allow these diseased homosexuals to go back to their perverted practices without any standards of accountability."[38]

Once questions of blame and responsibility for the disease intruded into public discussion, it was clear that AIDS would be political in a way that is unprecedented for a disease in modern times. The vehemence with which homosexuals were attacked for the disease far surpassed even Samuel Butler's satire and obscured the reality that this was a new and very dangerous epidemic disease for which no one could be held responsible in any real sense. Blame was both a political weapon used against gays and an internalized emotion that affected gay men, individually and collectively, and could act to prevent a rational assessment of what was going on.

More than lung cancer and cirrhosis, both of which are often clearly linked to personal behavior, AIDS was seen as the fault of the victim, "our" fault, "our" here being extended from the sick to gay men *in toto*. Peter Seitzman, a gay physician in New York, wrote:

> We all share the guilt that these men feel in a magnified, intensely personal form. What do the healthy ones do with this guilt? Weird things; different things. Most of us are able to deal with guilt in a healthy manner, and dispose of it. Some become obsessed with the idea that they have AIDS themselves. These people are miserable and deserve understanding, but their guilt is a purely personal burden.[39]

As non-gay moralists sought to blame gays for the disease—the Anglican Dean of Sydney was quoted as saying gays have blood on their hands[40]—so gays, too, found those to blame in their own community. An early article by Michael Lynch in the Canadian journal *Body Politic* saw guilt being created and fostered by the

gay media, and blamed people such as David Goodstein, publisher of *The Advocate* ("who concluded: 'our lifestyle'—and
wasn't it *The Advocate* that popularized this very word in our
vocabulary—'can become an elaborate suicide ritual' "), and Dr.
Dan William, who was one of the first to speak out against promiscuity.[41]

Neither blame nor guilt is a useful response to an epidemic.
Their prevalence in the discussions about AIDS underlines the
volatility and the political implications of the disease.

AIDS and Reaganism

Historians of medicine have sensitized us to the reality that the
course of an epidemic is shaped not just by the infectious organism and the medical response but also by the historical setting
within which it occurs. A typhoid outbreak in the nineteenth
century will be very different from a typhoid epidemic a hundred years later, when an effective medical response is possible
and when any suggestion of a health crisis triggers off a government response.

In the case of AIDS in the United States, the response involved
government at all levels and a considerable degree of buck-pass-
ing as to who was actually responsible for the various kinds of
responses demanded by a new and complex disease. The Public
Health Service found itself coping with a new epidemic at a time
when government austerity was slashing its budgets, and cuts in
social welfare had direct effects upon services available to AIDS
patients. In the words of President Reagan's Secretary for Health
and Human Services, Margaret Heckler, AIDS is the nation's
most important emergency health problem, yet it took the
widely publicized illness of Rock Hudson for President Reagan to
express concern for the sufferings of those dying from AIDS. The
Administration was remarkably slow to respond to the crisis, and
while it would be unreasonable to attribute these deaths directly
to them, it is also true that death and disease do not occur in a
sociopolitical vacuum. One of the central questions raised by
AIDS is the ability of the state to care for what both Hobbes and

Jefferson saw as the first requirement of government, namely the protection of life itself.

Both the social construction of and the governmental response to AIDS were clearly affected by the dominance of Reaganism in the eighties. In using the term "Reaganism" I am referring not only to the policies of a particular President but to an ideological syndrome which he epitomizes, based on the strengthening of the military while weakening the role of the state in protecting social welfare and civil rights. Such an ideology is an extension of that part of American liberalism which has stressed the legitimacy of individual selfishness and which turns the inequities of American social welfare into a positive virtue. As Alan Wolfe wrote:

> In America in the 1980's power is the ability to purchase the avoidance of risk. By that definition America is creating a vast group of powerless people which includes what used to be called the middle class. Fifty years after the greatest crisis in the history of capitalism, just about every aspect of American life is subject to the risks of the unrestricted marketplace. We are thus creating the first purely capitalist society in world history.[42]

In every other major Western country there exists some sort of national health insurance, so that people struck with catastrophic illness do not find themselves scrambling to pay for basic care. In most other affluent societies the sorts of basic welfare services required by the seriously ill are provided by the state.

But there is another side to Reaganism beyond the stress on economic individualism, and that is its strong sense of nostalgia. In the search to re-create the rest of the world in America's image and the domestic world in terms of traditional moral values, Reaganism seeks to escape the admittedly unpleasant realities of the present and to replace them with a mythical utopia of an America unchallenged in the world and held together by a common set of values at home. It is here that both Reagan's age and career, an object of bemusement to some foreigners, become positive virtues, for who is better qualified than an aging B-grade actor to lead the charge back to the 1950s? Nor was political discrimination and official disinterest confined to the United States; one found echoes of the Reaganite view in the reactions of politicians and press in Britain, in West Germany, in Australia (especially the state of Queensland).

This strand in Reaganism becomes relevant to the discourse on AIDS because it fueled the attempts by right-wing moralists to portray the disease as God's wrath and affected Washington's response in ways that went beyond restraints on government spending. As the French journal *Nouvel Observateur* commented sardonically: "Reagan, who would lead America back to the good old values, is justified from A to Z. Sex and drugs have become deadly. Nature itself is Reaganite. So far, no link has been established between AIDS and long hair."[43] Because AIDS hits the outcasts of society, because the double burden of being associated with not only sexuality but homosexuality made even concern for the dying seem politically suspect, it is remarkable that the response from at least some sectors of government and the medical profession has been as positive as it has.

The way in which AIDS is handled inevitably reflects the dominant ideology of the society. Much of the fear of discrimination among homosexuals and Haitians has been heightened by a general feeling that the Reagan Administration is not very interested in civil rights or unpopular minorities. "We have to look after our own because no one else will" is a frequently heard comment in AIDS circles, unconsciously echoing the Reaganite belief in transferring state responsibility to volunteer groups. For gay men this is not an impossible burden—though no private community can fund the Centers for Disease Control or the National Institutes of Health, nor should it. For the really marginal victims of AIDS, for Haitians, for black and Hispanic drug users, for poor women forced into prostitution, this becomes cruel piety.

AIDS hits those outside the mainstream of American society at a time when the generosity of that society to its outcasts is declining to a level previously unknown. Generosity is both economic and psychological; as one person with AIDS put it in an appeal to President Reagan:

> Like our first President, you are the father of this country. Do you hear me when I say your children are dying? This problem transcends politics. I ask for more than a simple release of funds; I am

asking for an act of love. If you are my father, Mr. President, I am your son. Please help me save my life.[44]

In a different sort of society AIDS would be perceived as a crisis of public health rather than a gay issue. In the United States in the first half of the 1980s the coincidence of a weak public health sector and a strong emphasis on community identity has helped shape the particular form the epidemic is taking. Once again the boundary between "medical" and "social" factors is blurred: the sort of research undertaken, the provision of health care, the response of hospitals and the medical profession, the way in which education of both the public and the "risk groups" is conducted, are all affected by political and cultural factors. The halfhearted response of governments, the considerable stigmatization of those struck by the illness and the politicization of the disease as revealed in the general assumption that AIDS is "the gay plague" all help to give the epidemic certain characteristics of Reaganism. As Stanley Marek, past president of the American Public Health Association, said of the Reagan Administration: "They tend to see health in the same way that John Calvin saw wealth: it's your own responsibility and you should damn well take care of yourself."[45]

CHAPTER THREE

The Conceptualization
of AIDS

I too think that these diseases are divine, and so are all others,
no-one being more divine or more human than any other; all
are alike and all divine. Each of them has a nature of its own,
and none arises without its natual cause.

—Hippocrates

Oddly enough, the closest parallel seemed to be the Andromeda
Strain. In the novel of this name, written in 1969, Michael Crich-
ton describes a deadly organism that comes from outside the
earth and wipes out a small town before mutating into a relatively harmless form.[1]

As we became aware of AIDS it had some of the science fiction
characteristics of the Andromeda Strain. Here was an apparently
quite new disease that was not even, in conventional terms, a
disease at all, but rather a syndrome that opened the body to the
ravages of a whole set of unusual bacterial, viral and fungal infections which in most cases proved fatal, and which was neither
airborne nor spread by casual contact but rather through blood
and semen. Researchers concentrated fairly quickly on the likelihood that it was caused by a virus, but until the French and
American discoveries of 1983–84 there was no conclusive evidence for this assumption.

The first cases of what can now be defined as AIDS were
reported in the medical literature in the late 1970s, although
there are rumors of even earlier cases. (One report in *The Lancet*
speculated that a case treated in 1960 could have been one of

AIDS.[2]) In Denmark, in France and in Belgium these early cases have been traced back to links with central Africa.[3] Dr. Frederick Siegal of New York reports that in 1979 he saw a woman from the Dominican Republic with "an inexplicable illness" that he now feels was AIDS. Siegal goes on to say:

> How many patients there were who slipped away unnoticed as she did before the disease reached the point of recognition will always be unknown, primarily because the sort of immunologic workup she received was not widely available to people of her background of poverty. At the time, most doctors wouldn't even have thought to inquire about the state of her immunity.[4]

(This case is particularly interesting in view of the subsequent insistence of the Dominican authorities that AIDS does not exist there, despite its shared border with Haiti.)

It was only in the spring of 1981 that reports from both coasts of unexpected illnesses among otherwise healthy young men—pneumocystis carinii (PCP) in Los Angeles, Kaposi's sarcoma (KS) in New York and California, severe anal herpes in New York—alerted physicians to the idea that something beyond individual cases was occurring. Probably the first to recognize that something new was happening were several doctors in Los Angeles.[5] In New York outbreaks of pneumocystis were noted at weekly meetings of infectious disease specialists sponsored by the city Department of Health, and in San Francisco nurses at San Francisco General noticed the same phenomenon.[6]

The ways in which signs of a new illness were picked up by the Centers for Disease Control in Atlanta reflect its sophisticated monitoring of the nation's health: requests for particular drugs, available only through the CDC, such as pentamidine for PCP and acyclovir for funguses, as well as networking among specialists, alerted the Centers that something unexpected was happening. A little more than a month after these first reports a CDC Task Force, headed by Dr. James Curran, then head of the venereal diseases section, was established, and has remained the pivot of American investigations into AIDS. Soon afterwards a working group on AIDS was established in Paris, where the first cases were being observed.[7] It may be significant that the CDC placed more emphasis on epidemiology than was true of the French, who were to make the most significant breakthroughs in virology and clinical research.

The scientific investigation of AIDS involved a number of disciplines: epidemiology, which involves the study of the incidence and history of disease; virology, which in the United States was dominated by work at the National Cancer Institute; and clinical medicine, which primarily involved those doctors with considerable AIDS cases. Of these, epidemiology, which provides invaluable clues to the nature of any new disease, is by its nature the most open to politicization, for epidemiologists must ask questions about the lifestyle and behavior of groups that are irrelevant to the laboratory scientist, and only raised in individual terms by the clinician.

The very first report on the new outbreak from the CDC stressed the homosexuality of those affected: "In the period October 1980–May 1981," read the report, "five young men, all active homosexuals, were treated for biopsy-confirmed P.C.P. at three different hospitals in Los Angeles."[8] A month later the CDC reported that KS had been diagnosed in "26 homosexual men." "It is not clear," said this report, "if or how the clustering of K.S., pneumocystis and other serious diseases in homosexual men is related."[9] However, by late August, when there were 108 cases of KS and PCP reported in the United States, over 90 percent among men known to be homosexual—at this stage there was only one known female patient—the CDC was suggesting strongly that the outbreaks were connected and that the underlying connection was immune deficiency.[10] Although, as the Siegals point out in their book on AIDS, "an argument can be made that Kaposi's tumor occurring in certain patients who don't develop opportunistic infections is not a part of AIDS but an independent event,"[11] there was little argument with the CDC's linking of apparently unrelated diseases.

It was not until the following year that the CDC began referring to "homosexual or bisexual men." It would have been clearer had the CDC used terms describing particular behavior rather than terms proclaiming identity. (In Canada, the Laboratory Centre for Disease Control talks of "homosexual/bisexual practices.") The crucial variable in determining infection is sexual or blood contact, and the CDC's terminology helped people overlook the very considerable amount of homosexual behavior that takes place among people who would vigorously reject any sort of homosexual identity.

The fact that the first reported cases were exclusively among gay men was to affect the whole future conceptualization of AIDS. The CDC's first report said that "the fact that these patients were all homosexuals suggests an association between some aspect of a homosexual lifestyle or disease acquired through sexual contact and pneumocystis pneumonia in this population." Soon the term "gay-related immune deficiency" (GRID) came into use, though not officially by the CDC, which to its credit preferred to use the clumsy but neutral phrase "Kaposi's sarcoma and related opportunistic infections."

It is ironic that the very success of the gay movement in claiming legitimacy for its "lifestyle" affected—and probably distorted—early research on AIDS. Instead of assuming that the culprit was a specific organism, researchers looked for factors in the "gay lifestyle" to explain what was going on; there seemed good reason to do this because, as the first report from the CDC concluded: "The patients did not know each other and had no known common contacts or knowledge of sexual partners who had similar illnesses."

Thus one of the first theories about the cause of "GRID" pointed to the use of "poppers," amyl and butyl nitrites, which were widely used by gay men, often to promote relaxation during intercourse. (Although amyl is illegal in most places, except on prescription, the closely related butyls are sold freely, usually as "room deodorizers.") One of the first CDC studies was "a quick and dirty survey," as Drs. Curran and Jaffe termed it, looking at the use of nitrites. However, while this study confirmed that their use was, indeed, widespread in the male gay world, it proved difficult to make any real connection between their use and the incidence of AIDS, although their effect on the immune system remains controversial.[12] More recently it has been suggested that the use of poppers may explain why Kaposi's sarcoma, unlike other AIDS-related diseases, seems almost totally confined to gay men.

There was also an almost immediate stress in research and writing on "homosexual promiscuity" (a term which was rarely defined). The first press report of the new syndrome appeared in the New York *Times* on July 3, 1981, and included the comment that "according to Dr. Friedman-Kien the reporting doctors said that most cases had involved homosexual men who have had multiple and frequent sexual encounters with different partners."[13]

If this claim had been clearly linked to the argument that "promiscuity" was significant because it increased the risk of exposure to dangerous organisms, it would have been self-evident. Unfortunately, however, the impression was fostered that "promiscuity" per se was the cause of the disease, an idea seized upon by both medicos and media. In May 1982 *The Lancet* published a paper which concluded that "amyl nitrite exposure and sexual promiscuity were associated with development of Kaposi's sarcoma, as well as histories of mononucleosis and sexually transmitted diseases,"[14] and as late as August 1983 the journalist Charles Krauthammer could write: "The one empirical fact we know about AIDS is that it is associated with promiscuity. AIDS victims have more than twice as many sexual partners as healthy homosexuals."[15]

The problem with such assertions is that people conclude not just that promiscuity is a risk factor but that everyone with AIDS has necessarily been very promiscuous, an assertion that has proved increasingly questionable. More significant, the stress on promiscuity meant that epidemiologists took a long time before following up on the health status of the lovers and longtime sex partners of gay men; I have heard of researchers who were genuinely unaware that such relationships exist among gay men and often coexist with frequent sexual adventures. Indeed, researchers seem so concerned with their ability to master the details of gay sexuality that they sometimes seem as willing as the media to believe that all gay men are full-time sexual athletes. (There are further problems in research; once AIDS had been established in the media as linked to promiscuity, that connection was likely to affect the answers people gave to epidemiologists seeking to establish patterns of transmission.)

During the first year of its recognized existence the new syndrome seemed linked exclusively to gay men. According to one account of the initial reaction: "The whole conversation on the

beach [at Fire Island] was about 'gay cancer,' even though the
Times had not used the phrase."[16] Three possible hypotheses
existed for this association: a genetic one, linked to some innate
homosexual predisposition; a lifestyle one, perhaps linked to particular locations frequented only by gay men; and transmission of
an infectious organism through activities confined to homosexual
men. The first possibility was not taken very seriously, although it
had an obvious appeal to those who like to regard homosexuality
as inborn.[17] Ann Fettner and William Check quote one prominent neurologist, Norman Geschwind of Harvard, as writing:

> Why are homosexuals susceptible? My own guess is that they do,
> indeed, have a special immune configuration based on the sex hor-
> mone status during pregnancy which probably has parallel effects,
> i.e. both in altering the sexual orientation and also affecting the
> immune system.[18]

(In correspondence with me Professor Geschwind denied writing this but he died before I could pursue the matter.)

The second hypothesis seemed more attractive, either in the
form of some organism lurking in specifically gay venues or in the
form of "immune overload." (Early street wisdom in New York
speculated on what might hide in the air conditioners at The
Saint disco or the hot tub at the St. Marks Baths, and there was
the seeming precedent of the role played by the air-conditioning
system in the Bellevue-Stratford Hotel in Philadelphia, site of the
outbreak of Legionnaire's disease in 1976.[19])

The overload theory was expressed by a number of doctors,
particularly in New York, who speculated that "recurrent bouts
of sexually transmitted diseases, especially those caused by viruses like CMV and other relatives of herpes, might 'overload' or
otherwise exhaust an individual's immune capacities."[20] Overload theories were linked to "lifestyle," as in the comment by Dr.
Larry Falk of Harvard that "overindulgence in sex and drugs"
and "the New York City lifestyle" were the culprits.[21] Sperm
itself was suggested as being immuno-suppressant, and some argued that it was particularly dangerous when it was received
anally, in what Jacques Leibowitch termed the "Sodom and
gonococcal theory" of AIDS.[22] As we shall see, variations of the

overload theory continued to prove important in the debate about the etiology and prevention of AIDS.

The evidence for an infectious agent was strengthened in June 1982, when the CDC reported on a "cluster" of cases in the greater Los Angeles area, in which sexual contacts among various members of the group had existed. Moreover, it began to be clear that lymphadenopathy and related general malaise were far more widespread, especially among gay men, than actual opportunistic diseases, and that this might well be a precursor to or a mild form of the syndrome itself. What is known as AIDS Related Condition (ARC) and sometimes as "pre-AIDS"—in Britain the term used is "persistent generalized lymphadenopathy" (PGL) and in Australia "lymphadenopathy syndrome"—is estimated to affect ten times as many people as are diagnosed with "full-blown" AIDS.[23]

The boundaries between ARC and AIDS are not always very clear, and I have heard heated debates about whether such and such an illness, combined with lowered immune functioning, is sufficient to classify someone as having AIDS. The CDC has retained a rigid demarcation between the two for definitional purposes, which has slowed recognition of the extent and gravity of ARC. But although people suffering from ARC can be very sick, relatively few go on to develop the full syndrome and die; one wonders whether the media reaction and resulting hysteria would have been noticeably less had the range of less serious illnesses been included in the conceptualization of AIDS itself from the beginning.

Non-homosexual Cases

In mid-1982 there was a major shift in the medical understanding of AIDS when it was discovered among other groups, first drug users and then Haitians and hemophiliacs. In June, the CDC reported that of the 152 known cases of PCP 21 percent involved drug users—probably an underestimate—and that these were a majority of the known heterosexual cases, then totaling twenty-six men and eight women.[24] Cases of severe illness discovered among Haitian refugees in Jackson Memorial

Hospital in Miami, especially toxoplasmosis, a parasitical infection, seemed to be linked to the same underlying factors as KS and PCP among gay men and drug users, which led researchers to go to Haiti in search of a possible source of the disease. At the same time the CDC announced that hemophiliacs also seemed susceptible, presumably because of their exposure to Factor VIII, a blood concentrate used to assist clotting and made from the plasma of thousands of donors. In September the CDC began using the term "Acquired Immune Deficiency Syndrome," following a conference on blood products sponsored by the Food and Drug Administration at which the term was suggested by Dr. Bruce Voeller, a former director of the National Gay Task Force.

In December 1982 the first case of AIDS possibly related to blood transfusions was reported—in a twenty-month-old boy, one of whose donors subsequently developed AIDS. This was to unleash the first major scare over AIDS in connection with contamination of the blood supply, and coincided with several reports of "unexplained cellular immunodeficiency and opportunistic infections" among infants.[25] By the beginning of 1983 some female partners of those belonging to risk groups were also showing up in the figures, although it was not yet determined whether only men could transmit AIDS. It soon became clear that AIDS could be transmitted by women, both to their sexual partners and to fetuses by way of the placenta.

As these reports of various non-gay cases came in, it suggested that one could interpret the statistics of AIDS to stress the ambivalent boundaries of the term "homosexual." An indeterminate number of people classified in reports as Haitians or IV drug users undoubtedly have had homosexual experiences, even if they strongly reject the definition of being gay. A number of the cases classified as "gay" have also used intravenous drugs; yet the CDC classifies them only under the "homosexual or bisexual" rubric, thus suggesting a lower number of drug users than is the case. There has been considerable debate about how many of the male Haitians with AIDS have had homosexual experiences, debate in which mutual accusations of racism and homophobia make accuracy particularly difficult to achieve.[26] The crucial point is what practices or situations facilitate the transmission of

AIDS, and in the interest of avoiding stigmatization stress should be placed on these rather than on particular identities. Dr. Curran of the CDC recognized this, albeit rather belatedly, when he acknowledged: "While it is true that members of some groups have a high risk of contracting AIDS, they are not a risk to others. Rather, risk factors—multiple sex partners, certain sexual practices, intravenous drug abuse and blood infusion—are related to contracting AIDS."[27]

The most striking indication that AIDS was in no intrinsic sense a disease of homosexuals came in the mounting evidence of its widespread existence in central Africa, where it seemed to have very little correlation with male homosexuality. The connection with Africa was known to researchers as a real possibility from 1982 on, but it took some time to be reported in the mass media, at least in the United States.[28] There is seriologic evidence that the virus believed to be associated with AIDS has been present in Zaire from at least 1977 on and is widely spread through central Africa.[29] One report claimed that "attack rates of the disease in Kinshasa, Zaire, and in Kigali, the capital of Rwanda, are running at rates as high as those recorded in New York and San Francisco,"[30] and more recent reports suggest the rates may in fact be much higher, with estimates of up to 7,000 cases in Zaire alone, eight times the United States incidence. About 40 percent of the cases reported from Africa are among women (which is also true for people with AIDS of African origin in Belgium and France), and there is evidence for considerable heterosexual transmission.

Let us suppose that AIDS had first been diagnosed in Zaire and Rwanda. Let us further suppose it had then appeared in the United States among Haitians and drug users, and only after them among gay men. Had this been the case, AIDS would undoubtedly have attracted less attention, less money—and probably less scapegoating. Or let us imagine that AIDS had first been isolated among "swinging singles" in, say, Los Angeles' Marina del Ray or New York's Upper East Side. In the latter case one suspects there would have been a greater sense of urgency about the disease, which would less easily have been perceived as confined to "the other."

Speculation about such scenarios—one could construct others

—underlines the fact that there is a great deal of social construction going on in our view of AIDS. Just how strong is the association between AIDS and homosexuality in the popular view can be seen in Belgium, where, despite the fact that most known cases are among Africans or people who have lived in Africa, the right wing press attempted anti-gay stereotyping around AIDS. The same is true in Italy, where as many cases have been reported among drug users as among gay men.[31] Ironically it was the comparative advantage enjoyed by gay men in access to medical care that meant the first cases were diagnosed among them, and probably means that there remains severe underreporting of AIDS, perhaps among other groups in the United States and Europe, but almost certainly in the Third World.

One of the reasons that the perception of AIDS has been so closely linked to gay men is that no other affected group has comparable political will and resources to deal with the issue. IV users, by reason of their addiction, are unlikely to form a political community, and while there are Haitian political and communal groups they have been hampered not only by limited numbers and resources but even more so by an ambivalence in acknowledging that they are at risk. Indeed, it is not too cynical to suggest that much of the Haitian rhetoric, encouraged by the government at home, claims simultaneously that it is racist to link Haitians to AIDS and racist to fail to provide adequate health and welfare services for those who have the disease. In this situation the very assertiveness of gay groups, which are comparatively well off in skills and resources, merely strengthens the image of AIDS as a gay disease, and the need to mobilize their own community means that gay leaders reinforce that connection. Gays, too, are ambivalent about AIDS, claiming that it should not be seen as a "gay disease" while tending to talk about it as if that's all it is.

Some AIDS researchers doubt that this perception can last very long. The growing number of cases that fit none of the "risk" categories, and the mounting evidence that AIDS can be transmitted not only heterosexually but also from women to men, are increasingly reflected in media reports, with claims that "AIDS is showing an increasing disregard for age, gender or sexual preference,"[32] and that "AIDS threatens to emerge as a standard vene-

real disease among American heterosexuals."[33] On the basis of
what is known at the time of writing, both of these comments
seem to me exaggerated; at least in the Western world heterosexual transmission seems fairly infrequent and inefficient. It is certainly true that there are more and more cases who are not gay.
Rather than this leading to more empathy with those who are
affected, there seems to be a move to find new scapegoats, of
whom female prostitutes seem to be the leading contenders.[34]

Homosexuality and Medicine

As AIDS was conceived as a homosexual disease, it strengthened, albeit in a new way, the role of medicine in determining
how we think about homosexuality. This was particularly salient
because of the historical link between concepts of disease in
general and of homosexuality. Indeed, one writer has suggested
that there may be more than a casual connection between the
social reactions to the Black Death and the hostility toward homosexuality that emerged in the Middle Ages[35] (although the
best-known historian of this change in attitudes, John Boswell,
locates the emergence of the hostility well before the plague of
the fourteenth century).[36]

We are on firmer ground when we look at the medicalization of
homosexuality during the latter part of the nineteenth century,
with the redefinition of what had been viewed as a sin and a
crime into an illness and a condition. The idea of "the homosexual" as a concept was codified when the word itself was coined by
the Hungarian doctor Kartbeny in 1869. This can be understood
as part of a general development in Western societies whereby
the professions gained power through their ability to name and
characterize ever-increasing areas of human life. The medical
profession provided the basis for increasing state control and
surveillance over sexuality, and also offered arguments for control through cure rather than punishment, which became the
basis for respectable arguments for the decriminalization of homosexuality over the next century. Not surprisingly, an important thrust of the newly energized gay movement of the 1970s
was directed against this medical discourse, and this thrust led to

the decision of the American Psychiatric Association in 1973 to relinquish the definition of homosexuality as an illness.[37] With AIDS the medical profession once again seemed to be embarked on the social control of homosexuality, although this time for somewhat different reasons.

To conceptualize a disease as linked to a particular group will have immediate effects on the way in which medical research proceeds. It is not merely that the resources available will reflect, at least in part, the political influence of that group. (It is frequently alleged that sickle-cell anemia has received insufficient attention because it afflicts only blacks.) Certainly there have been claims that AIDS would have received more immediate and benevolent attention from the government and the medical establishment had it first struck other, more respectable groups. Speaking of the first two years of the epidemic, Congressman Ted Weiss said: "Neither the government nor the medical community has accepted its leadership fully or devoted sufficient expertise in fighting this insidious epidemic."[38] (Less frequently one hears complaints that the power of homosexuals in America has ensured that too *much* attention is paid to AIDS, as in comments in the journal *Science* about "an unprecedented spending spree."[39])

More interesting is the way in which the very direction of AIDS-related research has been affected by the links to gay men. While the epidemiological evidence does point clearly to sexual transmission, this may have been stressed to the exclusion of other factors because of the emphasis on homosexuals rather than others with AIDS. (This point has been made by one of the best-known American AIDS researchers, Dr. Robert Gallo of the National Cancer Institute.[40]) The various research projects underway on psychosocial aspects of AIDS seem entirely confined to gay men, either because the researchers are themselves gay or because gay men are a much easier population to study than drug users or Haitian immigrants.[41] One scientist, in an article critical of the alleged overemphasis on AIDS research, claimed rather obliquely that: "It is likely that our attitudes towards AIDS are influenced by a variety of Freudian concerns for our sexual safety or identity."[42] The fact that so many AIDS researchers are themselves gay—though often not openly so—makes it particularly difficult to maintain scientific "objectivity." (Both prejudice and the desire to avoid prejudice can be involved. Some researchers may well have shied away from certain hypotheses because of a fear of being labeled homophobic.)

More than in most medical arguments it is possible to detect ideological positions in the debates over the etiology of AIDS, debates which were quite heated during the first several years of the epidemic. Those who argued, in a variant of the "immune overload" theory, that AIDS is essentially a response to frequent infection by already known organisms (cytomegalovirus was often mentioned) linked it very clearly to sexual "promiscuity," sometimes verging on seeing AIDS as self-inflicted. This view came to be echoed by some people with AIDS—"We both came to understand early in the game that it was promiscuity that made us sick and not some new mutant virus from Mars"[43]—and won considerable support within the gay world; ignorance of how diseases are transmitted still leads many to believe that the "fast-lane lifestyle" is per se the only problem. One can meet gay men who will seriously explain how they are not at risk because they are vegetarians, or take multivitamins, or work out frequently. On the other hand, those committed to the "new virus" theory are more likely to see AIDS as the result of bad luck, and argue that it was pure misfortune that caused it to surface first among gay men. Clearly factors other than the purely scientific are at work here; one encounters both those who want to blame themselves for being sick and those who would deny any responsibility.

It is not a simple matter of one theory being homophobic and the other not. (I have heard Dr. Jim Curran so characterize the "overload" theory because of the weight it places on individual behavior.) The dispute over a germ versus an environmental explanation of disease is a very basic one that surfaces in all epidemics, and is rarely best understood as an either/or situation; we know that there are many organisms which cause damage only under certain conditions.[44] To suggest that particular social conditions may have existed among certain groups so as to make a particular virus lethal, which is the basic argument of those who espouse a multifactorial explanation, is not in itself homophobic, anti-Haitian or whatever.

One of the consequences of seeing AIDS as a "homosexual disease" is to make it easy to construct conspiratorial views of AIDS, to see it as aimed intentionally at gay men. A leaflet distributed in 1983 by the Communistcadre, a self-styled scientific Trotskyist group, proclaimed: "AIDS is political germ warfare by U.S. government," and went on to argue that:

> The artificial nature of the origin and spread of AIDS convicts beyond any reasonable doubt the U.S. government as the creator and purveyor of the dread disease . . . with human intervention—made possible by modern scientific advances perverted to diabolical ends by the war-driven capitalist system of exploitation—it would be possible to guide the evolution of such a new virus as AIDS.
>
> In order to generate a serious epidemic of such a virus among gays one would expect the encouragement of the acceleration of sado-masochism and more violent forms of sexual expression in order to intensify venereal contact into more frequent blood contact. Gay males almost universally describe tremendous social pressure towards such a trend . . . in the late seventies—just before the AIDS breakout.[45]

Similar theories surface from time to time in the gay press; my favorite is the letter that suggested a chemical agent was "sprinkled like fairy dust on the floors of bathhouses where barefoot homosexuals would absorb it through their skin."[46] Former *Hustler* publisher Larry Flynt has been quoted as attributing AIDS to "a substance called Ogda-Ogda that has been put in the K-Y jelly by the Centers for Disease Control."[47] Even the president of San Francisco's Board of Supervisors, Wendy Nelder, joined the cries by suggesting that AIDS might be linked to fluoride.[48]

While such theories seem quite frankly crazy, other theories surfaced, claiming that AIDS may be the result of experiments in biological warfare that have got out of control. (It is worth remembering that CDC investigators of Legionnaires' disease a few years earlier had seriously explored a similar hypothesis.[49]) One character in Larry Kramer's play *The Normal Heart* refers to alleged tests on a virus that would destroy the immune system conducted by the Defense Department at Fort Detrick, Maryland, known as Firm Hand and first tested—on homosexuals—in

1978. As early as 1969 a Defense Department spokesman had acknowledged the theoretical possibility of such developments:

> Within the next 5 to 10 years it would probably be possible to make a new infective micro-organism which could differ in certain important respects from any known disease-causing organisms. Most important of these is that it might be refractory to the immunological and therapeutic processes upon which we depend to maintain our relative freedom from infectious disease.[50]

I frankly doubt any of these explanations, but one cannot totally dismiss their plausibility.

Ideology is also involved in the arguments that certain psychological characteristics predispose one to AIDS, rather like the suggestions of "cancer-prone personalities" that so infuriated Susan Sontag. At their most extreme such views were expressed in comments that AIDS was the result of "subconscious decisions by those who become ill as 'a dramatic form of protest.' "[51] In comments that bear out Sontag's warnings against seeking metaphorical portents in disease, David Black has suggested: "We need to entertain the mystical and find the link between Haitians and gays with AIDS not in their common tendency to suffer from hepatitis B but in their common tendency to conjure up those dark forces science holds at bay by pretending they don't exist."[52]

Some psychologists have argued that just as stress is a factor in the development of illnesses such as herpes, arthritis, diabetes and cancer, it is likely to be a factor in AIDS, and that internalized self-hatred may be a real factor in accounting for which of those exposed to the infectious agent will develop AIDS. A more likely link, it seems to me, is that stress will affect the way in which AIDS develops and manifests itself in an infected individual.[53] A related way of arguing this is to point to the way in which certain patterns of sexual behavior and drug use are related to low self-esteem, itself often the product of social stigma against homosexuality.

The particular nature of the AIDS crisis is affecting the practice of medicine as well as the direction of medical research. The emphasis on gay men as patients has produced numerous discussions and some literature aimed at the medical and therapeutic professions which stress the need to understand "gay lifestyles"; a major activity of many AIDS groups has been the provision of information and speakers at hospitals, medical conferences, nursing schools, etc. While AIDS has meant the re-medicalization of homosexuality, it has also brought about much greater sophistication in the medical profession's understanding of homosexuality than ever before.

At the same time AIDS has led to what may be unparalleled demands for accountability from the medical profession. It is hard to think of another illness where so much attention has been devoted to keeping a lay public aware of ongoing developments in research; public forums with researchers, continual conferences and meetings, interviews with the gay press, have all played a part in this constant scrutiny of medical developments. Two of the largest American gay papers, *The Advocate* and *The New York Native*, have employed writers with the specific task of keeping abreast of the voluminous literature on AIDS, and they have, in turn, developed their own networks (and bête noires) within the research world.

It is hardly surprising that demands for accountability go hand in hand with considerable suspicion of the medical profession. Added to the frequent horror stories of traditional medical attitudes toward homosexuals and of current practices in treating AIDS patients, the failure so far of orthodox medicine to treat AIDS effectively opens the way for a great deal of mistrust. Some of the fears induced by AIDS may be due to a feeling that it has revealed the limits of modern medicine and shown us an emperor without clothes. Whether accurately or not, many gay men claim that repeated treatments with potent antibiotics have contributed to immune breakdown—Flagyl, used against amoebas, is one drug frequently mentioned. "Perhaps," speculated one writer, "AIDS is just the first of a whole new class of diseases resulting from the tremendous changes human technology has wrought in the earth's ecology."[54]

Given these conditions, the field is ripe for almost any claim for alternative cures and preventive measures. (The same has been true historically of cancer.) Thus AIDS conferences have included workshops in acupuncture, vitamin therapy and the philosophy of macrobiotics; a pamphlet that circulated in San Francisco in 1983 promised relief through a mixture of diet and "positive thinking." I know of people with AIDS who have traveled to the Bahamas and the Philippines for therapy that is illegal in the United States, and people with AIDS in California and Texas often go to Mexico for drugs that are illegal in the United States. It is important to explore alternative treatments, some of which have produced promising results. More sinister are those organizations which seek to capitalize on AIDS fears by offering fraudulent "tests" and "cures" to the gullible. One advertisement in some California gay papers at the end of 1983 promised "21st century solutions to man's newest threat . . . unique ways to beef up your own immune system/practical ways to identify a potential AIDS carrier." A year later, for the sum of $385, one company was offering a "neutralizer/sterilizer" for use in the home: "Where an 'Andromeda' type syndrome occurs where both cause and cure are yet unknown, VIRALAID n/s produces a counter-attack on ambient environment germs, and maybe [sic] preventing the occasion of such unknown agents."[55]

In discussing the response of the medical profession to AIDS it is important to recognize that many of those involved in AIDS research and care are themselves gay. Before AIDS a gay/lesbian health network had already come into being, involving practitioners who were critical of the prevailing heterosexist biases of medicine. The Gay Nurses Alliance dates back to 1973, the National Gay Health Coalition was established in the mid-seventies, as was a caucus within the American Medical Student Association. The first National Gay Health Conference was held in a church basement in Washington in 1978, and starting in 1983 subsequent annual conferences included national AIDS forums. The Bay Area Physicians for Human Rights (BAPHRA) was founded in San Francisco in 1977, to be followed several years later by a national association, the American Association of Physicians for Human Rights (AAPHR).

AIDS provided an enormous impetus, leading many doctors and other health-care workers to come out and organize as openly gay practitioners. Local groups of AAPHR sprang up in many parts of the country, often as a direct consequence of AIDS. Many of the doctors who came into contact with AIDS patients were faced with a threat to the whole set of assumptions about detachment and objectivity upon which medicine prides itself. Many gay physicians, who had rarely encountered death among their patients, suddenly found themselves treating large numbers of men of their own age and social world who were dying, and seemingly resistant to all known therapies. Among some doctors the result was nervous collapse, among others a growing politicization and determination to develop an openly gay presence in medicine.

The Politics of Research

In testimony in the summer of 1983 to the House of Representatives subcommittee on Intergovernmental Relations and Human Resources, Dr. Edward Brandt, Assistant Secretary for Health, said: "AIDS has been officially recognized by Secretary Heckler as the Department's highest priority emergency health problem."[56] The declaration followed a summer of media hype in which AIDS was portrayed as the most serious epidemic since polio, even, in the words of an article in the New York *Times*, "the century's most virulent epidemic,"[57] a description which seems unfair to the 1919 flu epidemic. Clearly, once AIDS had been so identified by both media and government, this would affect not only the extent but also the direction of research.

AIDS research had begun among clinicians confronted with the disease—at Mount Sinai, Sloan-Kettering and New York hospitals, at the teaching hospitals of the University of California in Los Angeles and San Francisco—and was taken up by the CDC. Although the CDC is thought of as normally involved in surveillance and epidemiology, it does some laboratory work as well, and some of the research into retroviruses has been conducted at its laboratories in Atlanta. Although the CDC has been the most visible part of the Public Health Service in dealing with AIDS, the role of the National Institutes of Health, has been just as central. Based at Bethesda, Maryland, the NIH is the section of the Public Health Service responsible for most American medical research, both through its own work and through the funding of other institutions and projects. A number of observers saw NIH as very slow to respond to the need for AIDS research. Tim

Westmoreland, a congressional aide who has worked extensively on health issues, has talked of "the constant tension back and forth between Congress, authorizing specific public policy for biomedical research, and Bethesda, which in many cases is operating pure research . . . that kind of tension has produced a mentality whereby the Congress is, somewhat rightly, referred to as the Disease-of-the-Month Club, versus those people in Bethesda who think not only that pure science need not be relevant, but, if you listen to some of the witnesses on Capitol Hill, should not be relevant . . ."[58]

In fact, the National Cancer Institute and the National Institute of Allergy and Infectious Diseases, both parts of NIH, were involved in AIDS-related research within a few months of the CDC's initial alert, though largely because it tied into existing activities. (The National Cancer Institute had been conducting research into Kaposi's sarcoma since the 1960s.) The first AIDS patient was admitted to NIH hospital facilities in Bethesda in the summer of 1981. Much slower was the funding of outside research by the NIH, by far the largest source of such funds in the United States.

There were two major problems in funding AIDS research, the first being the question of how much money would be available, the second involving the very cumbersome processes whereby that money was made available to researchers. The first raises major questions of public policy and will be examined in a later chapter. As to the second, the NIH did not call for applications for AIDS-related research until August 1982, and the first funds were not allocated until early 1983, twenty months after the first alert. Frederick Siegal, one of the first immunologists involved in AIDS research, wrote: "The long delays in providing federal funding for AIDS prompted concern over the nation's ability to respond to new epidemic diseases in general."[59]

Further delays in the spread of information about AIDS resulted from the tradition that no research findings in medicine should be discussed until they were published in relevant journals, a precedent known as the Ingelfinger Rule, after a former editor of the *New England Journal of Medicine.*[60] The rapidity and extent of findings related to AIDS led Dr. Brandt to request the editors of the *NEJM* and other medical journals to expedite the publication of relevant articles. But the tension between the desire of individual researchers to keep control of their findings and the general need to know remained; at a scientific meeting in New York in 1983 a doctor from the National Cancer Institute was booed when he refused to give more details about pending work on the HTL virus.[61]

A number of people have suggested privately that homophobia was as powerful a barrier to initiating research as lack of money and bureaucratic delay. Such allegations are hard to pin down, although several researchers have told me they were "discouraged" by colleagues from becoming too involved in work on "a homosexual disease," and Dr. Brandt has referred to "some difficulty" in attracting researchers "because AIDS had become a gay rights issue."[62] In this atmosphere the sexuality of the researchers themselves inevitably becomes a subject for speculation, which becomes, in turn, a powerful disincentive for some to enter the field. One hears stories that the CDC deliberately excluded gay men from its AIDS Task Force and that the NIH has been influenced against supporting certain projects because review panels included closet homosexuals afraid of being revealed as such if they showed too much interest in AIDS.

It is certainly unfair to claim that anyone who is not gay is not capable of doing good research in this area, as was implied by one writer who sought to establish the potential homophobia of the CDC:

> Consider the composition of the AIDS Activity Group's full-time personnel. Those working exclusively at headquarters number ten —seven doctors, two public health professionals and one research sociologist. All of them are straight; one is an orthodox Jew and another a deacon in his church.[63]

On the other hand, there is real prejudice involved, as medical writer Ann Fettner has related:

> I've been to meetings at N.I.H. and heard really ugly stuff. One doctor got up and said: "Well, I can't refer to these people as gay, that's not a good word for it. I don't find it gay or charming." Another suggested that gays have their tubes tied. This is in the N.I.H.![64]

It is easy to dismiss the homophobia of researchers as irrelevant to scientific work. The problem is that a disease linked as closely to a stigmatized sexuality as is AIDS will cause considerable anxiety for most researchers. There is no guarantee that a homosexual researcher, particularly one who is closeted, will be more or less affected by unconscious fears or biases than a heterosexual one. Indeed, there is a whole story to be written on the way in which some researchers, particularly in the social sciences, have used AIDS projects to work through their own sexual feelings and ambivalences. (Sometimes this leads to strange tensions, as in meetings when researchers move uneasily between the terms "we" and "they" in discussing gay men.)

Following congressional pressure in 1983, government funding for AIDS research was greatly increased, and this, combined with the publicity generated by the media, ensured a sudden explosion in activity. Large amounts of money were now available—in California and New York from the state governments as well, though remarkably little from any private companies. Money was channeled not only into clinical and laboratory work but also into epidemiological studies; large-scale prospective studies of gay men were funded in five cities (two years after a workshop organized by the NIH recommended the need for such studies). A small amount of money was directed to psychosocial research, but it took a long time for federal funds to become available for any research into public education.

In broad terms the emphasis on research in AIDS was to concentrate heavily on etiology rather than cures, and this work was directed fairly quickly toward a viral agent. Cytomegalovirus (CMV), which is endemic in the general population and particularly widespread among gay men; Epstein-Barr virus, one of the herpes viruses, which causes mononucleosis and is associated with Burkitt's lymphoma, a cancer found widely in eastern Africa; adenoviruses and papoviruses were all examined. Increasingly attention was focused on human t-lymphotropic virus (HTLV), previously known as human T-cell leukemia virus, the first retrovirus to be fully isolated in human beings (in 1978) and one associated with certain forms of leukemia endemic in southern Japan and the Caribbean. (A retrovirus is distinguished from other viruses by its manner of replication.) Research on HTLV was led in the United States by Robert Gallo of the National Cancer Institute, who had originally identified the retrovirus, and in France by Luc Montagnier of the Institut Pasteur, whose work was made known to American researchers in early 1983 and who claimed that AIDS was caused by lymphadenopathy-associated virus (LAV), a different but related retrovirus.

In late April 1984, in an atmosphere more like that of a presidential announcement than a medical conference, Dr. Gallo stated that a variant of the t-lymphotropic retrovirus, which he termed HTLV-III, had been identified as the probable cause of AIDS. Flanked by various health officials, the Secretary of Health and Human Services, Margaret Heckler, claimed: "Today we add another miracle to the long honor roll of American medicine and science." Not since the announcement of a poliomyelitis vaccine twenty-nine years earlier had so much attention been paid to a medical discovery. The problem was, the discovery was not new.

Two days earlier the head of the CDC had attributed the discovery to the French team who had identified LAV the previous year. (The Atlanta *Constitution*, perhaps out of loyalty to the hometown boys in what appeared to be a nasty interagency fight, ran a front-page story stressing the dedication of CDC researchers—many of whom were said to be endangering their own health in their zeal to discover the virus—foreshadowing at the end the HTLV-III announcement.[65]) Mrs. Heckler, who, one assumes, could no more recognize a retrovirus than the rest of us, said: "We believe it [LAV] will prove to be the same." No wonder the New York *Times* in a lead editorial attacked "the fierce—and premature—fight for credit between scientists and bureaucratic sponsors of research," and in a very Foucauldian note added: "In the world of science, as among primitive societies, to be the namer of an object is to own it."[66]

In fact, it was something of a mystery why American researchers had been so slow to follow up the French findings, and the head of the CDC, Dr. James Mason, was quoted as saying he was not sure why this was the case.[67] Montagnier himself complained that the Americans had not paid sufficient attention to his work,[68] and considerable competition remains between the two institutes. It is easy to see this competition as part of the tradition of national rivalries in medical research—one classic example was that Wassermann's findings in serology which produced the test for syphilis named after him were due in part to pressure from the German government, which was concerned at being outdone by French scientists.[69] But the competitiveness and backbiting has been just as great within the United States, and there are American researchers who are prepared to insinuate that Dr. Gallo used the French findings without properly acknowledging them.[70]

Complaints against the National Cancer Institute have included both its alleged unwillingness to cooperate with other investigators and its lack of support for research that did not fit the retrovirus theory of AIDS, whether it was into multifactorial causes, bacteria or other viruses. A report by the congressional Office of Technology Assessment was critical of the failure of the NCI to make their culture samples available to researchers at the CDC.[71] (For examples of some of the less conventional research, see the *Journal of AIDS Research*, edited by Dr. Jo Sonnabend; even further from the mainstream are the suggestions by Alan Cantwell, 1983, that AIDS is a cancer caused by acid-fast bacteria[72] and several papers by Drs. Mark Whiteside and Caroline Macleod which posit a link between AIDS and several tropical diseases and suggest the possibility of insect transmission.[73])

A particular case of disinterest in unorthodox ideas is the fate of a hypothesis advanced by a Harvard pathobiologist, Jane Teas, concerning the possible involvement of African swine fever virus (ASFV). In a letter to *The Lancet* in April 1983, Teas pointed to the similarities between ASFV and AIDS, the appearance of ASFV in Haiti in 1978 and a possible cycle for its transmission to humans.[74]

Teas found little support—and no funds—from the medical establishment to follow up her theory. It has been alleged, above all in the pages of *The New York Native* and its sister publication, *Christopher Street* magazine, that this was due to scientific cupidity and the political influence of the pig industry. "What if your theory is right?" one veterinarian is claimed to have said to Teas. "It would destroy our $10 billion pork industry."[75] At least one writer has linked swine fever to a conspiratorial explanation of AIDS:

A *Newsday* article reprinted in the Boston *Globe* (1-9-77) reports that CIA operatives received the virus at Ft. Gulick (a CIA biological warfare training station in Panama), then travelled to Navassa (a U.S.-controlled island just off the coast of Haiti) and then to Guantanamo—the U.S. naval base on the island of Cuba—where the virus was spread to Cuban pigs. From there it spread to the Dominican Republic (1978), to Haiti (1979), and reappeared in Cuba in 1980.[76]

Both the CDC and the NIH insisted that there was no real evidence to support the ASFV hypothesis. But *The New York Native* persisted: "There is a rule in business about not betting the whole company. If Dr. Curran is . . . tying up all the C.D.C.'s time and resources on one hypothesis (e.g., retroviruses) then we question his judgment . . ."[77] In early 1984 the Department of Agriculture and the National Institute of Allergy and Infectious Diseases announced a research project to explore the possible role of ASFV in AIDS. (The medical columnist of a rival gay paper claimed to have been told that this was a move to humor *The New York Native*, which attributed more power to the gay press than most of us would have thought likely.[78]) Nothing seems to have come of this move, nor of plans for tests in several European countries,[79] but in July 1985 the New York State Health Department announced plans for testing the connection.

Few researchers are convinced by the ASFV hypothesis. What was crucial in the ASFV episode, however, was not that it disproved the HTLV-III hypothesis, but that it demonstrates the very tight control maintained over research by the medical establishment, at both the CDC and the NIH.[80] Undoubtedly part of the attraction of the ASFV hypothesis was that it appealed to considerable distrust of the CDC, at least among some sections of the gay movement. This was true, above all, of *The New York Native*, but criticism has been voiced by others, such as Virginia Apuzzo of the National Gay Task Force. A number of elements entered into this distrust: a feeling that the CDC's epidemiological work has been both insensitive and incompetent (for example, in allegedly ignoring the need for Creole-speaking interviewers to talk with Haitian patients), that there had been consistent underreporting of AIDS cases, as well as concerns about abuse of confidentiality and Dr. Curran's reported suggestion to compile a list of all those found to be "HTLV-III positive" (of which more later).

The CDC has been particularly vulnerable to criticism because it has tended to be more public about its work than other parts of the Public Health Service. This is not to deny the justice of some of the criticisms. The early epidemiological work was poor, according to most other researchers, though this was partly due to inadequate resources, and some recent work (e.g., in Zaire) is regarded skeptically by other researchers. Allegations of considerable underreporting are frequent, though it is not clear whether this is due to the reluctance of local physicians, failures by local and state officials or problems with the CDC's own procedures.[81] A report by the U.S. Conference of Mayors in 1984 found that in a quarter of the cities responding there was "significant variance" between the CDC figures and those compiled by local community groups.[82] Since leaving office Dr. Brandt has spoken of the delays and inadequacies of the American system for detecting and reporting disease, with its heavy reliance on the voluntary compliance of local doctors.[83] In a broader sense, the criticisms of the CDC were part of the scrutiny to which many AIDS researchers found themselves exposed. Irritating as it might be to the authorities, the demand that the ideological biases underlying medical researchers be exposed, and that researchers be accountable to those affected by their work, is one of the positive consequences of the politicization of AIDS.

Consequences of the Viral Discoveries

The hype that surrounded Gallo's announcement led to quite unjustified expectations. "Vaccine Against AIDS Is on the Way," headlined *U.S. News & World Report* (May 7, 1984), although even optimists thought three years would be the minimum time required, and some suggested that the nature of the retrovirus made the development of an effective vaccine unlikely. At least one gay newspaper is said to have claimed that a cure for AIDS had been found, although most of the gay press was more cautious in its reporting than the mainstream media. (Even so, I think David Talbot and Larry Bush are overstating it to say:

"Like an efficient tap, the press conference had all but cut off the flow of AIDS stories. Heckler had talked the media into believing that AIDS would soon become medical history."[84])

The discovery of a putative "AIDS virus," as it quickly came to be called, and even the mounting evidence that this was, in fact, the crucial agent in the disease, did not answer the question of under what conditions exposure to the virus would make one sick: "The distinction between infection and disease," as Montagnier has pointed out, "is of paramount importance."[85] Various co-factors—other viruses, drug use, genetic predisposition, stress—have all been suggested. As Jo Sonnabend and Serge Saadoun wrote, still insisting on a multifactorial etiology: "The important environmental factors are repeated exposure to multiple allogeneic semens, repeated infection with CMV, and infection with other sexually transmitted pathogens."[86] Other researchers warned more cautiously against attributing AIDS to HTLV/LAV alone. These questions became crucial as it appeared that very large numbers of people had been exposed to the virus: various studies suggested that the exposure rate was well over 50 percent among New York drug users and hemophiliacs and among at least some populations of gay men. (At the time of writing one heard estimates that up to one million people in the United States have been exposed, but such estimates are not very reliable.)

The discovery of the putative virus fitted into theories about the transmission of the disease that saw it originating in Africa, from where it was said to have spread, perhaps via Haiti, to the United States and the rest of the world. (It was speculated that the virus had undergone some sort of genetic shift during the 1970s, or had moved from animals to humans in this period, or had been spread widely with mass migration from the bush into the cities.) Complex theories of transmission have been suggested, such as one in which Cuban troops were seen as the link between Africa and the United States and/or Haiti, and it is true that there are AIDS cases among recent Cuban refugees to the United States, many of whom are gay. It is also possible that there are significant differences between AIDS in tropical and nontropical areas; the very high incidence of AIDS in the Everglades town of Belle Glade, Florida, whose population is largely Caribbean migrant workers, seems to support the arguments of those like Sonnabend, Whiteside and Macleod who claim that environmental and social factors play a role.

Growing information about the nature of the virus, and an understanding of its genetic code, provided the basis for more effective research on curing AIDS, and by early 1985 there were encouraging signs, with trials of various anti-viral drugs, in which, once again, the French researchers seemed to be in the lead.[87] Rock Hudson was only one of many Americans who went to Paris for treatments not available in the United States, leading to bitter criticism of the slowness of the FDA to license the French drug HPA-23. More significant was a feeling, expressed by a number of doctors and researchers, that not sufficient emphasis was being placed by the Public Health Service on developing treatments.[88] Even so, at the time of writing, trials with various anti-viral and immune-modulating drugs were taking place at a number of institutions in both the United States and Europe.

The most important consequence of the viral discoveries, however, was the development of blood tests for exposure to the agent and the possibility of developing a vaccine. The problems with the test were considerable; early tests produced a number of false results, both negative and positive, and their interpretation remains extremely controversial. As it appears that only a minority of those exposed to the virus will go on to develop "full-blown AIDS," it was not clear what a sero-positive test actually means. What did become clear fairly quickly were the explosive implications of making a test generally available and the likelihood that it would reveal that hundreds of thousands of people had been exposed to the virus. As the Office of Technology Assessment pointed out, Secretary Heckler's forecast of a blood test "did not take into account the social implications and ethical dilemmas that would have to be addressed when persons who might be carriers of HTLV-III were identified through a blood test."[89]

In fact, the development of acceptable tests took longer than the six months Heckler had predicted, and it was not until March 1985 that they were licensed by the FDA. The real pressure to develop large-scale testing came because of a desire to control the blood supply, and the full story is better taken up in the context of the next chapter. At the time of writing, the whole question of the provision, medical interpretation and social consequences of HTLV/LAV testing seemed the central issue in AIDS politics, and not only in the United States. One heard quite widely expressed fears that the test would be treated as a marker for homosexuality or drug abuse, and the basis for new forms of social control, with widespread blood screening and enforced discrimination and even quarantine of anyone found sero-positive. If this sounds farfetched, it is worth remembering that in the mid-nineteenth century the British Contagious Diseases Acts required the registration and fortnightly health inspection of prostitutes and "licentious women,"[90] and that an outbreak of plague in San Francisco in the 1900s led to the imposed isolation of Chinatown and proposals to raze the whole district and detain its inhabitants.[91] Even without such projections, it became clear that the implications of such testing were considerable. In a special report for the *New England Journal of Medicine* in early 1985, three AIDS researchers suggested: "It is possible that in the future health and life insurance could be denied or employment could be terminated. States may require compulsory reporting of HTLV-III positive results to their health departments for surveillance purposes. States may require HTLV-III testing before issuing a marriage license. Some people may consider a positive result as presumptive evidence that a never-married man 30 years of age or older is homosexual or that a minority person from the inner city is a narcotics addict."[92] These possibilities are taken up in the following chapter.

CHAPTER FOUR

Fear and Stigma

A joke in bad taste:

"What's the hardest thing about telling your mother you have AIDS?"

"Persuading her you're Haitian."

The most obvious effect of the conceptualization of AIDS as a gay disease was to scapegoat homosexuals. Others, particularly Haitians, have been caught up in the process, but it is gays above all who have borne the brunt of AIDS hysteria. As Dr. Mathilde Krim of the Sloan-Kettering Institute for Cancer Research told a congressional hearing in 1983: "The atmosphere of doom and total helplessness surrounding the problem of AIDS threatens to push us back into a medieval society, complete with the equivalent of colonies of pariahs and lepers and, since homosexuality is not going to disappear from the face of this earth, maybe we will also have colonies of heretics in hiding and an inquisition to find them out."[1]

AIDS has become a way of classifying an entire population. To many people "AIDS" and "homosexuals"—including lesbians—came to be synonymous. "Why aren't there more cases in England?" one well-meaning professor asked me in the States. "Isn't it the land of buggery?" Because of the way in which the disease has been conceived, the social impact of AIDS has become inextricably linked with the problematic and changing nature of homosexuality in Western society. Seymour Kleinberg has claimed:

> Since the late sixties we have all been living in a society at war, mostly with itself, under dire stress, and the sexual behavior of gay men has become the radical exponent of tension and disaffection widespread in all adult life. We have come to symbolize every confusion about sexuality in modern history, and thus, we are objects of fascination and abhorrence.[2]

In the hysteria around AIDS one sees rational fears of disease and contagion mixed in with irrational fears of sexuality and "otherness," which recall the irrationality psychoanalysts have uncovered in anti-Semitism.[3]

Across the United States over the past few years graffiti have symbolized this new and powerful way of stigmatizing homosexuals: "AIDS—America's Ideal Death Sentence" was scrawled across the poster of a gay organization at Stanford University.[4] The various press scares about AIDS have strengthened the association between homosexuals and disease, as in two columns in the Murdoch-owned New York *Post* written by Patrick Buchanan, a former speechwriter for President Nixon who was later hired to work for President Reagan. In these columns, entitled "AIDS Disease: It's Nature Striking Back," Buchanan invoked hepatitis and parasites as well as AIDS to argue that gays should be banned from food handling, donating blood and child care.[5]

It is important to distinguish between genuine fear of a dangerous and little-understood disease and exploitation of such fears to attack gays or other affected groups. To be stigmatized because of illness is hardly confined to people with AIDS; anyone suspected of carrying a disease will experience stigma, and it is a stigma that often extends to non-contagious diseases such as cancer and schizophrenia. It is not accidental that our language brands people as "lepers" or "typhoid Marys." Children born with herpes are the latest group to encounter such prejudice, having been kept out of schools and buses although the risks of contagion are slight.[6] In the case of AIDS the very considerable medical evidence that transmission cannot occur through casual contact seems to be screened out by large numbers of people. As two Danish doctors wrote: "What is most extraordinary about the

AIDS epidemic up to now is the high level of fear in a very large number of people in spite of the relatively small number of cases and deaths so far. Clearly there is no simple correlation between risk and fear."[7]

Examples of such discrimination are legion. They include refusals to serve on juries when the defendant had AIDS, despite assurances from public health officials that AIDS could not be transmitted by mere proximity,[8] the resignation of nurses who refused to care for people with AIDS and a proposal—subsequently withdrawn—by Delta Air Lines to exclude people with AIDS from their flights.[9] In Sydney, Australia, policemen objected to enforcing breathalyzer tests because they might come in contact with someone with AIDS, and in Britain all movement in and out of Chelmsford jail was halted after the prison chaplain died of AIDS, even though authorities acknowledged there was no good medical reason for the move.[10] (In 1984 I was stopped by a policeman in New York City. The cop, having looked through the newspapers I was carrying, which included the latest *New York Native*, asked me, in the usual charming way of New York police, "You don't have AIDS or any of that shit, do you?")

People with AIDS are neglected and abandoned by their friends, relatives and lovers; I know of one case where a mother has refused to have any contact with her two teenage children who live with their father, who has AIDS. There are reports of children with AIDS being abandoned in hospitals by their parents, being refused dental and X-ray services and being excluded from schools.[11] After considerable pressure by Dr. Arye Rubinstein of the Albert Einstein College of Medicine in New York, the state AIDS Institute provided money to establish a day-care center for pediatric AIDS.

In the period of peak hysteria in the United States in mid-1983, San Francisco firemen and police officers started wearing plastic resuscitation devices and rubber gloves when dealing with suspected AIDS cases, there was considerable panic in New York's jails and a call for the total isolation of prisoners with AIDS, and the city of Tulsa insisted on draining and disinfecting a public pool after it was used by a gay group. The Secretary of Health and Human Services had to issue a memorandum reassuring social workers that they ran no risk in interviewing or handling the papers of people with AIDS.[12] In New York City a doctor whose practice included a number of people with AIDS was threatened with eviction from his building; Dr. Jo Sonnabend, with the support of Lambda Legal Defense, a gay rights group, and the state attorney general successfully fought the eviction. This was the first clear-cut case of discrimination based on AIDS to reach the court, although by the end of 1983 Lambda reported that it was being approached with five similar complaints per week.[13] AIDS was invoked as a reason to deny access to gay fathers in several custody cases.[14]

Cases began to surface involving loss of jobs due to AIDS; in the case of two United Airlines stewards a labor arbitrator ruled that the airline could not summarily dismiss people merely because they were diagnosed as having AIDS.[15] There have been reports of dismissals from the armed forces due to AIDS (which was taken as prima facie evidence of homosexuality); in one case naval petty officer John Baskin was diagnosed as having AIDS and transferred to Bethesda Naval Hospital, where doctors recommended an honorable medical discharge. Naval officers made several attempts to circumvent this on the grounds of his assumed homosexuality, although in the end he remained at Bethesda.[16]

The most clear-cut example of job discrimination came from Broward County, which includes Fort Lauderdale, Florida, which at the beginning of 1985 was revealed to have a policy of firing any employee with AIDS. The courts have still to resolve the issue. Other cities and counties have taken opposite positions; in San Francisco the Civil Service Commission has ruled that employees may not refuse to work with someone simply because that person has AIDS.[17]

Least excusable was the quite considerable amount of discrimination and prejudice documented in the health-care sector, for here, above all else, one might expect the greatest degree of rationality. Yet as one doctor wrote: "AIDS is so relentlessly brutal that it has had a nefarious effect on the practice of medicine. According to some reports there have been physicians and medical students—only a few, one is led to believe—who have become so frightened that they have refused to treat AIDS patients."[18]

Surprising numbers of patients with, or suspected of, AIDS

have suffered indignities that go beyond the norm for even the worst of public hospitals; there are too many stories of patients not being fed, of beds not being changed, of abuses from doctors and nurses, to deny that, however real the fears engendered by AIDS, a certain degree of homophobia permeates much of the health system. (The experience of Haitians and drug users with AIDS is undoubtedly even worse. Unfortunately it is extremely difficult to get any documentation of this.) The New York *Times* quoted the story of Ron Doud, a prominent interior designer, as recalled by his lover:

> At Lenox Hill Hospital, Mr. Ruskay said: "He was paying $420 a day for a hospital room, and I couldn't get the porter to clean the room. I had to clean the bath myself." A public affairs official at Lenox Hill said, after talking with Mr. Doud's doctor, that she could not speak to this particular instance. She said the hospital was aware of fear of AIDS among its employees.
>
> When Mr. Ruskay moved Mr. Doud to Phoenix, his mother's home, at her request, "the pilot wanted to throw him off the plane," Ruskay said. At St. Joseph's Medical Center in Phoenix "they really were very afraid to handle him," Mr. Ruskay said. "They weren't even washing him."
>
> Finally when Mr. Doud died, the hospital staff "simply put his body in a plastic bag," Mr. Ruskay said. And the undertakers at the funeral home, "because of their fear all they did was to pour embalming fluid on top of the sheets he was in and close the plastic bag and put him in the casket."[19]

Confirmation that such practices were not isolated examples came from the journal *Emergency Medicine*, which in addition to itemizing such abuses pointed to the way in which medical staff, by using precautions far beyond those which are necessary to avoid contamination by bodily fluids—some staff would wear gloves and masks just to enter an AIDS patient's room—cause psychological and emotional problems for both those with AIDS and their visitors.

Similar problems have been reported in other countries, as in this account from Britain:

> Eventually Richard's temperature soared to 104. Still the doctors would not send him to hospital, despite repeated pleas. Only the intervention of a family friend—a doctor—led to his admission. In

hospital, Richard was immediately put in an isolation ward and visitors had to wear masks. For the first time his illness was treated seriously.

However, when Mrs. Hayes asked to see her son's consultant she had to wait eight hours for a three-minute impatient interview. Then she was told Richard had pneumonia and AIDS, which "should come as no surprise given his lifestyle" . . . Another 24 hours of pressing got Mrs. Hayes a second, even briefer interview . . . I was worried that my other son who shared a bathroom with Richard might get AIDS. The consultant just giggled and said: "Not unless he has been up to the same shenanigans and mixing with the same company." That was the level of his counselling.[20]

Fear and prejudice has not been confined to hospital settings; it has surfaced among dentists, morticians and pathologists. In England there was considerable press coverage at the end of 1983 when a leading pathologist, Professor Keith Simpson, refused to perform an autopsy on a man suspected of dying of AIDS. In New York there were reports of dentists refusing to treat not only people with AIDS but indeed all members of "risk groups," leading the state Health Department to issue guidelines which sought to balance their anxieties with the needs of patients for treatment. In the same way the department was forced to issue guidelines for undertakers in 1983 after a boycott on handling the bodies of those who had died of AIDS, the first time such action ever had to be taken. In Edmonton, Canada, technical staff at the University of Alberta halted a research project concerned with AIDS in the immunology department because of their fears of contamination.[21]

Under such conditions, it is not surprising that some authorities have raised the specter of quarantine, as a way of restricting the spread of AIDS. Quarantine, probably the oldest public health measure, developed from concepts of spiritual uncleanliness; in the Middle Ages it was used against those suffering from either leprosy or the plague, and quarantine of lepers persisted well into the twentieth century. Certain diseases are still regarded as potentially quarantinable, but it is a measure most often used to contain animal diseases. In the case of AIDS it has occasionally been put forward in an extreme form—at the peak of AIDS hysteria in Australia at the end of 1984, letters to the press spoke of confining "all homosexuals" to particular islands—but as a public health measure such draconian measures don't make very much sense. Nevertheless, Dr. Brandt has suggested that quarantine and mass firings of gays were seriously discussed within the Administration: "There was concern that since we didn't know for sure what the limitations of transmissibility were, we should protect against the worst case."[22]

A more limited proposal to quarantine AIDS patients was floated by the Chief of Infectious Diseases in California, Dr. James Chin, who raised the idea at the end of 1983 as a way of dealing with "recalcitrant" AIDS patients. (One assumes he had in mind the various stories about people with AIDS who allegedly were continuing to seek out new sexual partners.) After the acquisition of a copy of his memorandum by the National Gay Rights Advocates, a public-interest legal group, and the resulting press publicity, the idea was quietly dropped.[23] The following year there was a move to include AIDS under the provisions of the quarantine laws of Connecticut following considerable publicity over a New Haven prostitute who was believed to have AIDS. New legislation was passed, but ironically it didn't refer specifically to AIDS, and the prostitute in question was not affected by it, though she was forced off the streets by other prostitutes.[24] In both West Germany and Sweden there were calls for legislation to punish anyone with AIDS who had sexual relations with anyone not already sick, though no such laws were passed.[25] Britain did pass legislation in 1985 allowing local authorities to forcibly keep someone with AIDS in the hospital if he was thought to be a risk to others; the British government apparently found such measures necessary even though their case load was at the time less than 2 percent of the American.[26] With the introduction of blood testing for HTLV/LAV the potential for quarantine on a large scale obviously existed, and new voices surfaced to suggest it.

In most cases of AIDS-related discrimination it was clear that such discrimination was increased because of the homosexuality (or perceived homosexuality) of the sick, and that whole groups, Haitians and hemophiliacs as well as homosexuals, were stigmatized. As the CDC stated in the fall of 1983: "The classification of certain groups as being more closely associated with the disease has been misconstrued by some as to mean these groups are likely to transmit the disease through non-intimate interactions. This view is not justified by available data. Nonetheless, it has been used unfairly as a basis for social and economic discrimination."[27] Thus not only people with AIDS but large numbers of people thought to be at risk for AIDS have experienced the pariah status that AIDS is reintroducing into modern society.

Increasingly, even casual contact with homosexuals was seen as dangerous, especially after reports (rarely followed up when they were retracted) that "routine close contact" could cause AIDS. In San Francisco, it was reported that "when they miss a day of work, some gay employees must hand in medical excuses as proof they don't have AIDS."[28] One heard stories of people refusing to eat in gay-owned restaurants, and *New York* magazine reported that female models avoided male colleagues who "might" be gay.[29] Hostility and fear were particularly marked in the workplace and in prisons, where transmission of the disease was particularly feared; in New Jersey, prison authorities believe there are cases of infection via cell-made tattoo needles. The fear spread into families, as revealed in this letter to Ann Landers:

> My brother and his wife have two preschool girls whom I love as if they were my own . . . I make myself available as a free babysitter, and often spend my day off taking the girls places. My brother and his wife seemed pleased that I enjoy such a close relationship with my nieces, since it benefitted all concerned.
>
> Last week my brother told me as gently as he could that he thought it best that I don't come close to the children until more is known about AIDS. I am no longer welcome in their home.[30]

Luckily Ann Landers pointed out that there was no reputable evidence that close contact could transmit AIDS. Yet as AIDS—and AIDS hysteria—spread, increasing numbers of people faced similar dilemmas in their lives.

The Moral Crusade

Medicine and religion might seem quite distinct to us who live, despite the efforts of the religious right, in a largely secular age, but they have common origins and even after a century of "modern" medicine (often dated from the nineteenth-century work of Pasteur, Roux and Koch on microorganisms) it is all too easy for doctors unable to explain a disease scientifically to fall back on mysticism. There is a long tradition of explaining illness in terms of God's wrath; the Papal Bull of 1348 saw the Black Death as "the pestilence with which God is afflicting the Christian people" (while the doctors of the time explained it as being due to the triple conjunction of Saturn, Jupiter and Mars in the fortieth degree of Aquarius on March 20, 1345).[31] One wonders if current immunological theories will seem as odd several centuries hence.

Six centuries later, God is still perceived as wreaking punishment in much the same way. Perhaps the most extraordinary example of this in regard to AIDS came in an editorial by Dr. James Fletcher which appeared in the *Southern Medical Journal,* an official publication of the Southern Medical Association, in which biblical and scientific sources are melded to claim:

> A logical conclusion is that AIDS is a self-inflicted disorder for the majority of those who suffer from it. For again, without placing reproach upon certain Haitians or hemophiliacs, we see homosexual men reaping not only expected consequences of sexual promiscuity, suffering even as promiscuous heterosexuals the usual venereal diseases, but other unusual consequences as well.
>
> Perhaps, then, homosexuality is not "alternative" behavior at all, but as the ancient wisdom of the Bible states, most certainly pathologic. Indeed from an empirical medical perspective alone current scientific observation seems to require the conclusion that homosexuality is a pathologic condition.[32]

One wonders if the students at the Medical College of Georgia, in Augusta, where Dr. Fletcher teaches, might not get a more scientifically respectable education from medieval astrologers.

The AIDS epidemic in the United States coincided with the politicization of religious fundamentalism that began in the late 1970s and was expressed most clearly in the growth of groups like the Moral Majority. This coincidence was more than accidental; the spread of AIDS was linked to changes in sexual and social life which in turn were part of a general shift in mores which created anxiety among those who saw their traditional values under siege and were attracted to the certainties of the religious right. It is hardly surprising—though it may make one wonder about Christian charity—that the spokespersons for the new right, already prone to cite the acceptance of homosexuality as a sign of the current degeneracy, were quick to seize upon AIDS as fodder for their argument.

Perhaps because most people are not very receptive to attacks on those who are ill and dying, the new right has made use of AIDS less wholeheartedly than one might have expected. Indeed, Jerry Falwell, whose Moral Majority is one of the best-known components of the new right, has denied saying that "AIDS is the wrath of God upon homosexuals," although many reporters claim to have heard him.

Certainly Falwell has invoked AIDS a number of times, most strongly in July 1983, when he used the analogy of brucellosis to advocate the quarantine of homosexuals, acknowledging that this was unlikely because "homosexuals constitute a potent voting bloc and cows do not." He went on to advocate the closing of gay bathhouses and back-room bars, punishment for gays who donated blood and "firm guidelines" for those in contact with high-risk groups.[33] These views were taken up again in mid-1985, when Falwell launched a new campaign "to fight the spread of the deadly AIDS disease."[34] Falwell's views were to be echoed by a number of others, and not only in the United States; in Australia the leader of the local Festival of Light echoed the call for quarantine. In the United States an organization called the American Family Association sought support for a petition to the Surgeon General, Dr. Everett Koop, himself a sympathizer of the new right:

> Dear Family Member:
>   Since AIDS is transmitted primarily by perverse homosexuals your name on my national petition to quarantine all homosexual establishments is crucial to your family's health and security . . . If you want your family's health and security protected, these AIDS-carrying homosexuals must be quarantined immediately . . . These disease-carrying deviants wander the streets unconcerned, possibly making you their next victims. What else can you expect from sex-crazed degenerates but selfishness?[35]

Subsequent mailings from the Moral Majority also advocated excluding homosexuals from food handling.

Other religious-right groups made similar proposals. In the summer of 1983 a group called the Pro-Family Christian Coalition sought to prohibit the Reno Gay Rodeo from taking place, claiming it would cause a health crisis and using, once again, the argument that "close contact" could be contagious. A full-page advertisement in Nevada's papers was headed "AIDS Alert," but the agenda of the group was a broader homophobia; one of the group—a minister—was quoted as saying: "I think we should do what the Bible says and cut their throats." After considerable press controversy and a large public forum the local county commission refused to act against the rodeo.[36]

Some religious zealots have sought to "convert" homosexuals —both to Christianity and to heterosexuality—by playing on the fear of AIDS, and in one case a group entered the AIDS ward in San Francisco General Hospital under the guise of delivering toiletries and began to "witness" (i.e., proselytize).[37] Most involved in the work of sexual conversion is a New York-based group known as Aesthetic Realists, who claim to possess a "cure" for homosexuality and who invaded a panel on AIDS at a meeting of the New York Academy of Sciences in 1983 to promote their philosophies.[38]

Moralistic attacks inspired by AIDS have clear implications for the behavior of governments. In debates over decriminalizing homosexual behavior—still a crime in almost half the American states, in Israel, in New Zealand and in several Australian states— or in arguments over including homosexuals within the ambit of anti-discrimination laws, AIDS is increasingly invoked. Anti-gay doctors were paraded before the Virginia House of Delegates in 1984 to oppose the repeal of the state's anti-sodomy law, and in Duluth, Minnesota, voters repealed a human rights law in which fear of AIDS was an issue.[39] When the Australian state of New South Wales decriminalized homosexuality in 1984, a Liberal Party front-bencher attacked homosexuals as responsible for AIDS, adding: "I hope they do not find a cure for it."[40] AIDS was invoked in a ferocious campaign spearheaded by the New Zealand Salvation Army in 1985 to prevent that country decriminalizing homosexuality.

The best examples of the confluence of religious, medical and political stigmatization due to AIDS occurred in Texas, where the "Dallas Doctors against AIDS" have invoked the disease to sponsor legislation that would overturn a 1982 District Court decision *(Baker* v. *Wade)* which declared the state's anti-sodomy law unconstitutional because it infringed the right to privacy. (At the same time the Amarillo district attorney invoked AIDS in an unsuccessful argument against the decision before a U.S. Court of Appeals.) Using both medical and religious evidence, and equally careless with both, the group has been active in lobbying against gay rights. (They also supported a move to ban the gay student group of Texas A. and M. University.) In the campaign that led up to a referendum in Houston in January 1985 on the city's policy of non-discrimination against gays in employment, the threat of AIDS was frequently invoked: "The medical problems associated with homosexuality," began one pamphlet, "impact on us all. Since the diseases of one segment of society are often transmitted to others, it is in the collective interest to inhabit as disease-free a society as is possible."[41] The anti-gay position was upheld by a large majority, and AIDS clearly played a role.[42]

Prejudice against homosexuals sparked by AIDS ranges from the trivial, such as Joan Collins' attacks on homosexual "moral laxity,"[43] to the serious, as in reports of violence in which AIDS is the spark:

> They were chasing the gays with sticks and stones and shouting "unclean." Hate was in their voices. Their eyes were bloodshot. They were about 20 of them, all teenagers. They were macho and they were drunk.
>
> "Faggots got AIDS. Faggots got AIDS," they screamed, hitting gay men and lesbian women on the shoulders and legs with sticks.
>
> A big hulk of a kid with slow eyes threw a rock at a lesbian.
>
> "You're diseased," he said.
>
> It was a scene of gang brutality out of the movie *Clockwork Orange.*
>
> It happened in San Francisco, in bucolic Sigmund Stern Grove, on a Sunday afternoon last summer when a homophobic rat pack attacked a picnic sponsored by the gay Catholic group Dignity.[44]

In another incident in San Francisco the AIDS Foundation received an anxious call from someone who had helped beat up a

man with AIDS—and was worried about his chances of infection.
Other reports suggest a marked increase in anti-gay violence
since AIDS.[45]

Stigma and Non-gays

It is easy to pile up accounts of prejudice, discrimination, even
violence. Most significant is the cumulative effect of AIDS on the
social position of those groups associated with the disease. "AIDS
has acted as a snowplow," said Katy Taylor of the New York City
Commission on Human Rights, "pushing up and throwing into
relief the homophobia and heterosexism that exist."[46] But groups
other than homosexuals have felt the effects of what in a quite
different context Hunter Thompson called fear and loathing.

Least affected, perhaps, have been hemophiliacs, who have
been exposed in large numbers to the HTLV/LAV virus through
their use of Factor VIII, a product used to help clotting and made
from the plasma of large numbers of donors. (Plasma is the fluid
from which the red cells have been removed.) The real problem
for hemophiliacs is that fear of infection will lead them not to
take the blood products they require to help control bleeding;
there are reports of a considerable drop in the use of Factor VIII,
which could put hemophiliacs at grave risk. The subsidiary problem is that fear of disease will expose them to the same sorts of
stigma experienced by other risk groups. Speaking before a congressional hearing, Alan Brownstein, executive director of the
National Hemophilia Foundation, testified:

> In many respects excess fear of AIDS has presented more risk of
> death and disability than AIDS itself . . . How sad it was the other
> day when I learned from one of our chapters that their hemophilia
> camp enrollment was down 75% this year because parents of hemo-
> philiac children had fear of their children being exposed to other
> children with hemophilia. We are now beginning to get reports of
> instances in the workplace where fear of contracting AIDS is ex-
> pressed by those working side by side with hemophiliacs.[47]

Inquiries to chapters of the National Hemophilia Foundation
uncovered several cases of discrimination based on fear of AIDS,

and I have been told stories involving co-workers and students. (As evidence of the possibility of heterosexual transmission mounted, this introduced a new fear for hemophiliacs, who were being advised to follow "safe sex" guidelines even with their wives.) Just as fear of AIDS may be forcing some gays back into the closet, so some hemophiliacs are said to be more inclined to hide their illness than before. Even so, it is clear that the social position of hemophiliacs is rather different from that of the other affected groups; under questioning at the congressional hearings, Brownstein said: "hemophiliacs do not represent any particular group that has been stigmatized or against which there has been discrimination; we have received a very positive response from all the organizations we have been dealing with."[48]

In some ways even Haitians have been invisible victims of the epidemic. While journalists and researchers have rushed to examine every conceivable aspect of gay male life and how it has been affected by the epidemic, Haitians have attracted far less attention. This has been true even in New York, where there are significant numbers of Haitians with AIDS, as there are in Newark, Miami and Montreal. (Neither the New York *Times* nor *The Village Voice*, which have carried a number of "in-depth" stories on AIDS, has examined the impact on the Haitian community.) In part this neglect is due to the attitude of the Haitian communities themselves and their resistance to seeing themselves as at risk for AIDS. In part, though, it is a reflection of the low socioeconomic status of the half million or so Haitians in the United States and their lack of access to power or the media; most patients are poor, not well versed in English, and recent arrivals, in many cases illegal immigrants from one of the poorest and most brutal countries in the Caribbean. (There are parallels, though on a smaller scale, in the experience of Africans and Caribbeans with AIDS in Western Europe.)

Ever since the first cases of AIDS were diagnosed among Haitians in the United States in mid-1982, there has been controversy about whether to regard the group as a whole as being at risk for AIDS. Opponents of such a classification claimed that a large percentage of Haitians were, in fact, either homosexual or drug users, and that the CDC had ignored this because of a lack of interviewers skilled in Creole and aware of Haitian taboos.

"There is no scientific basis to classify a country or a people as a risk group," insisted Dr. Laine of the Haitian Medical Association. "If AIDS was a Haitian disease I think the Haitian population would already have been wiped out."[49] In response, the CDC insisted that the incidence of cases among Haitians that do not fit other categories far exceeds that among the population at large, and an explanation is required. This argument was bolstered by findings of quite widespread AIDS within Haiti.

Cases of AIDS in Haiti are believed to date back to the late 1970s and now number at least several hundred, though there are no reliable estimates. Information from Haiti is sketchy and obscured by poor medical services and political pressure to minimize the incidence of AIDS. However, there is considerable evidence that the majority of cases are neither drug users nor men with homosexual histories; the latest figures suggest that a third of known cases are women.[50] As in Africa re-using disposable needles and even contact with monkeys have been hypothesized as means of transmission. (One suggestion was that African monkeys, possible carriers of AIDS, were imported into Haiti and kept as pets in male brothels.[51])

This is not to deny the strong degree of racism in some of the claims that AIDS was a Haitian disease.[52] Certainly the effect of such claims on Haiti's tourist industry was catastrophic; one estimate is that the number of American tourists fell from 70,000 in the winter of 1981–82 to 10,000 a year later.[53] Alarmed at the effect of the connection to AIDS, the Haitian government responded with some scapegoating of its own, blaming the disease on homosexual tourists from the United States and local prostitutes. (In fact, the popularity of Haiti as a tourist mecca for homosexuals has been somewhat exaggerated in the media.) The Haitian government instituted a severe crackdown on homosexuals, proclaiming that "Haiti, under the direction of its president, Jean-Claude Duvalier, would not become the brothel of the Caribbean,"[54] and the Haitian ambassador to the United States wrote a letter to the *New England Journal of Medicine* protesting "the severe injustice" of "attributing the origins of AIDS to Haitians."[55] Under pressure, officials began to remove Haitians from the "risk group" classification. In August 1983 the New York City Department of Health ceased to so classify Haitians, and in

November Haitians were removed from the official "at risk" list of Ontario. In April 1985 the CDC finally dropped Haitians from their list of "groups at high risk," with the comment that "the Haitians were the only risk group that were identified because of who they were rather than what they did,"[56] and Canada's Laboratory Centre for Disease Control soon followed suit. The same comment, of course, could be made about the CDC's insistence on using "homosexual" as a noun rather than an adjective.

Whether there are significant differences between the Haitian cases and those belonging to other groups is not yet clear. (One study in New York City has suggested that the rate of HTLV-III sero-positivity among Haitian immigrants is much lower than among gay men, hemophiliacs and intravenous drug users; "from these data it does not appear that being of Haitian extraction by itself, in isolation from other risk factors, increases the relative risk of being exposed to HTLV-III."[57]) What has been distinctive about the classification of Haitians is that, unlike other groups, they protested their classification as a risk group, and even if without much clout domestically, their status as a nationality lent a certain support to their claim.

The official juggling of categories did nothing to alter the everyday discrimination AIDS has meant for Haitians in North America. Again, this is not as well documented as in the case of gays, but considerable anecdotal evidence exists. There are frequent reports from Miami, New York and Montreal of Haitians losing housing and jobs, especially in service industries, because of AIDS, and in 1984 the New York City Human Rights Commission received several complaints of this nature. The Haitian Coalition on AIDS was organized in March 1983 in New York and seeks to provide both services and information on AIDS for Haitians in New York. It receives some money from the state AIDS Institute, and has cooperated with other AIDS groups through the city's Inter-agency Task Force. Much of its activity has been aimed at persuading the public not to regard Haitians as a high-risk group for AIDS.[58] But unlike a group such as the Gay Men's Health Crisis, it cannot call on an affluent and politically sophisticated community for assistance, a contrast drawn with some bitterness by Haitian leaders who see the gay movement as very powerful and concerned only with itself.

One consequence of the poverty and illegal status of many Haitians—many are "boat people," denied refuge by an Administration that recognizes tyranny only when it waves a red flag—has been limited access to medical services and information. Even with the removal of the classification—most blood banks have continued to exclude Haitians from giving blood—discrimination remains. "It's more insidious than a person who has been fired or a Haitian who is brought into an emergency room and people get into their space suits," said one Haitian in Miami. "In the minds of a lot of people, Haitians and AIDS go together."[59]

The Fear of "Bad Blood"

AIDS really captured public attention when it became clear that it could be transmitted in blood and thus could strike anyone who might need a blood transfusion. The metaphorical weight of a disease believed to be not only spread through sexual contact but also passed on to "the innocent" through "bad blood" is enormous. The idea that the nation's blood supply was contaminated became a twentieth-century version of poisoning the wells (for which Jews were put to death during the Black Death), and with it was introduced a distinction between those who are somehow responsible for their disease and those whom Robin Henig in the New York *Times* termed "innocent bystanders."[60]

Fears connected with the blood supply were central to the great media panic of 1983; the right-wing weekly *Human Events* wrote: "There has even been speculation . . . that AIDS victims could deliberately contaminate the blood supply, thus spreading the condition into the general population, as a way to make certain that there is increased pressure on the federal government to find a cure."[61] There is a particular mystique to blood: "The blood is the life," says the Old Testament (Deuteronomy 12:23), and the doctrine of transubstantiation echoes this in Christianity. The prevalence of myths about vampires, the ritual bleedings in many cultures, the ceremonies of mingling blood in brotherhood, are all testimony to the universality of this mystique. That transfusions of blood could be used to save lives was first proposed in the seventeenth century, but it was only after

Karl Landsteiner's discovery of mutually incompatible blood types that it became a safe procedure. By now something like three million people a year receive transfusions in the United States, and the collection, storage and supply of blood has become big business.

Despite the popular belief that the American blood supply depends mainly on commercial transactions, almost all the whole blood used in the United States is now donated voluntarily, about half of it through the Red Cross, the rest through various community blood banks.[62] Commercially purchased blood is, however, largely the source of blood plasma, and about 80 percent of the world's plasma is collected in the United States.[63] Blood is not collected for money in Britain or Australia—when antibodies to HTLV-III were found in one-third of hemophiliacs tested in Britain, it was assumed this was because of the use of Factor VIII imported from America[64]—but in most Third World countries, as well as in such social democracies as Sweden and West Germany, payment is the rule.

The risks of contracting AIDS from transfusion as distinct from the use of plasma products are minimal; according to the testimony of Dr. Joseph Bove of the Yale–New Haven Hospital in 1983, the chances were equal to that of getting malaria and two hundred times less than the possibility of dying from an appendectomy.[65] Nonetheless, the number of recorded cases in the United States has passed the hundred mark, and the fear of such cases has engendered enormous publicity and several lawsuits against hospitals where transfusions took place. (One case, Kushnick versus Cedars-Sinai Hospital in Los Angeles, involving the parents of a four-year-old boy, has received national publicity.)

Once possible transmission through blood donations was suggested it was not long before there were moves to debar members of all "risk groups" from giving blood. In January 1983 the National Hemophilia Foundation called for such a measure, to exclude male homosexuals, IV users and those who had recently resided in Haiti. This move came ten days after a heated meeting of interested groups sponsored by the CDC at which representatives of the gay movement had urged the blood banks to "screen blood rather than donors" by using tests for hepatitis-B core antibodies and another, as yet experimental marker.[66]

The concern of the gay movement was clearly to prevent a general scapegoating of all gay men, but in the absence of a simple test for an AIDS agent, screening donors was much easier than screening blood. The Stanford University blood bank began using a T-cell test on blood donations in mid-1983, despite controversy about what the results meant.[67] One of the major plasmapheresis centers, Alpha Therapeutics, announced that it was excluding homosexuals, drug addicts and Haitians from selling plasma "because frankly we don't have anything else to offer at this time," and other blood-collecting agencies followed suit. In May 1983 France banned the importation of American plasma.[68]

The gay movement feared not only that such policies could create extremely dangerous stereotypes, appealing as they did to primitive fears of "bad blood," but that they were demonstrably unfair—for, given the prevailing assumptions about transmission, many homosexuals could not reasonably be classed as high-risk—and probably ineffective. Indeed, as the stigma of AIDS forced many back into the closet it was possible that a blanket exclusion of gay men would have an effect opposite to what was intended, leading some to donate blood, especially at the workplace, to dispel suspicion that they were homosexual. (This has been suggested as a particular problem in the armed forces, where blood donations are often required.) Only draconian investigations of private lives, it was argued, could enforce such a policy. In return for most blood banks adopting a policy of combining dissuasion with a number of face-saving devices—such as allowing blood to be donated during a company drive while stipulating privately that it should be used for research purposes only—leaders of the gay movement urged gay men not to donate blood. (The four makers of Factor VIII also agreed not to use plasma purchased in cities with high rates of AIDS.) In March 1983 the Public Health Service recommended that "as a temporary measure" members of groups at risk for AIDS—they were careful to specify "sexually active homosexual or bisexual men with multiple partners"—should not donate blood.[69]

Fear of contracting AIDS through blood transfusions was hardly allayed by these measures. Blood donations in the United

States fell 6 to 10 percent in 1983, although there was no conceivable way that giving blood could put one at risk for AIDS. (The following year this fear was still cited as a reason for the persistent shortage of blood donors;[70] when a similar shortage occurred in Britain, Prince Charles donated blood with a corresponding burst of publicity.) There were several attempts to establish private blood cooperatives in an attempt to avoid "contaminated blood"; a local case of AIDS triggered off such a move in the Roslyn County Club Association in suburban Long Island, whose members argued there wouldn't be many homosexuals "in a group like ours."[71] In both Florida and New Hampshire legislation has been proposed (unsuccessfully) that would make it an offense for members of any "risk group" to donate blood.

Probably the greatest hysteria in connection with blood and AIDS occurred in Australia at the end of 1984, following the deaths of three babies in the state of Queensland after transfusions with blood from a donor who turned out to be HTLV-III positive. The story led to national headlines for a month, was raised in the federal election campaign of December and led the Queensland government to seriously consider charging the donor with manslaughter. This has not happened, but Queensland did pass emergency legislation making it a criminal offense to give false information about one's eligibility to give blood, and there was a national campaign encouraging women to donate. The story received considerable international coverage, and was seen as "the crucial trigger" for a similarly nasty scare in Britain.[72]

Throughout 1984 there was feverish competition between American and several European firms to develop a reliable blood test for exposure to LAV/HTLV, and the FDA licensed such a test in March 1985 (testing had already been taking place for research purposes). As already indicated, the widespread use of tests created considerable doubt and fear. Dr. Frank Young, the Commissioner of Food and Drugs, warned that the test was by no means perfect.[73] Public health officials feared that people who felt themselves at risk might seek to donate blood as a means of being tested for "the AIDS virus," thus leading people to donate blood who would otherwise have stayed away, and the federal government made $12 million available to establish alternative

test sites to discourage the use of the blood banks for this purpose.
(The money was allocated via state health departments—but had
to be spent within ninety days, after which the sites would be
either discontinued or maintained by the states, which several,
most particularly California, have already indicated they will do.
The first results from blood banks suggested a very low level of
HTLV-III among those who volunteered to give blood.) Even so,
there remained considerable doubt about the efficacy and meaning of the tests and about the sort of information and counseling
that would be made available to those whose blood tested positive.

So great were the fears, both of false results and of their consequences, that various gay groups urged people not to take the
test except for research purposes, and Lambda Legal Defense
sought an injunction on the grounds that the test had a high error
rate.[74] The Pentagon decreed that all positive test results on
military installations must be reported to "the respective service
military health agency responsible for medical evaluation and
counseling of reactive donors," and subsequently ordered tests
for all recruits.[75] On balance, however, most public health officials seemed convinced that the test was justified—provided it
was used only for screening blood and not as a sole basis for either
diagnosis or characterizing people as members of a particular
group. The simplest way of ensuring this was outlined in a letter
from the Philadelphia Health Commissoner to Secretary Heckler:

> Blood banks should not be allowed to give donors the results of
> the HTLV-III antibody test, nor should they be allowed to maintain
> a deferral list of individuals with a positive test. In fact, the donated
> blood should be processed so that HTLV-III antibody positive blood
> can be discarded in such a fashion that no one knows who the
> positive individuals are.
>
> We must realize that we are at the *beginning* of the AIDS prob-
> lem, and we should not squander our resources or money doing
> things that actually benefit no one. The monies that would be spent
> on alternative testing sites should be used for future research, treat-
> ment of patients and educational efforts for all segments of soci-
> ety.[76]

Confidentiality

The concern was not only that the tests might be misleading, with unfortunate results for the individual and maybe even the blood supply, but that disclosure of results could have extremely dangerous consequences. It is common practice for blood banks to maintain lists of "deferred donors," and there was considerable concern at reported suggestions for a federal registrar of all "HTLV-III antibody positives." Fears were expressed that such a list would become a "surrogate marker" for homosexuality or drug use—"essentially what you would have is a list of sexually active gay men," said Rodger McFarlane of the Gay Men's Health Crisis[77]—but even more disturbing was the way individual doctors might handle such results. What if, for example, an HTLV-III test became a requirement for health insurance and/or employment, even though a positive result is not, by itself, proof of AIDS? To deal with this problem, at least one state, California, has adopted legislation that would make public disclosure of test results a misdemeanor.

The furor over blood testing and AIDS highlighted one of the main concerns of the gay movement—namely, confidentiality. Long before the test was available for use by blood banks, testing was taking place as part of research programs, and in general the need for epidemiological research and surveillance opened up possibilities for greater governmental intrusion into private life, a particularly touchy issue given the illegal status of drugs, prostitution and often homosexual behavior itself. "Never before," stated the Confidentiality Subcommittee of the New York City AIDS Network, "have so many gay men so willingly offered so much information about themselves and their lifestyles to government and private researchers." The subcommittee went on to point out:

> Suppose the FBI or the Drug Enforcement Agency were investigating drug trafficking and demanded information from the Centers for Disease Control on drug use by gay men, Haitians and intravenous drug users. Can we be certain that the CDC would not

share this information? Would subjects even be notified that the FBI
had requested this information? If so, would the subjects be able to
stop one agency of the federal government from providing information to another?[78]

Documented cases of breaches of confidentiality have occurred, as when the CDC turned over lists of AIDS patients to
public health departments and the New York Blood Center, or
when a list of people undergoing treatment for AIDS symptoms
was circulated among Seattle policemen. (There has been considerable argument as to whether declaring AIDS a notifiable disease requires the provision of names as distinct from the incidence of cases to public health authorities.) Questions of
confidentiality became increasingly important to gay groups after the controversies over blood donations began in early 1983.
In her testimony to Congressman Weiss's subcommittee in August, Virginia Apuzzo of the National Gay Task Force complained of the CDC's unwillingness to negotiate with gay groups
on the issue, and it took protracted lobbying to get any resolution
of the question. The following year the CDC announced new
safeguards on confidentiality of research findings, which would
prevent surveillance information from being made available to
anyone but public health agencies, and Dr. Brandt urged that a
model consent form be used by federally funded researchers.
Only in a few places, however, such as California and the city of
New York (whose Health Commissioner, Dr. David Sencer, took
a firm line on protecting confidentiality), did governments offer
any real protection against misuse of research findings.[79]

In some ways concern over confidentiality seems a particularly
American preoccupation; nowhere else is the right to privacy so
enshrined as a legal principle. On the other hand, similar problems have arisen elsewhere, and the potential abuses by governments, doctors and employers are the same. Thus in Britain there
was considerable argument over whether to make AIDS notifiable in a way that identified patients by name. (Ultimately the
government decided not to do so.) One consideration, as Cindy
Patton has pointed out in the American context, is that fear of
being listed may well make people hesitant to go to a doctor (as is
almost certainly the case for some Haitian immigrants who fear

discovery of their illegal status).[80] As with other aspects of the epidemic, the problem of how much information should be made available for research and surveillance raises difficult questions about the balance between individual rights and the public good.

CHAPTER FIVE

The Gay Community's Response

A plague is a formidable enemy and is armed with terrors that
every man is not sufficiently fortified to resist or prepared to
stand the shock against.

—Daniel Defoe,
A Journal of the Plague Years

"Among many gay men," wrote Seymour Kleinberg, "there is a
deep sense of shame and humiliation about AIDS. For some, to be
actively engaged becomes cathartic; work is a solace from anxiety and to make common cause with one's own a unique com-
fort."[1] As Kleinberg and others suggest, the idea of community
becomes central in the response to AIDS: "AIDS action has already begun to bolster and affirm the quality of gay life. It has
helped mobilize and involve many individuals who had previously seen themselves as apart from community concerns. And it
has once again shown lesbians and gay men the benefits of working together on a common cause."[2]

The term "community" has become ubiquitous in contemporary rhetoric; it is applied to any group, no matter how loosely
constituted, so that people speak of "the health-care community" or even "the straight community," as if the vast majority
who behave heterosexually are thereby linked together in a way
comparable to the Amish or the inhabitants of Chinatown. The
constant invocation of "the gay community—sometimes the "lesbian and gay community," which begins to point to the divisions
involved—hides the reality that even today most people who

engage in homosexual sex have little sense of being part of such a community, and may, indeed, be actively hostile toward "dykes" and "fags." Thus, for example, talk of "the gay community" acting to close sex venues overlooks the fact that many of the men who use baths or back rooms—not to mention some of the owners and operators—have no sense of belonging to the community being invoked. (This leads to attacks by some on "gay leaders" for failing to influence people who would reject their leadership if they knew about it.)

Nonetheless, the idea of community has powerful political and psychological implications, and has undoubtedly been strengthened by the AIDS crisis. Writing in a Los Angeles bar paper, the gay entrepreneur Buck Rogers spoke for many when he said: "Notice that I said Mormons take care of their own—they are not going to take care of us, they don't even like us, neither will any other section of society—except the gay community itself. It's up to us because no one else will bother."[3] It is this sense of being ignored by the larger society that has motivated thousands of gay men, and lesser but important numbers of lesbians, to develop communal organizations, hot lines and fund-raising events to meet the challenges of AIDS.

The rapidity of the gay response was possible because of a decade of organization-building among American homosexuals, involving national political groups, such as the National Gay Task Force and the National Gay Rights Advocates, local political groups like the Alice B. Toklas and Harvey Milk Gay Democratic Clubs in San Francisco or the Whitman/Stein Democratic and Log Cabin Republican Clubs in Washington, as well as literally thousands of communal groups offering social, religious, cultural, sporting and business activities. Almost all major American cities now possess extensive gay organizations catering to most conceivable interests, and this is increasingly true for other Western countries. There are gay marching bands and lesbian choruses, gay newspapers, publishers and bookshops, an international gay church (the Metropolitan Community Church), and in 1982 the first International Gay Games (known as the Gay Olympics until the title was denied by a court injunction sought by the American Olympics Committee) took place in San Francisco. The annual Gay/Lesbian Pride parades in most large cities are the most visible manifestations of this new gay visibility, and the largest, in San Francisco, draws several hundred thousand people onto the streets.[4] Although AIDS activities tapped new energies and leadership, they also built upon existing organizations and appealed to the existing rhetoric of gay community and solidarity.

The best-known organization to come out of the AIDS epidemic is New York's Gay Men's Health Crisis, which was founded in September 1981 when forty men, most of whom already had friends or lovers with the disease, met in the apartment of writer Larry Kramer. The early focus of GMHC was on education and fund-raising for research; several well-attended public forums on AIDS were organized, involving doctors researching and treating the disease, and the following spring the organization held its first major fund-raiser at a New York discotheque.

Within its first year the organization raised over $150,000, of which $50,000 was allocated to research (the largest amount going to a prospective study of gay men at St. Luke's–Roosevelt Hospital, thus anticipating the National Institute of Health's funding by two years), printed 300,000 health recommendation brochures and almost 100,000 copies of two newsletters and established a hot line to provide information and referrals to doctors.[5] In its second year, GMHC was able to provide financial assistance for the purchase of medical equipment at New York's Community Health Project, the National Gay Task Force's 800-number hot line and the newly established Federation of AIDS-Related Organizations (FARO). It also began major educational programs aimed at health professionals.

In mid-1984 GMHC moved to a two-story headquarters in the Chelsea district, painted in industrial gray, where it is the center of an expanding range of activities and a growing professional and volunteer staff. "We started off trying to find services to which we could refer people with AIDS," one of the founders of GMHC told me. "We discovered we had to create them ourselves." As Rodger McFarlane, executive director for two years between mid-1983 and mid-1985, said: "We were forced to take care of ourselves because we learned that if you have certain diseases, certain lifestyles, you can't expect the same services as other parts of society . . . We're there primarily to handhold and troubleshoot, and help these people get some control over their lives."[6]

To do this GMHC developed both therapeutic and practical support services for people with AIDS, most particularly through crisis counseling and a buddy system whereby someone is assigned to spend time with an AIDS patient as his companion, confidant and helper. This is an important experience for "buddies" as well as for those who are sick: "I felt compassion for these guys' loneliness and despair," said one volunteer. "I heard that they had been neglected by their family and friends, even other gays, and that they had been treated badly by some hospital personnel."[7] By early 1985 there were some 300 people working as either buddies or crisis counselors, some of them women and an occasional straight man. More basic services are provided, such as assistance in dealing with the welfare bureaucracy. (The city of New York's first real contribution to GMHC was to pay the salary of GMHC's financial assistance coordinator.) Such work can be complex and time-consuming, given the bureaucratic labyrinth of the welfare system:

> Take the case of a Haitian woman who contracted AIDS and was denied a home and access to her three children by her family. Her hospital wanted to discharge her to a shelter, but GMHC intervened, prolonging her stay for over four weeks until all the paperwork needed to get her a place to live and money to live with was completed. A single volunteer committed herself to the case, and she didn't rest until mother and children were reunited.[8]

Many of the people helped by GMHC are not gay, which is also true of some of the volunteers. But as the name suggests, GMHC sees itself as very much a gay organization, "a family of healers," to quote one of the directors. (It is interesting that its house organ, *The Volunteer,* carries a note warning that mention of an individual in its pages does not necessarily imply anything about his or her sexual orientation.) Inevitably, such a large and rich organization—for the past several years it has spent close to $800,000 a year, of which only 20 percent came from government funds—has had to adopt a bureaucratic structure, and it is seen by some as overly cautious politically, too conservative in its attitude toward medicine and sometimes too inclined to see people with AIDS as no more than victims in need of professional guidance. (These feelings have spawned several smaller groups, such as Wipe Out AIDS, which has concentrated on "positive alternatives" to mainstream medicine.) In response, the men who established and administered GMHC say that they found a vacuum which had to be filled and that dealing with so much money and government agencies requires a certain professional expertise. This position was not established without considerable rancor, discussed at length in Kramer's play *The Normal Heart*, with Kramer himself pushing for what Rodger McFarlane terms the prophetic as against the pastoral role.

One of the major problems that neither GMHC nor the city of New York has been able to address satisfactorily is housing, which is critical for many people with AIDS (long illness often leading to a loss of income and hence housing). Nursing homes are forbidden to accept patients with infectious diseases, and most residential hotels won't. Housing has become the major preoccupation of another volunteer group, the AIDS Resource Center, which in 1985 was able to establish the first housing facilities for people with AIDS in New York. (The city's welfare workers had been struggling to meet the need through YMCAs and single rooms, though all too often people were discharged from hospitals to city shelters, which in New York are Dickensian facilities. As Rodger McFarlane observed, probably without too much exaggeration, sending someone with compromised immunity to a shelter is "as good as homicide."[9])

Historically, New York, while possessing a large and visible gay population, has not had a strong gay movement. Although the movement seemed strong in the early 1970s, when the Gay Activists Alliance mobilized large numbers to take part in direct action, New York seemed unable to develop the sort of organized gay political activity that exists in San Francisco, Los Angeles, Washington or Houston, although it was the seat of both the National Gay Task Force and the largest gay legal organization, Lambda Legal Defense. This has begun to change in the 1980s, in part due to the impact of GMHC, which touched thousands of gay men, predominantly white and middle class, and brought them into the organized gay community. Above all, the enormous success of GMHC in tapping gay money has boosted gay communal organization across the board; in April 1983 GMHC organized a sold-out benefit at Madison Square Garden attended by 18,000 people, and later that year another function—a benefit at food writer Craig Claiborne's house—raised $100,000. This is more than most gay organizations spend in a lifetime. The example of GMHC has inspired other organizations, and over the last few years New York has seen a growth of gay communal activity and fund-raising to a level previously found only in Los Angeles, symbolized in mid-1984 by the purchase from the city of a building to serve as a Gay and Lesbian Community Center and David Rothenberg's campaign for the City Council in 1985.

One of the unique features of GMHC, a reflection of both its origin before the number of AIDS cases had reached present levels and the wealth it has been able to generate, was its commitment to raise money directly for research. In most places the need for education and basic services has made any question of funding research a luxury, although in Chicago the Howard Brown Memorial Clinic, a gay community organization, offers grants for pilot projects. As David Harris of AID Atlanta argued:

> Many people in our community feel that whatever money is raised should automatically go to research. Whereas the sentiment is well-intentioned, it is naive. To believe that the few thousand dollars that we raise in our community can even partially finance such a massive research effort is to ignore the facts . . . Your money can better be used in lobbying efforts, such as the FARO lobbying project which is mandated to lobby for $100 million for AIDS research.[10]

Raising private money for medical research is an American tradition, and groups like the American Heart Association and Cancer Society sponsor a great deal of research. This model was adopted by the AIDS Medical Foundation, whose chair, Dr. Mathilde Krim, an interferon researcher, has been able to use her extensive medical and political contacts to do some major fund-raising and draw attention to the epidemic. The AMF has been able to underwrite a number of research projects, but even it has felt pressure to provide some of the services not made available by government, and in 1985 was raising funds to create an AIDS Health Care Facility to help with testing, treatment and information.[11] (As a consequence of its research activities the AIDS Medical Foundation also became involved in helping Americans with AIDS go to Paris for treatment.)

As the crisis expanded there was both a growth of volunteer organizations and increasing recognition that only a combination of communal and government efforts could provide the very complex welfare and educational services that AIDS demanded. (By 1984 even GMHC was finding that its ability to raise money could not keep pace with the increasing demand for services.) In some cities there already existed an organizational basis for AIDS education and support work, as in the Whitman Walker Clinic in Washington, D.C., the Fenway Clinic in Boston, the Howard Brown Memorial Clinic in Chicago and the Gay and Lesbian Community Services Center in Los Angeles. These two themes, communal organization and government support, came together most clearly in San Francisco, where the AIDS Foundation and the Shanti Project together provide the most comprehensive range of AIDS services anywhere, backed by considerable city support and money.

The AIDS Foundation grew out of the Kaposi's Sarcoma Research and Education Foundation, which was established in early 1982 with close ties to the University of California and San Francisco General Hospital. For a short time it sought to become a national organization; it has evolved into the central body for AIDS education and lobbying work in the city, with a large paid staff and considerable government contracts. (It also operates a certain number of direct services for people with AIDS.) Its main focus is on public awareness and information, and here it can claim to be in the vanguard:

> There have been many firsts over the past two years: the first MUNI and BART informational campaigns [these are public transport systems serving the Bay Area]; the first TV public service announcements; the first educational efforts in commercial sex establishments; the definition of and education around safe sex; the successful formation of community AIDS prevention partnership; the first major random-sample survey of the city's gay/bisexual male community and much more.[12]

In the *de facto* division of responsibilities in San Francisco, the Shanti Project is responsible for most of the direct contact with people with AIDS. Shanti existed before the epidemic; it was founded in 1974 by Dr. James Garfield to provide peer support for the terminally ill, but a decade later reconstituted itself to deal exclusively with AIDS. Shanti provides the kind of direct services and counseling that GMHC offers, but with considerably more support from the city government. Shanti volunteers— over one hundred at any given time—are put through a vigorous training, in the course of which unsuitable applicants are winnowed out; the training reflects the experiential bias of Californian psychotherapy.[13] The volunteers work both as counselors and in practical support, akin to GMHC's "buddy" system. Volunteers will go to enormous lengths; one, a lawyer, accompanied (on his own funds) his client to Manila for therapy, and had to call back to San Francisco for instructions on inserting feeding tubes when his client's condition worsened. Shanti-trained counselors work directly on the AIDS ward and in the clinic at San Francisco General Hospital.

It is through Shanti that San Francisco offers a housing program for people with AIDS; the city has made several houses available and they are administered by Shanti. (Their location is kept secret, which says something about the stigma attached to AIDS.) Home-care services are also provided through Shanti, and by all accounts have been much more successful than an attempt to provide similar services in New York through a contract with the Red Cross, a program which was remarkably ineffective due to lack of outreach and bureaucratic red tape.[14] Overall, the experience of San Francisco suggests a model for care of those with a complex disease that requires both hospitalization and home care—namely, the provision of community-based services with government money and support, and the use of both professional and volunteer staff. It is a model that has impressed non-Americans; the Australian Health Minister, Dr. Neal Blewett, visited San Francisco in early 1985 to study it. Like GMHC, Shanti has inspired other groups across the country to follow its lead.

As AIDS spread, so, too, did volunteer groups providing services, counseling and information. Outside New York and San

Francisco, the largest group is probably AIDS Project/LA (which also provides some housing for people with AIDS).[15] AID Atlanta provides a hot line with information and referrals and a range of services to people with AIDS, from emergency funding to counseling and public education, throughout the Southeast; in Texas large organizations are active in both Dallas and Houston; Kansas City has a hot line and a support group, and local bars have raised money to assist with medical costs for people with AIDS.[16] In most of these cases there has been virtually no support from city, county or state government. As Harold Daire, founder of the Oak Lawn Counselling Center in Dallas, told Congress:

> Unlike New York City, San Francisco and Los Angeles, organizations in Dallas and Houston are entirely dependent upon private contributions to fund support services. The KS/AIDS Foundation and Committee for Public Health Awareness of Houston, the Oak Lawn Counselling Center AIDS Project, the Dallas Gay Alliance and the Dallas AIDS Action Project have been hampered in their efforts to petition for state and municipal funds because time and energy must be devoted to combat groups such as Dallas Doctors against AIDS and Alert Citizens of Texas.[17]

Similar problems were experienced by the Health Crisis Network in Miami, with the additional problems of trying to work with members of the Haitian community—35 percent of local cases are found among Haitian immigrants—who are extremely suspicious of what they see as a white gay organization. In general, AIDS groups have found it very difficult to establish themselves as non-gay, even where they have deliberately presented themselves as such and made very real attempts to reach out to other affected communities. At the same time, non-gays with AIDS have often had nowhere else to turn when state and family support has failed. Of the other groups affected only hemophiliacs had an already existing network of organizations able to offer the sort of services and information required. Those who are prone to attack the selfishness of gay men should remember that almost 40 percent of GMHC's clientele have been people who are not gay, the same proportion as in the city's overall incidence of the disease.

Since Tocqueville, it has been a cliché to observe that volunteer organizations are one of the strengths of American society. In general, the American model of establishing gay communal organizations to respond to AIDS has worked best in those countries, such as Australia and Canada, with similar traditions; it is far less popular in, say, Mediterranean Europe. An angry letter in the French journal *Le Gai Pied* in late 1984 deplored the "fragility of the French gay world . . . There is not yet in Paris a group or association which has undertaken to struggle against this illness and to provide help for the sick."[18] (Such an organization, known as AIDES, was established shortly thereafter and has involved up to five hundred people in providing education and services.) In Berlin at least two AIDS organizations existed by the end of 1984, one of which, the Selbst Hilfe Gruppe (Self-Help Group), was advocating a hospital for AIDS patients.[19] Where there was an already existing gay movement with strong ties to government, as in Denmark and the Netherlands, organization around AIDS followed automatically.

Britain is an interesting case, for at the time AIDS struck, it had a weak gay movement and one that enjoyed no recognition from the national government (although the London County Council and other local bodies had implemented a number of pro-gay programs). The Terrence Higgins Trust was established in London in 1982 in memory of one of the first people in Britain to die from AIDS; like GMHC, by whose structure it has been considerably influenced, it was founded by men who were in many cases new to the gay movement. By late 1984 it had established itself as the leading source of public information on the disease in Britain, and organized a national conference with hundreds of delegates coming from a wide range of gay groups across the country. (AIDS in Britain is largely a London phenomenon, and owing to the centralization of British politics it is practical to think of one national organization, which is less possible in federal systems.) By mid-1985 it had 250 volunteer workers and had received funding from both the British government and the Greater London County Council.[20]

Concern about the question of blood donations was the spark for the establishment of the Toronto AIDS Action Committee in 1983, which was soon followed by active groups in other Canadian provinces. The existence of a fairly large gay movement was a significant resource in Ontario (although the committee was careful to seek out non-gays to take part in the organization); in its first year it was able to raise considerable sums of money through the help of the Gay Appeal, an existing Toronto organization that specializes in funding gay communal activities. The organization drew on both movement veterans and new activists; with the influx of government money it developed a full-time staff, as well as some of the structural rigidities associated with GMHC. In Vancouver the impetus for organization came from gay doctors; in Montreal several groups came into existence, reflecting the fragmentation of the movement between the two language groups. In May 1985 groups from across the country—including one representing Haitians—established a Canadian network on AIDS. In Australia the development of large-scale AIDS hysteria in 1984–85 led hundreds of people to attend organizing meetings in Melbourne and Sydney. (AIDS groups in Australia date back to 1983 and grew out of existing political and communal activities.)

AIDS organizations fulfill a number of needs. They provide information for both the general public and "risk groups" and increasingly have focused on prevention education, as in the Houston KS/AIDS Foundation's AIDS Play Safe Week in September 1983. They offer practical help to those with AIDS to bridge the enormous gaps in the American health and welfare systems; a lot of time is spent "walking" people through the bureaucratic maze, which often seems designed to exclude people from benefits through their sheer complexity. And they offer support and counseling to those with AIDS and their families.

This last is particularly important because of the special problems experienced by many people with AIDS: they are often forced to "come out" as gay while sick and to deal with rejection and guilt due to their sexuality at a time when they are already under great stress. I was told in Miami of one man who had no friends when he fell sick, because he had been so scared of being found out as a homosexual that he totally separated his social and his sexual life, not allowing emotional involvement to occur in either. Such experiences are by no means uncommon. Ken Wein, who headed GMHC's clinical services, a job he came to after being sacked for "coming out" at work, claims that the loss of self-esteem and the fear of abandonment are greater among people with AIDS than among those with other life-threatening illnesses. And AIDS organizations, no matter how much they may wish to eschew politics, are often caught up in battles over civil rights and struggles for elementary government recognition and support.

I once asked Rodger McFarlane where the gay movement in New York could be found. "Here," he answered, pointing to the building where he worked, and it is clear that the burgeoning AIDS organizations are evidence of a developing sense of community among the many thousands of gay men (and some others) who have become involved as volunteers, donors and clients. The National Gay Task Force estimated that gay groups raised almost $7 million for AIDS work in 1984,[21] and McFarlane estimates the value of volunteer work for GMHC as worth over $3 million a year.

There are certain parallels here to the women's movement; during the 1970s health issues became a major concern and women's health centers were often the most visible focus of feminist activity, in other countries as much as the United States. The feminist critique of health care became for many a starting point for an overall analysis of the place of women in society.[22] Despite considerable health problems—STDs, hepatitis, alcoholism and drug abuse, psychological stress—a similar movement never really developed among gay men. Most gay men, even most activists, failed to incorporate health issues into any overall political analysis, and while the groups that made up the National Gay Health Coalition were well aware of these links, they made little impact on the burgeoning gay commercial world. Far too many of us assumed that modern medicine could cure any of the illnesses that seemed to accompany "fast-lane" living, and the closest most gay men came to a critique of health care was a vague (and usually ill-informed) attack on psychoanalysis and psychiatry.

In some ways AIDS has changed this. Groups like GMHC, AIDS/LA and the AIDS Action Committee in Boston seem to represent a development among gay men similar to that which took place earlier among feminists. Yet, partly because of the need for immediate practical responses, partly because of the major role played by medical professionals themselves, the growth of AIDS organizations has not meant a corresponding growth in analysis of medicine and health as a social and political issue. Where such analysis has occurred, it was often due to the work of lesbians, many of whom had already been active in feminist health groups.

AIDS is said both to have increased a sense of community between gay men and lesbians and to have sharpened the divisions. Many lesbians have responded with enormous energy and generosity to the crisis; I know of few AIDS groups where lesbians do not play an important role (GMHC is more male-dominated than most). At the same time many lesbians feel resentment that gay men, who never showed any interest in questions of women's health, now seem to expect total commitment to AIDS activity from them. As Karen Peteros of the Lyon-Martin Clinic, a lesbian health center in San Francisco, wrote:

> I've just opened the mail at the clinic. We've received a notice from [City Supervisor] Harry Britt's office announcing a $900,000 appropriation from the City's budget for AIDS services. My feelings are mixed. On the one hand, I feel elated that some funding for AIDS work is finally here. On the other hand, I feel resentful. I feel resentful because this crisis already overshadows many others, and because men's issues always take precedence over women's . . . What about women's health? What about lesbian health services? I feel incredibly angry, but guilty too. It's hard to be supportive of anyone else's issues, particularly men's, when the history of support is not reciprocal.[23]

In the same way, Pat Maher, for a time acting director of New York City's Office of Gay and Lesbian Health Concerns, has pointed out that while the office was established in response to AIDS, the city has no office of women's health concerns.

Lesbians are involved in several ways: as workers in AIDS projects, as victims of increased homophobia as a result of the epidemic, because of the special problems posed by the disease for artificial insemination, a concern of growing numbers of lesbians, and because, like other women, they are not immune to the disease. A network of women involved in AIDS work grew out of the second AIDS Forum in Denver in 1983, and brings together

women who need to deal with other lesbians—and gay men—
who see AIDS as exclusively a gay male issue. (Such perceptions
can surface in unpleasant ways. The lesbian who told the New
York *Times* that "in a way we're more so much more advanced
than men" was hardly contributing to mutual empathy between
gay women and men.[24])

An example of women's involvement was the Blood Sisters of
San Diego, a drive by the women's caucus of the local gay Democratic club to donate blood as a way of expressing solidarity with
gay men whose blood was suspect. (A similar move was made by
women members of a San Francisco gay Jewish congregation,
Sha'ar Zahev, the year before.)[25] A Blood Sisters movement also
exists in Vancouver, although, as in most countries outside the
United States, few lesbians seem involved in AIDS organizations
in Canada.

A very special variant of community created by AIDS is organization among people who have the disease themselves. Indeed,
AIDS may be unique as an illness in which some of those who
have it have responded by organizing politically, a response possible because of a pre-existing sense of belonging to the gay
community. The People With AIDS movement grew out of support and counseling networks, and has had a complex and not
always very happy relationship with mainstream AIDS organizations. Michael Callan has recounted the development of a group
in New York that grew out of one established for AIDS patients
by GMHC, and the bitter arguments among those present about
cause, treatment and attitudes toward sex. In 1983 the media
began searching for people with AIDS to interview, and made
stars of a few, including Michael himself. Through press coverage
and involvement with AIDS groups a political perspective developed:

> At the [New York AIDS] Network we began to see that we could
> use the insights gained from our personal struggles with AIDS to
> contribute to the larger political battle against AIDS. We were mak-
> ing connections between racism and homophobia and the govern-
> ment's totally inadequate response to this crisis which was devastat-
> ing the gay and Haitian communities.[26]

Similar groups were forming elsewhere, especially in San Francisco, where Bobbi Campbell played something of the role Callan played in New York. (Campbell died in August 1984, almost three years after being diagnosed. His death had an enormous effect upon San Francisco gays, for many of whom Campbell had been a symbol of the will to live in face of the epidemic.[27]) At the 1983 AIDS Forum in Denver, members of some of these groups came together, taking the name People With AIDS, a name attributed to Mark Feldman, and claiming the right to be included in the leadership of all AIDS organizations. The following year in New York, an attempt was made to establish a national association of people with AIDS, with its own hot line and newsletter, and the latter began appearing in June 1985.

In several cities people with AIDS have been key figures in the AIDS movement and have been involved in support, educational and lobbying work. Since 1983, members of People With AIDS have been prominent figures in Gay Pride marches across the country, often including many who can march only with great pain and difficulty. They assert a particular expertise that doesn't sit very well with authoritarian doctors and academics, who too often remind one of the famous "nerve specialist" Dr. S. Weir Mitchell, who told Charlotte Perkins Gilman that he didn't want information from his patients, he wanted complete obedience.[28] Yet the expertise of those who have experienced the disease brings a dimension to our understanding of AIDS not usually touched by academic science and medicine. I have spent time with some remarkable men with AIDS, and have listened to their presentations at conferences, and I am struck by their capacity to understand the social and political implications of their illness and to communicate this to others.

Ten years ago, I was sick for a long time—ironically, with toxoplasmosis, one of the opportunistic diseases now associated with AIDS. My doctor put me in touch with other people with the disease, and I found a real solace in talking with them by telephone. On a much larger scale the forging of community among people with AIDS is of enormous psychological and probably therapeutic value; the opinions of doctors on the benefits of social support in dealing with stress and illness are echoed in the words of one person with AIDS, Glen McGahee:

Don't try to go it alone. By being together, we can share feelings and experiences without the hassle of being analyzed or pitied. We already have a lot in common. We are blood brothers and sisters. It is to our advantage to share information regarding our experiences. What we learn can benefit others and make our lives easier. Through our sharing and open communication we will live better, fuller lives.[29]

For the healthy, people with AIDS are often an inspiration and a model; it is common for their presentations to release considerable sorrow and anger, which helps uncover all sorts of deeply buried fears about disease, disfigurement and death. While only a minority of those with the disease, almost exclusively gay men, have been involved in these groups, the counseling and support work of AIDS organizations has helped bring together large numbers of the sick, who find solace and strength in constructing their own sense of community and working with others with AIDS.

Inevitably, the proliferation of organizations concerned with AIDS produced demands for more coordination and contact. The gay movement, as is true of most American movements, is strongest at the local level, and the few national organizations that exist, most significantly the National Gay Task Force (NGTF), have limited resources and membership. The first national AIDS Forum took place in Dallas in August 1982, but at the time it was overshadowed by a simultaneous change of leadership within NGTF. The following year, however, at the second national AIDS Forum, there was a move to establish a national AIDS organization, the Federation of AIDS-Related Organizations (FARO), which would be independent of the gay movement (though the only non-gay group to join was the Haitian Coalition on AIDS). FARO moved to set up a national clearinghouse for information and to appoint a Washington lobbyist, reflecting dissatisfaction among some of its constituents with the lobbying work already going on. The federation proved less successful than had been hoped, partly because it never raised the projected budget, and the following year it was reconstituted so as to concentrate on lobbying and assistance to organizing people with AIDS.

AIDS and Gay Identity

To be a Haitian or a hemophiliac is determined at birth, but being gay is an identity that is socially determined and involves personal choice. Even if, as many want to argue, one has no choice in experiencing homosexual desire, there is a wide choice of possible ways of acting out these feelings, from celibacy and denial (the position advocated by the Catholic Church) to self-affirmation and the adoption of a gay identity. This last is only one possibility, and a fairly recent one.[30] Because AIDS occurred in a historical epoch which had seen increasing numbers of men and women adopt this identity as a central part of their sense of self, it inevitably had a major effect upon both individual and social conceptions of homosexuality.

AIDS seems to have affected gay men in two contradictory ways, making some more likely to come out and incorporate their homosexuality more centrally into their lives, while others have become less willing to associate with the gay world, more guilty and denying of their homosexuality. Thus it is difficult to say with much certainty just how the epidemic has affected gay life, despite the frequent comments that it has led gay men to go beyond a preoccupation with sex and partying to a new evaluation of community and family. "This disease marks the end of gay life as we know it," said one person with AIDS in Los Angeles. "It's over. All that disco shit is over . . ."[31] Sometimes the gay community is compared to an adolescent now coming into middle age and taking on responsibility for others and for future generations.

Rhetoric aside, AIDS has begun to alter the shape of gay male life in America, not just in terms of individual behavior (of which more later) but also in terms of creating genuine community. The combination of a desire to help one's "brothers and sisters" and the anger generated by a sense that no one else cares has given renewed life to gay organizations and brought thousands of new activists into gay communal activities: "I feel we need our own institutions to protect us because no one else will. We have to create a psychological state like Israel that gays can depend on."[32] (Of course, there are other reasons why people become involved as volunteers, including guilt, boredom and, not least, a superstitious belief that this is a way of warding off illness for oneself.) Over the past several years this spirit has been reflected in events like the National Gay/Lesbian March that preceded the 1984 Democratic Convention in San Francisco and in the expansion of the gay movement across the country, so that cities like Lubbock, Texas, and Des Moines now have Gay Pride celebrations. One sees similar developments outside the United States, such as the 1985 Gay Mardi Gras in Sydney, which was a great success despite considerable media panic and attempts to prevent it from happening at all.[33]

It is easy to be carried away by a Pollyannish view of "gay community." AIDS has also occasioned disillusionment, burnout and fighting among gay organizations, as in San Francisco, where the political clubs have disagreed bitterly over the appropriate response to the epidemic.[34] Not surprisingly, the passions that surround AIDS often lead to bitterness between erstwhile allies, in part because so much is at stake and also because genuine disagreement and struggles for control become intermingled. Some lesbians are resentful of the emphasis AIDS has attracted within the gay movement, and many men have been forced back into the closet because of AIDS; I suspect there is more self-repression going on than was true a few years earlier.

It is difficult to disentangle the influence of AIDS on gay life from that of a changing political and economic environment, in particular the growing conservatism in the United States and a number of other Western countries during the 1980s. It became common for gays to say that AIDS marked the end of the Stonewall era, that period, beginning in 1969, when major social transformation and even liberation for homosexuals seemed possible. ("The seventies began with the pill and ended with AIDS" is one remark that sums up this view.) Yet even without AIDS the ideology of the times would have made the optimism and generosity of the Stonewall period seem out of place. Indeed, it is probable that without AIDS the gay movement would be much weaker than it is now.

But the impact of the epidemic has been uneven. Above all, concern over AIDS seems to have failed to mobilize black, Hispanic and Asian gays, despite the high incidence of AIDS among at least the first two groups. Both within and outside the gay world, AIDS is seen as largely a white disease (when AID Atlanta lobbied for city money this was one of the myths they had to work to dispel). Some attempts have been made to reach out to non-white groups, especially in New York, Washington and Phila-delphia (where Black and White Men Together have made a "rap record" on AIDS), but the reality remains that virtually all AIDS forums, conferences and organizations involve an extraordinary overrepresentation of whites and a real failure to involve others. (Ironically, Jesse Jackson was the only major presidential candi-date in 1984 who acknowledged AIDS as an issue and even men-tioned knowing someone with the disease.) In San Francisco it took the intervention of the city's Human Rights Commission to get the AIDS Foundation to translate literature into Spanish.

This is a reflection of a larger reality—namely, the tendency of both the gay and the non-gay press to conceive of homosexuality in largely male, middle-class and, above all, white terms. It is instructive to look at *Newsweek*'s 1983 cover story on "gay Amer-ica." In the eighteen accompanying illustrations it is impossible to find one non-Caucasian face.[35] The same is often true of the gay media. It could be argued that the gay movement and the gay press are doing no more than reflecting the social segregation that persists in the United States, several decades after the end of *de jure* segregation. In many cities the commercial gay world, particularly the bars, echoes this *de facto* segregation. In San Francisco the Castro district is largely a mecca for white gays, thus furthering the myth that there are few others; in Atlanta there is one large and almost exclusively black gay bar set among a string of predominantly white gay bars on Peachtree Street. It is sometimes argued that many black and Hispanic gays are com-fortable with this sort of segregation, that they prefer to stay in their own communities, which is an odd argument from those who also argue that sexual identity is, by itself, the basis for a sense of community.

But even if this assertion were true—which ignores the extent of plain old-fashioned racism, to which gays are no more immune to than anyone else—the fact remains that AIDS does not distin-guish by race, and that the number of blacks and Hispanics with

AIDS, many of whom are gay, is perverse testimony to the extent to which there is sexual contact, at least, across racial lines. A few groups, such as the National Coalition of Black Gays and Black and White Men Together have sought to raise consciousness among non-Caucasians; some AIDS literature—although far less than is necessary—has been distributed in Spanish, and a very small amount in Creole. The larger problem, of integrating those who are not white into the gay community, remains, and, if anything, has been accentuated by AIDS.

What will AIDS mean for gay life if, as pessimists believe, it continues to grow unabated for a number of years? There are those who argue that we will come to accept premature death as one of the risks of being gay, as we have accepted other, less lethal risks. If this seems farfetched, reflect on the extent to which young ghetto black men live with death as a real possibility, whether from violence or drug overdose. I have heard it suggested that gay male culture is obsessed with death, as in the fantasies of Genet, Mishima and Fassbinder, or the cult of performers who died tragically, like Monroe and Garland. I find this suggestion unpersuasive; modern culture in general is obsessed with images of death, as, indeed, it is with youth, and in America this has been accentuated by a series of assassinations over the past twenty years.

It is true that AIDS has introduced a new sobriety to gay life that is affecting us in as yet uncharted ways. It is a Christian myth to believe that suffering is ennobling; more often it is crippling. The novelist John Rechy, who for twenty years has chronicled the underside of gay male life, has caught the current feeling among many gay men, especially those who are not part of institutionalized communal activities:

> And these men who would come here to cruise and connect for sex, instead keep raising the volume of their radios as if to throttle the sound of their own bruised laughter, and in that lot off Santa Monica Boulevard, in the darkest hours of night and early morning, they drink and smoke grass—and they dance, clap, twist their bodies. There is the atmosphere of dead euphoria, of despair flailing to find its shape in a dance tinged with danger and defiance and deep sorrow.[36]

AIDS and the Gay Movement

On the whole AIDS organizations developed independently of existing gay political groups, even where gay activists were involved in establishing the organizations. The political nature of the epidemic, however, has meant that AIDS has increasingly come to dominate the agenda of the gay movement as a whole and, in turn, to affect the nature of that movement.

There are few areas where the ongoing redefinition of homosexuals as a legitimate minority has been as marked as in mainstream American politics. Gay groups have come to play a significant role in city politics in San Francisco, Los Angeles, Washington, Houston, Boston, Minneapolis, Chicago and Philadelphia; one congressman (Gerry Studds), one ex-congressman (Bob Bauman) and several state legislators have publicly declared themselves gay; a gay presence has been officially recognized within the Democratic Party, and in 1984 all major candidates for the party's nomination made overtures for gay votes; there are four openly gay judges in California and at least three cities have had openly gay mayors, including the city of West Hollywood, which was established by referendum in 1984 and has an openly gay majority on its City Council; the black civil rights leadership publicly endorsed gay rights, and a black lesbian was included as a speaker at the 1983 March on Washington.

These are developments which predate AIDS. The National Gay Task Force was founded in 1973, the Gay Rights National Lobby in 1978. Harvey Milk was elected an openly gay city supervisor in San Francisco in 1977, and openly lesbian and gay legislators were elected to state houses in Minnesota and Massachusetts during the 1970s. What AIDS has done is to increase the demands of the gay movement and to politicize many thousands, particularly men, so as to make gay representatives, for the first time, players in the battle over allocating governmental resources.

The AIDS crisis has been as powerful a force in mobilizing gays to take part in the political arena as were the Stonewall riots of 1969, the Anita Bryant campaigns of 1977, aimed at repealing protection of gays under anti-discrimination laws in Miami and other cities, and the Proposition 6 campaign in California in 1978, an attempt to ban homosexuals or "supporters of homosexuality" from teaching in the schools. The difference is that whereas earlier rallying points required a certain perception that homosexuality was a political issue best dealt with by an organized response, a perception resisted by many gays, AIDS is literally a life-and-death issue that can affect every gay man, no matter how wealthy, powerful or closeted. Nothing short of such a crisis could produce the sort of support that has funded Gay Men's Health Crisis and led thousands of people to volunteer for AIDS work across the country, and even AIDS has not been sufficient to mobilize most homosexuals. The gay movement after AIDS is a larger and politically more diverse movement, but it has a long way to go before it encompasses most of the people for whom it wants to speak.

AIDS is producing a fundamental shift in the nature of the movement, as new people, many of them previously apolitical, become involved and as the focus of the movement shifts from an emphasis on rights to the allocation of resources. For if demands concerning rights tend to be symbolic and call for expressive politics and expressions of solidarity with other groups, a focus on resources tends to make a movement more akin to a traditional interest group, more concerned with professional leadership and access to the back rooms of power.

The most obvious impact of AIDS has been to produce a new professional leadership in the gay movement, one whose legitimacy is based on expertise rather than on either movement experience or popular representation. Increasingly, people with medical and scientific credentials come to speak for gays in public forums, and to influence the overall direction of the movement, as is true of the leaders of the various gay medical groups that have come to prominence during the epidemic. Sometimes, as with Dr. Bruce Voeller of the Mariposa Foundation and one of the founders of the National Gay Task Force, such people are also movement veterans; more often they have come to political activism via the AIDS crisis. The best examples of such new leaders are found in New York, where with a few exceptions the men who established the Gay Men's Health Crisis were new to the movement—"We'd be out partying on Fire Island during the Gay Pride marches," one of them told me—and are now among the prominent leaders of the New York gay community. Mel Rosen, the first executive director of GMHC was tapped by the state to administer the AIDS Institute; together with Roger Enlow, the first head of the Office of Gay and Lesbian Health Concerns, and Rodger McFarlane of GMHC, he became for a while one of the most prominent gay spokespersons on AIDS in the city. Because groups like GMHC and the AIDS Foundation in San Francisco have budgets large enough to employ full-time staffs, they inevitably develop leadership with time and resources that can't be matched by people without full-time movement jobs, and this in turn increases their access to the media and their clout within the gay movement.

AIDS stories have increasingly come to dominate the gay press, and the epidemic could be said to have ensured the success of the first long-lived gay newspaper in New York City, *The New York Native*. *The Native* was founded in 1981 by the publishers of the gay literary magazine *Christopher Street* and very soon became the major gay organ in which news and discussion of AIDS appeared, to the point where some referred to it as "The New York Review of AIDS." Its medical articles, first by Larry Mass, then James d'Eramo, combined with its free personals to make it very successful and second only to *The Advocate*—which also has a health columnist, Nathan Fain—in influence among the gay media. Even outside the east coast, *The Native* is relied upon for information on the epidemic; one straight epidemiologist in San Francisco told me in 1984 that he regarded it as having the best overall coverage of AIDS available anywhere.

Major political activities of the gay movement since its energizing in 1969–70 and the emergence of gay liberation have involved large demonstrations, such as the annual Gay Pride parades, the 1979 March on Washington and the San Francisco "White Night Riots" later that year in protest at the very light sentence passed on Dan White, the assassin of Harvey Milk and Mayor George Moscone. There have been a few echoes of this heritage in connection with AIDS—in May 1983 there were several large candlelight rallies, involving perhaps 8,000 people in both New York and San Francisco and 3,000 in Houston, and more funding for AIDS was the first demand of the very large gay march that preceded the 1984 Democratic Convention in San Francisco. Most AIDS politicking, however, has involved the lobbying of federal, state and local governments rather than large street demonstrations. (A national vigil on AIDS funding in the fall of 1983 drew 12,000 to Washington rather than the 100,000 the organizers had hoped for.) Inevitably this has meant dependence upon professional leaders able to talk the language of politicians and bureaucrats. Even under the Reagan Administration, AIDS has produced more contact between the gay movement and federal officials than ever before. Both Heckler and Brandt have met with gay groups, Brandt quite frequently, and the various levels of the Public Health Service have established considerable contact with the gay movement. It is revealing that one of the early meetings scheduled by Dr. James Mason when he became head of the CDC at the end of 1983 was with representatives of the National Gay Task Force. As Virginia Apuzzo, executive director of NGTF from 1982 to 1985, said: "The Public Health Service now doesn't take too many steps without at least informing us. We may disagree violently with the steps they're taking, but we've institutionalized our presence in that process . . . We had the first 800-number crisis line in the country for dealing with the AIDS crisis. When the Public Health Service was instituting its crisis line, it came to us to be trained in how to do it."[37]

In general, AIDS has made the gay movement more sophisticated in its approach to government and more savvy in the ways of getting things done. As part of the need to influence governments, groups such as NGTF, the Gay Rights National Lobby and the Federation of AIDS-Related Organizations have developed close working relations with organizations such as the American Public Health Association and the American Psychological Association. Unfortunately, organizations representing other affected groups—Haitians, drug users and hemophiliacs—have often been reluctant to work together with gay groups, due to their own homophobia. (The only North American city where I have heard gay leaders express satisfaction at their relations with Haitian groups is Toronto.) The National Gay Task Force, in particular, has been important in mobilizing support for greater commitment to AIDS by the federal government; its perseverance, together with that of Lambda Legal Defense, was described by one congressional staffer as the "fox terrier" approach.

At the local level, gay political clubs have been important in the lobbying process, especially in California; a major reason for the generous response of San Francisco is undoubtedly the clout of the two major gay Democratic clubs in that city, one of which, the Harvey Milk Club, published one of the first brochures on "safe sex" back in 1983. In New York, gay groups across the state played an important role in winning funding for the AIDS Institute. (The existence of a gay group in Binghamton meant that both the Senate Majority Leader and the chair of the Assembly Health Committee could be approached by their own constituents.[38]) The National Coalition of Black Gays was able to persuade Congressman Stokes of the House Appropriations Committee to designate an aide to work with the coalition on AIDS.[39]

The other side to these developments is that the pressures to respond to the constant crises posed by AIDS divert attention from other matters of concern to the gay movement, such as discrimination in general, violence, immigration and even other health issues. For all the work that has been done by both national and local groups, the American gay movement is not yet a mass movement with a firm base of large membership and financial resources; it cannot begin to compete, in terms of personnel and resources, with the forces that can be mobilized by the fundamentalist right. After the burst of media publicity in the spring and summer of 1983, the influx of new people and money into AIDS work couldn't keep up with the increasing size of the problem. By the following summer volunteers from NGTF were soliciting money on New York's Christopher Street to operate their national hot line. Even some established groups within the gay movement have been slow to fully use their clout for AIDS lobbying, a criticism then *Advocate* publisher David Goodstein leveled against MECLA (the Municipal Elections Committee of Los Angeles), the first gay political action committee and one that has raised very considerable funds for political campaigns.[40] The gay movement lacks nationally known leaders able to galvanize and articulate demands for the entire "community." The closest to such a leader is probably Virginia Apuzzo, executive director of NGTF from 1982 to 1985, who has been a major voice in raising awareness about AIDS and who has tried consistently to relate the issue to broader questions of health policy (she once served as Assistant Commissioner in New York City's Health Department).

Perhaps the greatest gap in AIDS politicking is the lack of a genuine mass mobilization behind demands for a greater government response to AIDS. Preoccupied with the exigencies of dealing with immediate problems, the AIDS leadership has not been able to sufficiently educate their potential constituency to an awareness of the government's failures (of which more in the next chapter) or to develop effective ways for large-scale participation in pressuring government. In the 1984 presidential elections, it was striking how many gay men supported Ronald Reagan, despite the fact that gay leadership is almost unanimous in agreeing that his administration's response to the AIDS crisis has been woefully, if not criminally, inadequate. (As the gay movement expands, it has lost any claim to ideological coherence; one finds gay activists who claim to be conservative Republicans, with no sense that this may pose a contradiction.) The development of a more professional and expert gay leadership carries with it the risk of isolating that leadership from those it represents, who are seen as sources of funds and recipients of advice rather than potential actors in a political movement. In early 1985 a group of activists in San Francisco, many of whom came out of earlier mass movements, began organizing precisely the sort of grass-roots political activity around AIDS that has so far been lacking. Out of this came the Mobilization Against AIDS, which organized a nationwide candlelight vigil on Memorial Day in 1985 and a broad-based petition calling for a "moon-shot mentality" in the fight against AIDS.

As AIDS spread to other Western countries, gay movements have organized to make demands on governments for greater expenditures on research and services. Non-Americans are less experienced in using pressure-group techniques, but at a European AIDS conference organized by the COC (the Dutch national gay organization) in January 1984, Lisabeth Baarveld, a Dutch member of the European Parliament, called for pressure by the gay movement to obtain necessary funds for AIDS research.[41] In Canada some funds have been forthcoming from both federal and provincial governments; in Britain the Terrence Higgins Trust began pressing for government support in late 1984 and subsequently received a small amount; in Australia, where the gay movement developed certain political skills in the protracted struggles for decriminalization, it succeeded in getting financial support for AIDS programs from state and federal governments. The New Zealand government has been particularly generous in supporting that country's AIDS Support Network. Outside of Scandinavia and the Netherlands, there are no European countries where the gay movement has institutionalized itself in the political process as in the United States, and in most countries the gay movement is more clearly aligned with the left, if not always the conventional left (as in the case of the large gay presence among the West German Greens). It is possible that AIDS might alter both these characteristics.

Apart from intensifying lobbying at the various levels of government, AIDS has highlighted the perception of the gay movement that one of its major problems is sensationalism and misreporting in the media. AIDS has had the effect of greatly increasing gay visibility in the media, but hardly in ways that are particularly positive. Dissatisfaction with media treatment is a long-standing grievance of gay activists, and some of the earliest gay liberation demonstrations were aimed at the press. AIDS has rekindled these dissatisfactions.

A particular grievance has long been felt against the New York *Times*, which has consistently refused to use the term "gay" and has been very remiss in its coverage of gay political and cultural events. The *Times*'s attitude seemed typified in its failure to report GMHC's April 1983 Madison Square Garden fund-raiser, which was attended by 18,000 people, including Mayor Koch. This omission led to pickets, calls for a boycott and a meeting between gay leaders and the vice-chairman of the newspaper. Similar meetings have occurred elsewhere, for example with the Boston *Globe*. In Britain the AIDS Action Group, led by Julian Meldrum, has been active in attacking untrue and sensationalistic media coverage and has made official complaints on several occasions to the Press Council.

The modern gay movement grew out of the radical and liberationist ideology of the late sixties and early seventies. It shared with other movements of the time a concern with the symbolic and the dramatic, and saw itself as part of a greater movement for overriding social change. Much of this impetus had died before AIDS became a major issue, especially in the United States, where the gay movement was already developing into a more professional and traditional interest group, with increasing numbers of activists who do not share the leftist politics of early liberationists. In the United States in the mid-eighties, two contradictory tendencies exist within the movement; in many ways it has moved in directions that reflect the larger ideological shift to the right within society, but this is counterbalanced to some extent by the fact that AIDS has the potential to radicalize many people who previously have not been politically involved. Whether this occurs or not will depend in large part on the extent of the epidemic and the government's responses over the next few years.

CHAPTER SIX

Politics and Money

Medicine is a profession that deals in costly magic.
—Morris West, *The World Is Made of Glass*

One of the features of modern medicine is that it demands ever-increasing resources. In most Western countries the growing costs of health care have become a central political question, and nowhere more so than in the United States, where the role of the state in providing for the health care of its citizens is smaller than in any comparable society, and the private sector plays a major role in the control and regulation of medical care and in medical research. This does not necessarily mean, as Reaganite ideology would have it, that American medicine is better or more efficient than elsewhere; it is certainly more expensive and the growing importance of health-care corporations means there is a vested interest in certain kinds of expensive treatment rather than prevention, which is less easily commercialized. According to some estimates, only Israel spends a greater percentage of its GNP on health care.

Thus to talk of government and AIDS is to talk primarily, though not exclusively, of money. Of money available for research and surveillance, for hospital and medical care, for services to people with AIDS, for public health education and prevention. It is further to talk of the fight for government spending in these areas, in an era when government spending on everything but defense was under attack. Pressure for spending on AIDS-related research, treatment and services came from within the Public Health Service and its state and local equivalents, to some extent from the media[1] and above all from the gay movement and some of its allies in Congress and such organizations as the American Public Health Association and the American Psychological Association.

Until recently, gay politics involved demands for recognition and legitimacy, not for economic resources. (A professor of mine once remarked that ceasing to treat homosexuality as a crime was the most cost-effective policy available for a government that wished to show itself as progressive.) With the emergence of AIDS the gay movement found itself thrust into conventional pressure-group politics and discovered, as have other movements before it, that power and money are inextricably intertwined. At the same time, the AIDS epidemic revealed, perhaps more sharply than most examples, the real shortcomings in the American medical system, a system that combines highly developed technology with a grossly inequitable distribution of health care, in which the role of government is dispersed in a very confusing way among federal, state and local levels.

The Response in Washington

The onset of AIDS coincided with major cuts in most federal domestic spending, as part of the Reagan Administration's overall budget priorities. The first calls for money for AIDS were for specific amounts to be allocated to research, traditionally the responsibility of the federal government, and early lobbying concentrated on this issue. As the epidemic grew there developed an interest in monies for treatment and education, and an awareness of the responsibilities of the different levels of government in health care.

Just how much money has been spent on AIDS research is a more complex question than it might appear, for as Administration representatives have stressed, a great deal of ongoing basic medical research has considerable implications for the understanding and treatment of AIDS, and some money has been made available by state governments and private sources. The funds for AIDS research allocated to the Public Health Service (which means primarily the Centers for Disease Control and the National Institutes of Health, with lesser amounts going to the Food and Drug Administration and the Alcohol, Drug Abuse and Mental Health Administration) increased from $5.5 million in fiscal 1982 to a peak of $96 million in 1985.

By the standards of any other country this was enormous, and means that the great bulk of AIDS-related research in the world continues to take place in the United States, but it remains a very small proportion of total outlays; in 1985 the National Institutes of Health alone spent over $3 billion and AIDS expenditure has been less than 1 percent of the total expenditure of the Public Health Service.

In recent years as much attention has been directed to the amount spent on AIDS as to much larger research programs. In part this is because over a period of several years it was Congress that insisted on increasing resources for AIDS work at both the CDC and the NIH against the wishes of the Reagan Administration. As Congresswoman Barbara Boxer of California remarked: "It was the strangest thing. Normally in an epidemic, health officials come begging Congress for more money. It seemed that we had to beg them to say they needed it."[2] Certainly, compared with previous medical emergencies—a frequent comparison is with President Ford's request for $135 million in 1976 to develop a national immunization campaign against swine flu—the Administration's response was extraordinarily halfhearted.[3] More than anything else it was scrutiny and pressure from a few members of the House of Representatives in 1982 and 1983 that forced a reluctant federal government to allocate more money to AIDS research.

The first significant congressional response came from Henry Waxman, a Los Angeles Democrat who has considerable clout in California politics and whose subcommittee of the House of Representatives Committee on Energy and Commerce included, odd as it might seem, oversight of the Public Health Service. As his aide, Tim Westmoreland, recounted it:

> At the time of the initial hearings by the Congress on AIDS we had just come through the 1981 period when the Stockman black book had made tremendous cuts in every public health agency in

the Public Health Service . . . We were watching, after a 25% budget cut in the C.D.C. and a 30% cut in the Food and Drug Administration, to see what the first disaster would be . . . AIDS happened to be the first accident to come along after the Stockman black book.[4]

Waxman's staff had been alerted to AIDS some months previously by Dr. Jim Curran of the CDC Task Force, and in April 1982 a one-day hearing was organized at the Gay and Lesbian Community Services Center in Los Angeles, thus ensuring that future congressional response would be intimately connected to the perceived importance of the gay community. In his opening address, Waxman, the only member of the subcommittee present, made it clear that he was appalled by the government's response to health emergencies and that this was worsened in the case of AIDS: "There is no doubt in my mind that if the same disease had appeared among Americans of Norwegian descent, or among tennis players, rather than among gay males, the response of both the government and the medical community would have been different . . ."[5]

The Waxman subcommittee could hold hearings; it could not, however, authorize funds. The first congressional move to beef up spending on AIDS research came a few months later when a Republican senator, Harrison Schmitt of New Mexico, requested that an extra half million dollars be added to the CDC's appropriations for AIDS work. This provision was accepted by both houses, and upheld despite a presidential veto of that section of the budget. During that year there was a mounting feeling among gay organizations and some members of Congress that the funds available for research were totally inadequate, and moves for a major increase were initiated by Representative Phillip Burton, a powerful liberal Democrat from San Francisco. Slowly pressure mounted, and Congress added a further $2 million for AIDS to the budget of the CDC.

In retrospect, everyone agrees that the process was too slow. It was not until 1983, eighteen months after research had begun, that political mobilization behind the issue began to be effective. The gay movement began lobbying seriously, both via the National Gay Task Force, newly energized after Virginia Apuzzo became executive director in late 1982, and the Gay Rights National Lobby, which until then had been primarily concerned with building support for a federal gay rights bill. The relevant House Appropriations subcommittee was receptive, with support not only from liberal big-city representatives like Edward Roybal, Democrat from Los Angeles, and Bill Green, Republican from Manhattan, but also from Chairman William Natcher of Kentucky and the ranking Republican, Silvio Conte of Massachusetts, who was enraged at what he considered the Administration's dishonesty. Conte's anger also revealed something of the internal disputes within the government's ranks:

> I am personally very distressed with this situation where the administration comes before the subcommittee and states time after time that sufficient resources are available and then changes its tune suddenly, at a time when it is very difficult for the committee to consider this position. Now, this borders on not dealing with the subcommittee in good faith, and I, for one, must express my disappointment . . .[6]

In March 1983, Representative Waxman, with the support of ten members of Congress, all Democrats, introduced a bill to provide for a special fund to allow the Secretary of Health and Human Services to meet unforeseen health emergencies. Discussion focused heavily on the alleged failings of the Administration in dealing with AIDS. The Administration opposed the bill—despite a similar proposal the year before by then Secretary Richard S. Schweiker—and stressed its ability to meet emergencies by shifting funds within the CDC and NIH, despite evidence that this shortchanged other programs, including, at the CDC alone, surveillance of hepatitis, studies of chlamydial infections and pelvic inflammation, studies of influenza and purchases of supplies and equipment.[7] This legislation was subsequently passed but has never been funded. Representative Ted Weiss of New York has sought to establish a similar fund that would cover prevention, treatment and public education, as well as research and surveillance.

Just as several hearings by Waxman's subcommittee put effective pressure on the Administration, further progress on research funding followed hearings held by Representative Weiss's sub-

committee on Intergovernmental Relations and Human Resources in August 1983. These were the most extensive hearings
to date on AIDS, and allowed representatives of almost every
affected group, including three people with AIDS, to appear
before a congressional committee. They also made public dis-
agreements within the Administration over AIDS funding and
led the Administration to sharply increase the amount it proposed to spend. From testimony to the subcommittee and docu-
ments acquired by the San Francisco *Chronicle* it is clear that the
CDC had been consistently pressing for more money, and
equally consistently had been knocked back by the budget makers. The CDC, for example, was unable to establish a national
surveillance system for AIDS for several years after the outbreak
of the epidemic. (The block was in the White House rather than
the Public Health Service; there is evidence that Dr. Brandt,
Assistant Secretary for Health, pushed hard for more resources.[8])
Within two weeks of the Weiss hearings, Health and Human
Services Secretary Margaret Heckler announced that the budget
request for AIDS research would be increased from $17.6 million
to $39 million.

But the Weiss hearings were significant for more than raising
questions of resources and embarrassing the Administration into
raising its requests for funding. The device of congressional hearings—to which there is no real counterpart in the parliamentary
system—allows interest groups to put public pressure on bureaucrats, and in the course of these hearings there was considerable
criticism of both the CDC and the NIH, as well as a sharp exchange between Weiss and representatives of the Public Health
Service over their policies on confidentiality.[9] These hearings
helped shape a congressional perception that here was a major
health crisis which the Reagan Administration was treating far
too lightly, and ensured that considerable sums were allocated to
AIDS research over the next several years. The Senate played a
lesser role in the battle, largely because Republican control made
it a less fertile place for initiatives, although some measures were
pushed by Senators Weicker (Rep., Conn.), Kennedy (Dem.,
Mass.) and Cranston (Dem., Calif.). Insight into the Senate's role
comes from Dr. David Sundwall, an adviser to the Labor and

Human Resources Committee chaired by Senator Orrin Hatch
(Rep., Utah):

> Sundwall says that he and Hatch took pains to make sure that
> their important Senate health panel did not get its hands on an
> AIDS funding bill, because of the intensely homophobic make-up of
> the committee. Included on the committee are such stalwarts of the
> Right as Senators John East (Rep., N.C.) and Jeremiah Denton (Rep.,
> Ala.). When the House sent over an emergency funding proposal to
> the Senate in 1982, he and Hatch "finessed it" so that the bill
> bypassed the committee and went directly to the Senate floor "in
> the quiet of the night."[10]

The irony of this statement is that most lists of right-wing
stalwarts in the Senate would include Hatch, a Mormon from one
of the most conservative states in the nation.

Bizarre are the ways of Congress. By concentrating power in
the hands of committees, and within these of chairmen and subcommittee chairmen, they allow certain groups and individuals
extraordinary influence (examples are the stranglehold of
Southerners over civil rights legislation for so long, and the ability of senators such as Joe McCarthy and William Fulbright to
become national figures through their control of committee
hearings). Occasionally an unpopular or relatively insignificant
group benefits from these arrangements, and in the case of AIDS
funding it was crucial that Henry Waxman and Ted Weiss chaired
two of the potentially relevant subcommittees. Without the work
of both of them and their staffs it is doubtful if anything like the
amount spent on AIDS research would have been made available.

Congressmen such as Waxman and Weiss undoubtedly have a
genuine commitment to do something about a very nasty and
fatal disease. It is not questioning their goodwill to point to the
reality that congressional action on AIDS was instigated by members representing large and visible gay communities: Weiss and
Green (Manhattan), Waxman (West Los Angeles and West Hollywood), Burton, and after his death in 1983, Sala Burton and
Barbara Boxer (San Francisco). Here one sees the effect of the
mobilization and organization of gays already discussed; it is salutary to imagine the tardiness of the response had IV users and

Haitians been the only victims of AIDS, had Republicans controlled the House of Representatives as well as the Senate (and hence chaired the relevant oversight and appropriations committees) or, indeed, had AIDS struck ten years earlier, before the existence of an organized gay movement, openly gay professionals who could testify before the relevant committees and openly gay congressional staff.

Following the Weiss hearings and the greatly increased Administration request for funds, the major battle had been won; as Mike Walsh of the Gay Rights National Lobby put it, AIDS had been institutionalized, meaning that Congress had established the principle that there should be adequate funding for AIDS research. This does not mean, of course, that everyone was satisfied with the amounts provided; continuing Administration pressure to cut domestic spending ensured that struggles for funding would continue. Following the HTLV-III announcement Dr. Brandt lobbied hard within the Administration for an extra $55 million to be allocated for AIDS research in the 1985 budget; his requests were ignored by Secretary Heckler but after leaks to Congress were acted upon by the legislators.[11] The 1986 budget request from the Administration—one of the vagaries of the American budgetary process is that it is an almost continual process, involving very complex three-way disputes among the Administration, the Senate and the House—was for over $10 million *less* than was allocated for 1985, despite increasing demands for greater resources to be devoted to research into treatment and prevention, but was subsequently increased. The pattern described in a report of the Office of Technology Assessment which had been commissioned by Representatives Weiss and Waxman seemed likely to continue:

> Through the Assistant Secretary for Health individual Public Health Service agencies have consistently asked the Department of Health and Human Services to request particular sums from Congress; the Department has submitted requests for amounts smaller than those suggested by the agencies; and Congress typically has appropriated amounts greater than those requested by the Department . . . Of greater impact than holding general funding of PHS agencies about even or decreasing it have been budget requests for

decreases in personnel ceilings. At critical times, several of the PHS agencies have actually experienced decreases in personnel.[12]

The struggle to institutionalize AIDS was a good example of the workings of American pressure-group politics, in which a public health emergency was increasingly perceived as a gay issue in response to the reality that the gay movement was the only organized group consistently pushing for a response. In this their major allies were researchers and some of their bosses within the Public Health Service, up to and including Dr. Brandt. Secretary Heckler's concern is harder to evaluate; there is some evidence she went against White House wishes in declaring AIDS the number one public health priority, and in her widely publicized visit in August 1983 to a hospital patient with AIDS, she aimed at reducing some of the hysteria surrounding the disease.[13] But there is also evidence that she has not been prepared to do battle with the Office of Management and Budget, center of the Administration's budget cutting, for greater spending, and her priorities have clearly stressed a blood test ahead of either treatment or prevention education.

Whether Reagan himself had ever shown an interest in AIDS before his get-well call to Rock Hudson is unknown. (Heckler claims to have spoken to him about it.[14]) Certainly he never mentioned it in public during his first term, though as President he used his access to the media to appeal for help for a liver transplant, not to mention his frequent invocations of the rights of the unborn. It is clear that several measures were taken by the White House to prevent too close an identification of the Administration with AIDS. This was most apparent when Dr. Brandt canceled plans to speak at a dinner of the Fund for Human Dignity, the foundation that finances some of the work of NGTF. This cancellation followed a demand by the American Life Lobby for Dr. Brandt's resignation after it was announced that he would present an award to the Blood Sisters Project of San Diego. The Lobby's spokesman called Brandt's participation "an outrageous legitimization of an unnatural lifestyle that is repugnant to the vast majority of Americans."[15] (Brandt's office attributed the cancellation to an "unexpected meeting."[16])

From available evidence it appears that the Administration,

particularly the White House, has collaborated in fostering the idea that AIDS should be seen as a gay issue rather than a health emergency which should transcend the characteristics of those involved. Ironically, this is also the view of large segments of the gay media and movement; while there have been some attempts to de-emphasize the gay aspects of AIDS, it has been very diffi-cult to escape it. Thus one finds observers as astute as David Talbot and Larry Bush writing that "since Congress as a whole is not inclined to be sympathetic to gay issues, the challenge has been to package AIDS funding in less than obvious ways—as part of general public health appropriations for example," although it is hard to see why this is not a totally appropriate way of provid-ing for AIDS.[17] But Talbot and Bush are pointing to a real prob-lem, which Nathan Fain identified:

> Hardly anyone knows, outside the community of gay men, that more than $17 million has been spent to track thousands of gay men over four years in New York, Baltimore, Chicago, San Francisco and Los Angeles . . . presumably if Jerry Falwell ever found out what is, after all, public record, he would split a polyester seam.[18]

Fain's judgment is probably correct, which shows how perverted the rhetoric of interest-group politics becomes when research undertaken to understand and control an epidemic disease can be seen as a response to "special interests" and the encourage-ment of unpopular lifestyles.

The Costs of AIDS

The total costs of AIDS, if one includes medical and hospital expenses, the cost of information, testing and support services and the loss to the economy of large numbers of able-bodied people, is staggering. It is by its nature a difficult cost to reckon; one study up to November 1984 estimated that the direct costs of the epidemic in the United States amounted to $955 million, that one million days of work and $650 million in output had been lost and that the total cost to that date must be about $1.5 billion.[19] The study of these costs must examine not only the overall bur-den but the way in which that burden is distributed.

Perhaps the most striking aspect of American health care when viewed from an international perspective is the absence of any sort of national health scheme, whether this be through national insurance (as in Australia, Canada and France) or a direct government service (as in Britain). Medical costs in America are covered by a complex mix of private insurance (usually linked to employment) and government programs, designed, at least in theory, to provide for those who are not adequately insured. Suggestions for a national health insurance scheme have a long history; it was proposed in Theodore Roosevelt's Progressive platform of 1912. During the seventies various schemes for expanding health insurance were proposed, ranging from an American Medical Association plan for tax incentives to Senator Kennedy's proposals for government-regulated insurance.[20] In the more conservative eighties such proposals have retreated into the background, and as Paul Starr put it: "The failure to rationalize medical services under public control meant that sooner or later they would be rationalized under private control."[21] Moreover, the thrust of the Reagan Administration's health policies has been to limit expenditure on Medicare and Medicaid (government-financed care for the old and the poor, respectively) and to force greater responsibility onto local governments. Medicaid is estimated to cover only half the poor in the United States, because of variations among the states (which play a major administrative and financial role in these programs) and the exclusion of able-bodied persons between the ages of eighteen and sixty-four, regardless of their income.[22]

The rapid expansion of medical costs in the past decade—health care now takes up 10 percent of the GNP and almost 12 percent of the federal budget—has resulted in real pressure to contain costs, but the responses of the Reagan Administration moved away from the attempt to provide equal quality medical care for all regardless of income, which had been the original aim of Medicare and Medicaid. California, traditionally one of the most generous states in its administration of the program in 1982 turned over responsibility for its 280,000 Medicaid (which it called Medi-cal) "medically indigent adults" to the counties, while providing less than 70 percent of the funds it had been spending on the programs, and adopted measures to cut costs for other Medi-cal patients.[23] Other states took more drastic action; testimony from health-care workers in Tennessee claimed that "in some cases indigent patients were denied hospitalization until their conditions deteriorated, and testimony indicated that some critically ill patients could not obtain hospital care."[24]

The AIDS epidemic occurred at a time when city and county governments were already feeling the strain of caring for large numbers of people denied coverage by federal and state programs, and the concentration of cases in a few areas has meant enormous stresses for these systems. Well over 10 percent of the population—25 to 30 million people—have no medical insurance at all, and these include a disproportionate number of young unmarried adults, the group most likely to contract AIDS (how many IV users or illegal Haitian immigrants are likely to enroll with Blue Cross?), but even those who have insurance are not necessarily fully covered for the costs of major illness.[25] The fact that most insurance is linked to employment means that protracted illness will entail the loss of insurance at some point, thus forcing even those who have been prudent and sought coverage to rely upon the various government programs, with all the uncertainties and delays that these involve. Some states make it mandatory for insurance companies to provide continuing coverage on an individual basis, but this is a major expense when people can least afford it. In the panic over AIDS some gay employees fear losing their jobs at a time when the associated health benefits are particularly important. Such questions are not problems in countries where there is universal health insurance, unrelated to employment, a powerful argument for its introduction in the United States, although the Thatcher government's cuts in hospital facilities might well affect Britain's capacity to respond to a growing epidemic.[26]

One of the great fears associated with the HTLV-III antibody test is that a positive result, even in a healthy individual, will become a reason for insurance companies to deny insurance or to claim that they are exempt from covering a case of AIDS should it arise later on. Already one case has been referred to Lambda Legal Defense of someone who was refused insurance because he was considered at high risk for AIDS on the basis of his existing medical history. No insurance company will admit to a policy of excluding members of "high risk" groups, but what informal restrictions and "persuasion" might exist is more difficult to evaluate. (I have heard the story of one insurance salesman who was told not to sign up any more young single men; one wonders whether gay businesses, or those assumed to have considerable numbers of gay employees, will find it increasingly difficult to arrange group health coverage for employees.) It is not surprising that by 1985 several insurance companies were offering coverage expressly for AIDS.

In theory, someone without insurance—provided one has also exhausted virtually all one's assets—is picked up by the federal government via Supplemental Security Income benefits, which also qualify one for Medicaid. (Some policy makers have speculated on the possibility of getting Medicaid to pick up health insurance premiums before these policies expire.) It took some time and effort to get AIDS recognized by the Social Security Administration as qualifying for disability benefits, and even so, the very complex patchwork of local, state and federal rules is extremely complicated and often requires long waits, particularly hard in the case of a disease that can strike suddenly. As one person with AIDS, Tony Ferrara, told Congress:

> Unless you have looked into the tortured face of a person with AIDS and seen the terror, not only at the thought of dying, but at the thought of being tossed out of their homes because they haven't the money to pay their rent, or of having their phone service, electricity or heat terminated because they cannot work and therefore have no income with which to pay these bills, you cannot fully appreciate the tremendous need that exists . . .[27]

It has taken longer, and considerable lobbying, to get AIDS-related illnesses (ARC) recognized by the Social Security Administration, although the Administration has often been helpful in the way it interprets existing regulations. Because state and county governments are involved in these programs, provisions are very different from one jurisdiction to another; for example, access to home care, which may be crucial in determining whether one can be discharged from a hospital, varies enormously across the United States. A further problem has been coverage for "experimental treatment." As a considerable amount of the treatment for infections associated with AIDS can be so regarded, this has been an enormous escape hatch for insurers. It took the threat of a lawsuit to get Medi-cal to pay for pentamadine, the drug often used for pneumocystis.[28] Another example was given by Sandra Panem, involving the use of interferon, which has been tested in several hospitals for AIDS but is not paid for by Medicare because it is not "established and standard treatment."[29]

The ultimate burden on city and county hospitals is immense. By the beginning of 1985 figures like $1 billion in hospital costs were being mentioned,[30] and New York City Health Commissioner David J. Sencer claimed the city was spending $1 million a week. Even so, there were increasing reports that New York, with the highest case load in the country and a very high hospital occupancy rate, was reaching a point where it would literally run out of available beds for AIDS patients by the end of 1985: "It is now routine for me and my colleagues to wait days before finding a bed for a seriously ill patient, often with a life-threatening infection. As I have said, at the rate the disease is progressing, by this time next year there will be an additional 3,000 cases of AIDS reported in the city. The hospital beds for these patients do not exist."[31] In London about a third of the national total of cases have gone to St. Mary's Hospital in Paddington, which clearly places a great strain on that particular hospital.

Preliminary studies in San Francisco suggest that the average lifetime cost for hospital care for AIDS patients is between $25,000 and $32,000, lower than the figures usually quoted—and seemingly lower than costs in other parts of the country. As Peter Arno of the Institute for Health Policy Studies pointed out: "The higher cost of treatment at other hospitals around the country may be due in part to a much larger proportion of patients utilizing intensive care facilities than the ten percent of AIDS patients who do so at San Francisco General Hospital. One may speculate further, that this relatively low level of utilization of intensive care facilities at SFGH reflects the high quality of social support and counselling activities that are part of the patient care given on the AIDS ward."[32]

Not only is the expense of AIDS treatment considerable; the standard available is remarkably varied. Because there is no clear

cure, much treatment is experimental, and many patients receive care as part of ongoing medical experimentation. The particular problems of stigma and prejudice, already discussed, affect treatment considerably. In a few centers there are first-class
hospital facilities available for AIDS patients, and at least in San
Francisco and New York, after some agitation, hospice facilities
have been made available to some of those who are terminally ill.
More commonly, however, patients experience the problems
common to overcrowded public hospitals. In San Francisco, concern over these problems prompted the establishment of a separate AIDS ward and clinic in 1983, which has subsequently
treated about half the city's total case load and has become the
most visible sign of that city's commitment to do everything
possible to deal with the epidemic.

The proposal for an AIDS ward was originally opposed by some
on the grounds that it would ghettoize AIDS patients and further
increase their stigma. There was also concern, which I have
heard echoed in New York, that it would be undesirable for the
hospital to become known as an AIDS center. The basic rationale
was that only in a specialized ward could patients receive opti-
mum care and escape the homophobia that many had experienced in general hospital treatment. Moreover, as Dr. Mervyn
Silverman pointed out, there were certain medical reasons for
separation: "The last thing we want to do is expose these patients
to any infectious agents. Hospitals have a lot of them . . ."[33] Two
years later several hundred people with AIDS had passed
through the ward, and patients were having to be housed in
other areas of the hospital. There is general agreement that the
ward and accompanying outpatient clinic offer a level of compassion and humane treatment unparalleled in most other hospitals,
indeed in other parts of San Francisco General. The staff, many of
whom are openly gay, have all volunteered for this assignment
and have an extraordinary dedication to the patients with whom
they are working. The strain on them is enormous; ultimately
they can do little more than help make death a little less painful
and traumatic. The decision of when to discontinue life-support
systems is an everyday one on the ward.

Ward 5B has become a fixed point on tours of San Francisco's
AIDS efforts; when I was there in January 1985 both the Austra-

lian Health Minister (flanked by television cameras) and a delegation from New York City passed through on inspection visits. Other cities have considered similar facilities; one was mooted for New York's Bellevue Hospital, and there was talk in London of reopening a disused hospital for AIDS cases. In 1985 an outpatient clinic opened in Sydney for screening and treatment. Many other cities will face a need for greatly expanded facilities within this decade, and similar strains exist with prison systems. New York's Sing Sing has a special ward for AIDS patients. The pressure on San Francisco General is considerable; by late 1984 there were times when all the respiratory-care units in the hospital were required for AIDS patients. As numbers mounted, there was increasing talk of seeking direct federal aid, of pressuring other hospitals to admit more AIDS patients and even of converting a former federal hospital to accommodate new AIDS cases.

The load on San Francisco has increased because people from surrounding areas come to the city for treatment and hospitalization. Two cases of "dumping" of patients have created a considerable furor: the first in late 1983 when a hospital in Gainesville, Florida, chartered an airplane to send a critically ill patient to San Francisco, allegedly because the hospital could not provide adequate treatment, the second in mid-1984 when a doctor at San Luis Obispo, a town several hundred miles south, ordered a patient who was critically ill sent in a private car to San Francisco General. In both cases there was no attempt to request assistance before dispatching the patient.[34] That San Francisco's burden should be increased by the failure of other localities to provide adequate facilities is testimony to the inequities imposed by a decentralized health-care system.

Philip Lee, now chairman of San Francisco's Health Commission, has summed up the dilemmas posed by the escalating costs of AIDS treatment:

> The emphasis at almost every level of government and in the public sector is on deregulation, which is hostile to health planning. Can such a strategy meet the challenge of the AIDS epidemic? The overriding concern of those who question the strategy of decentralization, deregulation and increased price competition in health care is with the adequacy of resources at the state and local levels to

assume full responsibility for the programs, including the costs that would be transferred to state and local governments, or to individuals. Underlying the whole debate is a very clear but controversial question of the federal role and national responsibility. Is AIDS a national problem? Is it a problem where the federal role is primarily in biomedical research and disease surveillance? What is the federal role in public health education and AIDS prevention? What is the role in financing health care for AIDS patients?[35]

State and Local Governments

The problems of jurisdiction to which Philip Lee referred have been pointed up very clearly in the AIDS epidemic. No other system is as decentralized, although in Canada health is largely a provincial matter, and in Australia the state governments play a large role. (In Britain the greater county councils, slated for abolition in 1986, have also been alternative sources of funds for certain welfare projects.) By early 1985, 60 percent of all United States cases had been reported in just five cities—New York, San Francisco, Los Angeles, Miami and Newark—and this accentuated the importance of decentralization. In a few cases, most notably New York, California and New Jersey, some state monies and programs were forthcoming. In most cases the onus for care, information and services was placed on local county and city governments.

Such decentralization makes it very difficult to generalize about government responses to AIDS in the United States. Much of the response has depended on existing health and welfare programs, and these in turn often have depended on the relative roles and resources of city and county health departments. (In general, counties play a larger role in smaller and newer cities. Because they cover larger areas than cities they are likely to be less responsive to the needs of AIDS, which has so far tended to be heavily concentrated in urban centers. This phenomenon has affected government response in both Los Angeles and Houston.) A survey by the U.S. Conference of Mayors in 1984 assembled information from fifty-five local governments on their AIDS efforts. Of these over 40 percent of cities with populations over

200,000 and almost 25 percent of those with less than 200,000 reported AIDS-related local public spending; two-thirds of the larger cities had established task forces on AIDS by late 1984.[36]

What does seem apparent is that the response of both state and local governments is largely a function of the strength of the gay movement. In some cases, most particularly in San Francisco, this has meant a more generous response from governments than might otherwise have been the case. Elsewhere, however, this linkage has been more likely to hamper a full-scale response to a medical emergency, as politicians are prone to dismiss AIDS as no more than the concern of a "special interest." In the fifty-five cities that responded to the Conference of Mayors survey—notable non-respondents were New York, Philadelphia, Detroit and Boston—gay communal groups were more heavily involved than any of the public health agencies in providing hot lines, home care and, by a much narrower margin, counseling.[37] Too often city or state responses have become bogged down in arguments about giving money to gay organizations or politicians' fears that they might be seen as favoring an unpopular minority. As AIDS spreads outside those cities where gays do have some real clout, the perception of it as a homosexual disease becomes more and more of an obstacle to the provision of adequate services.

These points can be nicely illustrated by reference to the politics of AIDS funding in three of the cities where the case load is highest—San Francisco, New York and Miami. In the first two, city governments have spent large sums of money on AIDS-related activities, but in very different ways. New York has operated via existing government agencies, primarily within the Health Department, while San Francisco has been far more willing to fund new programs through volunteer groups and to underwrite a much wider range of activities, especially in education. This difference is at least in part explicable by the far greater influence of the gay movement in San Francisco and the tradition of city support for gay-related activities. (Before the epidemic the city was already supporting gay social welfare services such as the Pride Foundation and Operation Concern, a counseling agency for lesbians and gay men, and had established an office of Lesbian and Gay Health within the Health Department.) Not only does San Francisco have a much larger and more

effective gay political movement, it also, since 1977, has had a
gay supervisor and a mayor with ties to at least some parts of the
gay movement. (In San Francisco the City Council is synonymous
with the county government, a correspondence unique in California, and one that avoids much of the jurisdictional buck-pass-
ing that has dogged provision of AIDS services in Los Angeles.[38])
In addition, the mainstream press in San Francisco has provided
a coverage of AIDS that is far more detailed and politically sophisticated than is true elsewhere.

In New York, on the other hand, the gay movement has been
surprisingly weak and disorganized, and it seems probable that
the decision of the city administration to work through existing
structures is due, at least in part, to a desire not to be seen as too
supportive of homosexuals. Mayor Koch has, after all, been subject to constant rumors that he himself is gay (in one mayoral
primary he was smeared by a slogan that ran: "Elect Cuomo, not
the homo") and his attempt to include gays in the purview of city
anti-discrimination provisions sparked off considerable controversy with the Catholic archbishop and other hard-line churches
in 1984.[39] The New York City Council has consistently refused to
include gays within the provisions of anti-discrimination laws,
despite a campaign to achieve this for over a decade.

Other factors have influenced San Francisco's response: the
city government is richer, with fewer ongoing crises than New
York (which is still haunted by memories of near-default in the
late 1970s); it has traditionally placed considerable emphasis on
health concerns; and the University of California's Medical
School, UCSF, is an important influence in a way that no one
medical school can match in New York. For all these reasons, the
overall response of the city and its volunteer organizations and
medical profession has made its management of AIDS a model
for dealing with a medical emergency. The city first moved to
allocate money for the epidemic in October 1982, when a funding package for AIDS was put together by Supervisor Harry
Britt's office, and the following year the Board of Supervisors
unanimously approved a $2.1 million allocation for AIDS ser-
vices, which was more than tripled by 1985. Included in these
expenditures were certain programs that have yet to be matched
by any other city. As already discussed, the city has funneled

much of its funds through Shanti and the AIDS Foundation, while maintaining considerable coordination and oversight through an AIDS office within the Department of Health and, since 1984, a mayoral task force.

Other than the provision of the AIDS ward and clinic, the most controversial aspect of San Francisco's programs has been the decision to fund public education projects aimed at high visibility (for example, billboards and subway advertisements) and at directly changing sexual practices among gay men. The battle over what sort of programs and under whose control was one of the more ferocious in the AIDS story; its flavor was caught in the newspaper story headlined "Possible Truce in AIDS Wars."[40] Despite this conflict, the city has been willing to allocate considerable resources to the development of education programs, which have gone far beyond printing informational brochures and posters to providing therapeutic counseling and self-help groups to assist gay men in coming to terms with the very real fears and difficulties involved in radically altering sexual behavior. (These will be further discussed in the next chapter.) Some disquiet has been expressed by a couple of supervisors over the way in which educational funds were being spent, but in general the city has been supportive of almost every program proposed. The almost total concentration of AIDS among gay men in San Francisco meant that the problems of education posed in cities such as New York, Newark or Miami, with more diverse case loads, seemed less significant. Still, fear of heterosexual transmission led the city to expand its "safe sex" campaign to a broader population in 1985.

The response of the city of New York has been far more guarded and hesitant. It took some time for the Gay Men's Health Crisis to approach City Hall for assistance, and even longer for Mayor Koch to meet with the group and make any statement about the epidemic. The Office of Gay and Lesbian Health Concerns was established by Mayor Koch in March 1983, an odd response to the epidemic in a city where almost a third of the cases are not gay. More importantly, unlike the AIDS office in San Francisco, the New York office has had no real power, either to initiate programs or to coordinate the city's overall efforts. The original director, Roger Enlow, resigned in August 1984 and it took over six months for a successor to be appointed.[41] The Health Commissioner, Dr. David Sencer, did appoint an Interagency Task Force, which provided a useful forum for bringing together city and private officials concerned with AIDS work, but it had none of the real clout a mayoral task force could bring to bear. Dr. Sencer has taken a strong position on matters of confidentiality, and the city has been a leader in attempts to prevent misuse of the HTLV-III test.

The city has spent considerable sums on hospital care, on surveillance and epidemiological work, but until mid-1985 its response to the need for patient-support services and large-scale education and information was meager to say the least; in mid-1983 State Senator Roy Goodman described the city's response as "going after a monster with a fly-swatter."[42] To a number of activists the city's response has been a disgrace. Larry Kramer described the city's failure to provide money for AIDS screening and diagnosis as "particularly shocking and offensive,"[43] and by early 1985 so little had changed that Rodger McFarlane was moved to describe the city's lack of planning as "criminally irresponsible."[44] Criticisms of the city fell into three major areas: a lack of planning and coordination, a failure to provide support for the work of volunteer AIDS agencies and the absence of a large-scale educational campaign.

As the scope of the crisis increased there was a growing awareness that the city had failed to make comprehensive plans to deal with the strain on medical and welfare services posed by the epidemic, and from the end of 1984 on, criticism of the city administration became more vocal. As Mathilde Krim of the AIDS Medical Foundation pointed out: "The response in New York has been totally different than the coordination, the planning you have in San Francisco. There is no chronic care, no hospice, no meals on wheels, nothing to keep people at home instead of in a hospital."[45] The services that in San Francisco are largely city-funded were for the most part established in New York by volunteer organizations with private money, though the city did fund the position of financial services coordinator at GMHC and in 1983 provided considerable funds for a Red Cross-administered home-care service which did not prove a success. And the city's educational efforts were almost entirely confined to professional groups, leaving mass education and information to GMHC, which did not have the resources to mount campaigns on anything like the scale attempted in San Francisco.

The comparisons with San Francisco became official when New York City sent a delegation to that city in early 1985 to report on its response, and its report provided the basis for a number of new initiatives. In March, Mayor Koch announced a slew of programs involving housing, outpatient and hospital care and education, which the city estimated would amount to $6 million a year, as well as the establishment of a high-level policy and planning committee.[46] There seemed to be two major reasons for the city's actions: the scope of the problem had become too great to be ignored, and enough pressure had been put on the mayor and his advisers to force action. The pressure came from a number of areas—within the city administration, from sections of the press, from AIDS organizations and from a couple of City Council members. (It was not without significance that 1985 was an election year in the city.) I suspect that had New York possessed a more organized and vocal gay movement the response from the city would have been faster.

Until this announcement, Mayor Koch's strategy had seemed to consist largely of claiming that someone else—usually Washington—should take responsibility for the epidemic, and in fact some of the programs financed by the city government in San Francisco were taken up by the state government in New York. Initially, the state seemed even less likely to act than the city. At hearings called by Senator Goodman, Republican chair of the State Senate Investigations Committee, in mid-1983, David Axelrod, State Commissioner of Health since 1979, not only admitted he had not sought extra funds in the two years the disease had existed—with almost half the known cases in his state—but made several extraordinarily confused statements, in the course of which he suggested: "AIDS is not a new disease . . . there are unique features of this disease that suggest it may not be related to an infectious agent, but may be related to other environmental or occupational conditions . . ." What these might be was not explained.[47]

Following these hearings and considerable gay lobbying, Goodman proposed a state AIDS Institute with funding of over

$5 million; as in Washington, the legislature proved more amena-
ble than the executive branch, and agreed to the proposal.
(There have been public arguments over the extent of Governor
Cuomo's support for the Institute.[48]) The Institute was a unique
idea, possibly the most innovative institutional response of any
government to the AIDS crisis. It was unusual in that it represented a major state commitment to medical research, usually
assumed to be an exclusive federal responsibility. It was even
more so in that through its Advisory Council it allowed for the
direct participation of affected groups; half the membership of
the Council is drawn from the gay movement, People With AIDS
and the Haitian Coalition on AIDS. The largest sums go to research, but the provision of money for services and education has
enabled the creation of community service organizations across
the state. Thus, under the impetus of the Institute, there are
groups doing AIDS education, counseling and service work in
every region of New York State. (The state has given some financial assistance to groups such as GMHC, providing something like
20 percent of their budget in 1984 and 1985.) The AIDS Institute
has been concerned with education and information, and has
sought to develop a number of programs targeted at special
groups.

In California, on the other hand, the state was slower to provide money, and it is a reflection of the power of the University of
California that all research money has been channeled into that
system. Under pressure from a few liberal politicians money was
also made available for educational programs, and outside San
Francisco the educational and informational work in California
has been largely state-financed. During 1985 initiatives taken by
several assemblymen led the state to develop a larger role, and
despite the veto of some proposed programs by Governor
Deukejian, California now leads the nation in state AIDS activities. In New Jersey, which has a heavy concentration of non-gay,
primarily drug-user cases, money for research and education has
been provided, and several other states have begun to fund similar items.

What happens when city, county and state governments all fail
to recognize that AIDS is a particular problem that requires
special medical, welfare and educational responses? The simple

answer is that many of the programs that have been found necessary in San Francisco and to a lesser extent in New York, Los
Angeles, Boston and Washington are not provided, unless volunteer organizations step in. The worst neglect is found in southern
Florida, where there is a heavy case load (about a third Haitian)
and an almost total lack of interest at all levels of government.
There was a move by the state legislature in 1984 to provide
special monies to the University of Miami for AIDS research and
treatment (this would have covered Jackson Memorial Hospital,
where most AIDS cases are found), but it was vetoed by the
governor. The political climate in southern Florida is hardly fa-
vorable to AIDS funding; Miami was the scene of Anita Bryant's
first successful anti-gay campaign in 1977 and the gay movement
remains weak, the growing Cuban population tends to be very
conservative and homophobic (a characteristic they share, ironically, with the Castro government) and Haitian refugees are
regarded with great suspicion. Nor is Miami the only place in
Florida where AIDS is a problem; the heaviest concentration of
AIDS per capita in the United States is in the town of Belle Glade,
a migrant workers' town on Lake Okeechobee in Palm Beach
County, one of the wealthiest counties in the United States and
one, it would seem, completely oblivious to the squalor, poverty
and burgeoning health crisis in its midst.[49] Although the Health
Crisis Network in Miami and other groups in Key West and Fort
Lauderdale have been able to mobilize some support and
money, virtually all gay, and there has been a certain amount of
organizing among local Haitians, no level of government has
accepted any responsibility for dealing with the epidemic. When
a small amount of money became available in 1985 for a health
education program among local Haitians, it was from federal
sources.

Money and Experts

The growing costs of modern scientific research have clearly
affected the ways in which medical research is conducted. It is no
longer possible for individuals working alone in their laboratories, or doctors working in their surgeries, to undertake signifi-

cant research. Inevitably, this means that research becomes bureaucratized and centralized, not only within large medical schools and research institutes but internationally as well, so that the United States has come to dominate a great deal of medical research because of its resources. (It is striking, for example, how large a global role is played by the CDC in tracking and researching epidemics.) The need for considerable funds, most of which will ultimately come from government, means that politics will often determine the priorities of research; as one writer put it: "The politics of biomedical research have been the politics of the appropriations process."[50] In 1983 it was estimated that almost $10.5 billion was spent on health research and development in the United States, of which 60 percent came from government sources and the largest amount of this through the National Institutes of Health.[51]

Equally, what areas are researched will often be determined by non-scientific criteria. Whether it be the National Foundation for the March of Dimes demanding action on polio, or public and media pressure several years ago in support of interferon research, medical researchers respond to pressure groups in much the same way as do governments. Just as the Supreme Court is said to read the election returns, so the scientific establishment reads the newspapers. In the competition for resources, illnesses develop their own constituencies, with groups that raise money, provide support services and lobby for research funds. The apparent independence of the National Cancer Institute within the National Institutes of Health is a direct result of the campaign in the early 1970s that led to President Nixon's "war on cancer." In this respect the politics of AIDS are not very different from the politics surrounding other diseases, such as muscular dystrophy and arthritis, which also have their lobby groups.

Once a disease becomes "fashionable," it generates its own establishment and vested interests. Aided by politicians, lobbyists and the media, the money and attention focused on AIDS in the United States since mid-1983 have ensured the development of an AIDS industry, involving researchers, doctors, therapists, social workers and administrators, who have taken control of the definition and management of the disease. This is most obvious in the political arena, where a number of positions have been created to deal with the epidemic—in San Francisco alone perhaps fifty new jobs have been created to deal with the non-research and non-medical side of AIDS—but is equally true in science and academia, where the pattern resembles that of other diseases. As Dr. Herbert Dickerman of the AIDS Institute in New York put it: "Money is merely a telegram that must get to the proper recipient to be used effectively. Scientists are faddists—when they see a good idea they flock to it."[52]

As the stakes in both money and scientific prestige increase—one hears frequent rumors that some of the leading figures in AIDS research are preoccupied with the lure of a Nobel Prize—so, too, does the fight to control AIDS. I have already referred to bitter disputes between the Institut Pasteur, the CDC and the NIH over "the AIDS virus"; even within the NIH there is conflict between different agencies, especially the National Cancer Institute and the National Institute of Allergy and Infectious Diseases, where the bulk of AIDS research has been carried out.[53] Suspicion about the competence and the commitment of the Public Health Service in general is quite widespread, and there have been a number of suggestions for some sort of overall master-planning authority for AIDS research. This was a proposition put before a congressional hearing in 1983 by the American Public Health Association: "The nation's single most urgent current need is the prompt development of a comprehensive AIDS research, surveillance and monitoring plan. Without such a plan we will unwittingly waste much of whatever time, talent and money are applied to the AIDS program."[54] Similar calls have been made on several occasions by the National Gay Task Force. The report of the Committee on Government Operations that followed the 1983 hearings recommended (with ten of the fourteen Republicans dissenting) that "an independent panel of appropriate professionals be convened to facilitate the coordination and farsighted planning of our national response to AIDS." The panel was to include "expert scientists, health professionals and lay individuals."[55]

Similar demands had been made some years earlier in support of cancer research, when the analogy of the moon shot was used to call for a national plan to wipe out cancer,[56] an analogy that has surfaced again in the rhetoric surrounding AIDS. Critics of this approach could point out that it was not evident that better research would result from placing it under the aegis of a national panel. On the other hand, as the report from the Office of Technology Assessment suggests, considerable competition and refusal to cooperate among agencies of the Public Health Service had slowed down some research,[57] and even Dr. Brandt, since leaving the Administration, has said there needs to be more centralized direction of AIDS efforts. That part of the committee's recommendation which involved "surveillance, treatment and prevention" was even more easily defended, especially if it would be a way of increasing federal contributions to the escalating costs of these programs (which was clearly one reason why a majority of the committee's Republicans opposed it).

Fights over the control of research become clearly political in the disputes—between the upholders of orthodox medical research, including the Public Health Service, and those with different priorities, particularly People With AIDS and groups who have been influenced by feminist and other radical critiques of health care—over whose and what "expertise" is important. This is particularly acute in discussions of epidemiological and psychological research, but because of the conceptualization of AIDS as a gay disease all sorts of criteria not normally thought of in medical discourse become involved. Conflicts arise, too, between the priorities of laboratory researchers and those whose primary concern is patient care and prevention. Following a large public forum on AIDS in Sydney in 1984, several revealing critiques were published in a local gay paper, suggesting that the medical experts were concerned more with "creative research" than with helping those afflicted with and exposed to the disease: "Towards this end, the researchers are loath to interfere with their 'unsullied' sample, but gratefully receive hundreds of thousands of our dollars. Meanwhile, the subjects of their research languish in their hospital, treated like plague victims, their basic human rights ignored and even their lives endangered by the attitudes and treatments of the people entrusted with their care."[58]

Such concerns became particularly crucial once the question of understanding—and, more important, changing—sexual behavior was raised as a central factor in the discourse about AIDS.

The role of sexual transmission was not immediately obvious (remember the search for "lifestyle" factors, such as "poppers"), but by mid-1982 it was being strongly argued. "In my own view," wrote Dr. Dan William, "the available evidence is already sufficient to classify AIDS as an infectious disease that can be spread sexually."[59] Arguments such as these provided the basis for growing moves to develop educational campaigns for "risk reduction." (One should note that there were risks other than sexual in the transmission of AIDS, for example the sharing of needles, but not surprisingly it was the sexual ones that dominated discussion.) Quite apart from the substance of these campaigns, and what they meant for sexual behavior, their existence raised the question of whether those concerned to prevent the spread of AIDS were reintroducing, from the best of motives, a re-medicalization of homosexuality. As Michael Lynch, a critic of William, wrote later that year: "Like helpless mice we have peremptorily, almost inexplicably, relinquished the one power we so long fought for in constructing our modern gay community: the power to determine our own gay identity. And to whom have we relinquished it? The very authority we wrested it from in a struggle that occupied us for more than a hundred years: the medical profession."[60]

A perfect example of this reassertion of medical power over homosexuality occurred in the spring of 1984, when several researchers at the University of California's Medical School in San Francisco organized a conference on "intervention strategies for high-risk behavior." Those invited to participate were researchers from universities and public health services, with a couple of public relations men included on the "media and health education" committee. This professional elite angered a group of invited observers from various AIDS organizations, who felt *their* expertise had been totally slighted. The organizers apparently felt no compunction at allowing a closed gathering of "experts," some of them closeted homosexuals, to define how gay men should behave. For many of the observers it was all too reminiscent of the way in which homosexuality had been traditionally defined by doctors and psychiatrists.[61] What was at issue was not whether there should be some attempt to educate people about "high-risk behavior," but rather who should control and determine the information and its dissemination. As we shall see, a number of AIDS groups had already launched such campaigns, usually with medical participation. An extreme position was taken by the French gay medical group, the Association des Médecins Gais, who refused for a long time to follow suit lest they be accused of exercising *"le pouvoir médecin."*[62] Similarly, at the 1985 International Conference on AIDS in Atlanta there was considerable anger from the large number of people present from AIDS groups and gay organizations at what was perceived as attempts by government scientists to use the HTLV-III antibody test to control the expression of gay sexuality by dividing men into "positives" and "negatives."[63]

The rewards of expertise are considerable. They involve prestige, jobs and often, quite directly, money. Nowhere is this clearer than in the commercial offshoots of the LAV/HTLV-III discoveries. Licenses to develop a blood test for the retrovirus were granted to five companies in 1984, of which at least one had significant connections with NCI investigators. But other companies both in and outside the United States were involved in developing tests; one estimate was that the American market alone would be worth $80 million a year.[64] The competition for leadership in virus research is so intense that one company, the Chiron Corporation of California, hired a public relations expert to publicize its success in cloning the genes of HTLV-III, rather than waiting for formal publication.[65]

The American free enterprise system thus allows private companies to make enormous profits from biomedical advances that have been achieved with government money. Despite this, there is no obligation for commercial firms to release their research findings, even when they might be of direct use to other researchers or doctors.[66] In this tradition, vaccine development and manufacture is often left to private enterprise: "I don't think the government will want to be involved this time," said Dr. Peter Fischinger of the National Cancer Institute. "It should be done by a commercial entity."[67] One assumes that private companies would see vaccine development as an attractive proposition—Dr. Jim Curran has spoken of the need for universal vaccination—but the problems of indemnification should such a vaccine produce dangerous side effects, as has been true of the vaccine against whooping cough, make this by no means a certain proposition. It is conceivable that reliance upon private manufacturers could lead to considerable delay or the production of a vaccine that is so expensive that it is unavailable to many of those most in need, as has been true of the hepatitis-B vaccine. (The same problems apply to drugs which may be developed for treatment of AIDS.) As one observer wrote: "The country may soon be in the ludicrous position of developing a vaccine for AIDS and of not being able to find a manufacturer to produce it."[68]

Indeed, trying to get information on relative responsibility for vaccine development is a case study in the gaps left in the American health system by the quite remarkable deference to private industry. In 1981 the National Institute of Allergy and Infectious Diseases, the section of the Public Health Service most directly involved in vaccine development, appointed a committee to investigate priorities in vaccine development. The very detailed (and expensive) report of that committee, published four years later, concluded: "This committee understood that it was probably not aware of all pertinent vaccine-related activity in the private sector. Given this situation, no formal attempt was made to incorporate the level of industry interest in individual vaccines into the mechanism designed for selecting priorities for accelerated development."[69]

Does it not seem extraordinary that a top-level committee, designed to establish national priorities in a central area of health care, can go no further than "suggest" that "NIAAD decisions on how to implement the program of accelerated vaccine development should incorporate a review of relevant activity in the private sector"?[70] Given the public money and concern involved in vaccine development it would seem that this is a perfect case for greater centralization of information and activity. It is no wonder that some researchers in California, most particularly Professor Marcus Conant, have been trying to figure ways of using the state government to make vaccine development attractive to local biotechnical companies. Once again, the lesson is that political will as much as scientific discoveries affects the progress of our health.

CHAPTER SEVEN

Contagious Desire: Sex and Disease

Can't it be like the fantasy?
Can't it be like it used to be?
How to have sex in an epidemic
Without getting caught up in polemic

—Michael Callen and Richard Dworkin,
"How to Have Sex in an Epidemic"

Once AIDS was clearly linked to sexual transmission, largely—
though not exclusively—through male homosexual acts, it was
inevitable that further discussion of the disease would become
inextricably connected with fears, fantasies and beliefs about
sexuality. Indeed, much of the time a preoccupation with AIDS
as a sexually transmitted disease has tended to totally dominate
discussion and to give a metaphorical weight to AIDS as "the
wages of sin" that no disease since syphilis has achieved.

The parallels are actually quite remarkable. In the period
when syphilis first became widespread in Western Europe, the
early sixteenth century, it was regarded, as Sir William Osler
wrote in a famous essay early this century, "as a mysterious epidemic, hitherto unknown, which had struck terror into all hearts
by the rapidity of its spread, the ravages it made, and the apparent helplessness of the physicians to cure it."[1] The attempts to
blame syphilis on American Indians, and the claim that it was
brought back to Europe by Columbus, charges now largely dis-
credited, remind one of similar claims about AIDS. It did not take
long for syphilis to be linked to sexual contagion, and hence to

punishment by God. This attitude persists right into the present era; venereal diseases are still seen by some as divine retribution. As the chaplain in John Horne Burn's story "Queen Penicillin" says: "My boy, if there were no disease in the world there would be no decency. The fear of God. Our illness is the sign of the disapproval of God for what we did."[2]

One historian, Stanislav Andreski, has even claimed that the widespread outbreaks of syphilis in Renaissance Europe were an important influence in the rise of Puritanism. While he is not incautious enough to ascribe too much to the one event, he suggests that the existence of syphilis and the recognition of sexual transmission was a powerful reason for men to listen with sympathy to the Puritans.[3] Fear of venereal disease was a potent weapon in promoting sexual restraint until the discovery of antibiotics, which, together with reasonably safe and efficient means of contraception, allowed for the "permissive revolution" of the 1960s and 1970s. (This was foreseen by some physicians who feared that the discovery of penicillin would open the way to a "promiscuity that is rotting the family at its roots."[4])

The "permissive revolution" saw a marked increase in genital herpes, and for a time this seemed to echo syphilis as a warning against promiscuity. "Perhaps it's current sexual practice that is the real epidemic," wrote Lois Draegin, "and the rash of sexually transmitted diseases raging through the city simply a symptom."[5] Amy Wilentz has analyzed the way herpes was presented in a *Time* cover story that was illustrated with a large scarlet letter H so as to link "promiscuity" to both disease and radicalism. "But perhaps not so unhappily," wrote *Time* of the disease, "it may be a prime mover in helping to bring to a close an era of mindless promiscuity. The monogamous now have one more reason to remain so. For all the distress it has brought, the troublesome little bug may inadvertently be ushering in a period in which sex is linked more firmly to commitment and trust."[6]

Herpes is, of course, trivial beside AIDS, a factor ironically foreshadowed by Wilentz:

> No wonder that in the midst of an epidemic of cancer, *Time* is fanning the fires of fear about something as piddling as herpes. Cancer, some of the causes of which have long been linked to the

industrial environment, is a less attractive disease than herpes, with
its supposed ties to the 1960's, and what used to be rather fondly
thought of as the left. Cancer is a disease that the state can inflict on
the citizenry, while herpes seems more a disease of choice, that is a
democratic affliction.[7]

That AIDS was in all probability transmitted sexually was
grasped fairly rapidly, despite the simultaneous branding of it as
a new form of cancer, which is rarely thought of as contagious.
Some gay men continued to resist this claim, arguing that it was
an unproven hypothesis that had been adopted more for moralistic than scientific reasons. Thus as late as October 1984 an editorial in the Los Angeles gay paper *Frontiers* claimed: "There is at
this time no documented proof that AIDS is a sexually transmitted syndrome."[8] But even among those who accepted the very
strong evidence for sexual transmission there was no automatic
consensus on the implications of this. One of the continuing
stories of the AIDS epidemic has been the struggle, above all by
gay men, to find ways of adopting sexual behavior and ethics that
would include an awareness of how to prevent transmission of
AIDS.

To understand just how difficult this adjustment has been requires an understanding of the way gay men have developed a
particular set of values and behavior around sexuality which
AIDS seemed to throw into question. During the 1970s the
growth of both gay assertion and a commercial gay world meant
an affirmation of sex outside of relationships as a positive good, a
means of expressing both sensuality and community. In some
ways this was no more than adopting and pushing further general attitudes toward "liberated" sexuality that developed during
this period. In others it was taking one of the most characteristic
features of homosexual life as it had existed before such assertion
—promiscuity, often in fleeting and anonymous encounters due
to fear of discovery—and making of it a virtue.

A few gay men fretted that there were problems in this es-
pousal of unrestrained sexual encounters ("So many men, so little
time" was the logo of a T-shirt of the time), but in general sexual
adventure became a central tenet of gay life. "Whenever I threw
my legs in the air," one person with AIDS subsequently re-

marked, "I thought I was doing my bit for gay liberation." The search for new and hotter partners became the thrust of much of the new gay male literature of self-assertion, as in the writings of Andrew Holleran *(Dancer from the Dance)*, Renaud Camus *(Tricks)*, Edmund White *(States of Desire)* and, above all, John Rechy, who praised what he termed "the sexual outlaw" as the symbol of the homosexual as revolutionary. Interestingly, one of the few critics of this ethos of continual sexual adventure was Larry Kramer, whose novel *Faggots* attempted a critical examination of gay "lifestyles" (and was much attacked for this) before such lifestyles were implicated in AIDS.

The most striking failure of this ethos was the refusal of so many gay men—and medical professionals—to deal with the extent to which sexually transmitted diseases accompanied "liberated" sexuality. AIDS, after all, was preceded by a growing awareness that both hepatitis and enteric parasites were passed on sexually, and unlike most venereal diseases were not easily treated. The fear of echoing the traditional moralistic condemnations of homosexuality, indeed of sexuality, meant that most doctors were unwilling to think through the implications of these diseases and that many gay men accepted frequent medication with strong antibiotics. Being responsible about one's health was equated with having frequent checks for syphilis and gonorrhea, and such doubtful practices as taking a couple of tetracycline capsules before going to the baths.

The stress on sexual adventure and excitement did not necessarily mean a lack of meaningful relations—many gay men, like some straights, wanted both, and many a man on his stomach at the baths for a night would then go home to (or with) his lover. For some it involved an attempt to integrate a freer, guiltless sexuality into a larger sense of being gay, as was true for the Fairies, gay men who sought spiritual, cultural and sexual community with each other.[9] Others more closely approximated the stereotypes of the straight press, combining a constant search for sex with too much alcohol and drugs, and resisting the restraints of any sort of emotional commitment.

Because to talk of AIDS and sex means confronting two taboos, that against promiscuity and that against homosexuality, it is difficult even to find non-emotive language to deal with it. The very word "promiscuity" is loaded, and means very different things to different people; to a small-town Christian it may mean several partners outside a lifelong marriage, to some gay men it means more than this in one night. Discussion of sexual practices is equally difficult. After a decade of putting down curious straights for asking: "But what is it you do anyway? How can two men . . . ?"—suddenly the most intimate details of sexual congress were being discussed in newspapers and street language appeared in publicly funded pamphlets. Finding a balance between prurient voyeurism and legitimate concern is always difficult, and under the stresses of death and disease it was all the harder.

The temptation aroused by AIDS is to reverse one's whole world view of sexuality, rather as some thought Germaine Greer recanted her feminism in writing about motherhood in her book *Sex and Destiny*. I have myself written at various points in defense of cruising, promiscuity and the baths, though being an optimistic romantic, I have never seen these as excluding love and commitment. As late as 1982 I wrote a piece in which I argued that "gay men are developing new forms of sexual relationships that make it possible to reconcile our needs for commitment and stability with the desire for sexual adventure and experimentation . . . I do not think it too fanciful to see in our preoccupation with public sex both an affirmation of sexuality and a yearning for community, which may be one of the healthier ways we can devise for coming to terms with a violent and severely disturbed society."[10] This occasioned me some embarrassment the following year as it became increasingly clear that major modifications in gay male sexual behavior were becoming necessary.

But what sort was not immediately clear. The early reports stressed promiscuity and the need to reduce the number of partners, ignoring the fact that the relevant question was what acts were performed, not where or with how many. Indeed, some of the most stigmatized forms of gay sexuality may well be among the safest—sadomasochism, insofar as it involves ritualized nongenital contact; pederasty, which often amounts to no more than acts of mutual masturbation; and "public sex," for example in parks and on beaches, where again mutual masturbation is common. (As the eighties moved on, masturbation was being increasingly touted as the only guaranteed form of safe sex, with considerable controversy surrounding the protection afforded by condoms in other sexual acts.)

In retrospect, doctors and AIDS organizations have been blamed for being slow to stress the implications for behavior of the epidemiological evidence about the spread of AIDS. (Note that so far we do not know precisely how and under what conditions the disease is spread. Considerable anxiety was sparked off in late 1984 when reports appeared of the presence of HTLV-III antibody in saliva, allowing the press to proclaim a "saliva scare."[11]) Randy Shilts has claimed that gay men have on the whole been extremely irresponsible in adjusting: "Like the dancers in Edgar Allan Poe's 'Masque of the Red Death,' gays partied on, blithely ignoring the plague and its implications for the gay community."[12] In fact, discussion of changing sexual behavior began relatively early, and by late 1982 had become a central topic in at least some of the gay press, above all *The New York Native*. Indeed, the extent of writing and discussion about gay sexuality provoked by AIDS offers a unique case study of how social and political factors help shape sexual behavior.

By the summer of 1982, Neil Alan Marks could reflect:

> It is extremely difficult to write about sexuality in 1982. If the Christopher Street Liberation Day Committee has indicated that this year should mark a "Heritage of Gay Pride," many sexually active gay men are now negatively obsessed with a heritage of promiscuity . . . The one connection that has made us the unique community that we are leads to the one attack that we all respond to: the attack against life itself.[13]

During that same summer Dr. Jim Curran made his first public appeal to gay men to limit their sexual partners, and was supported by gay doctors such as Dan William and Jo Sonnabend in New York.[14]

In November the *Native* published what was to become a landmark article in the AIDS debate, "We Know Who We Are," by Michael Callen and Richard Berkowitz, identified as "both 27 years old, have both been excessively promiscuous, and are both victims of AIDS." For many readers the article was irritating

because of its absolute commitment to the "overload" theory of
AIDS (both writers were patients and protégés of Dr. Jo Sonnabend). But its central point was to denounce promiscuity as the
basis of AIDS, an argument which, with some variations, could
also be argued by those who believed illness could result from
one encounter with "an AIDS virus." As they wrote:

> Disease has changed the definition of promiscuity. What ten years
> ago was viewed as a healthy reaction to a sex-negative culture now
> threatens to destroy the very fabric of urban gay male life. What we
> have in the 1980's is a positive political force tied to a dangerous
> lifestyle. We must recognize the self-hating short-sightedness in-
> volved in knowingly or half-knowingly infecting our sexual partners
> with disease, only to have that disease returned to us in exponential
> form.[15]

Callen and Berkowitz laid out a position they were to maintain
through the next few years, arguing for education rather than
state action to radically change gay sexual practices:

> We are not suggesting legislating an end to promiscuity. Ulti-
> mately, it may be more important to let people die in the pursuit of
> their own happiness than to limit personal freedom by regulating
> risk. The tradition of allowing an individual the right to choose his
> own slow death through cigarettes, alcohol and other means is
> firmly established in this country; but there is also another Ameri-
> can tradition represented by the Federal Trade Commission and
> the Food and Drug Administration which warns people clearly
> about the risks of certain products and behaviors.

In 1983 Callen and Berkowitz published a pamphlet called "How
to Have Sex in an Epidemic," which achieved some considerable
attention (it was even reviewed in *The New York Review of
Books)* and was one of the first attempts to lay down the new
rules for sex.

But even in decrying state intervention, Callen and Berkowitz
foreshadowed what would become a major debate—namely,
whether the state should act to close down baths, back rooms and
other places where casual homosexual contacts took place. (This
possibility was soon being discussed in other articles, in both *The
Native* and the Canadian journal *Body Politic.)* The analogy with
the famous Broad Street water pump in London that John Snow

demonstrated to be the cause of cholera in 1857 began to surface in relationship to the baths.[16]

No such simple analogy could hold. There was no evidence that sexual transmission was affected by where it occurred (although transmission of other diseases might have been increased by the poor sanitary conditions of many clubs and back rooms). And there was a strong argument that the required education and changes in behavior could be facilitated through existing sex places where homosexual men—including many who never read the gay press and didn't identify themselves as gay—were to be found. The basic argument for closure was that without the presence of such places there would inevitably be a decline in the number of sexual partners—one would have to be very determined (or very lucky) to find as many partners on the streets as are available to one man in a bathhouse. Moreover, it was argued, perhaps naïvely, that any barrier that extended the time before sex took place (hence allowing for more reflection, perhaps even for discussion of medical histories) was desirable.

The spring of 1983 marked, as already indicated, the peak of AIDS coverage in the American media. Not surprisingly, this sparked off renewed debate about the need for changing sexual behavior, debate increased within the gay community by pieces like Callen and Berkowitz's (which was reprinted in several papers in California) and Larry Kramer's *cri de coeur,* "1,112 and Counting."[17] Already claims of changing attitudes in gay sexual behavior and attitude had been reported,[18] but it was not until mid-1983 that they really started to show up in measurable ways.

Closing the Baths?

For various reasons a debate which had begun in New York was to play itself out in San Francisco, where from May 1983 on, the city's responsibility for public health versus the right of individuals to control their own sex lives became a central issue. It is ironic that the first serious move to close gay bathhouses came in the city that had become universally regarded as a symbol of gay liberation. (Raids and closures of homosexual baths and sex clubs have, of course, long been common for moralistic reasons, and in some cities, such as Toronto in 1978 and Sydney in 1982, have been important events in rallying the gay movement.)

The first shots came in the lead-up to the annual Gay Freedom Day parade in June, the first time that Dr. Mervyn Silverman, head of the city's Health Department, spoke of pressure on him to close the baths. "I hope," he said, "that the people coming here will realize that they can't do the sort of things they might do at home."[19] The parade program carried risk-reduction announcements on its back cover (paid for by the city), and following consultations with gay groups Dr. Silverman announced that he would require bathhouses to post warning notices on AIDS. The various businesses involved were reported to agree,[20] but not all were happy; one bathhouse (fairly soon to go out of business) took out ads in the gay press proclaiming:

> If AIDS is indeed sexually transmitted, why have there been so FEW cases? Yes, I say few because if an estimated 20,000,000 gays have an estimated 200 "contacts" per year this means that in 4 and a half years we have seen 1279 AIDS cases in 4,000,000,000 contacts, or odds of 3,127,443 to 1 against getting AIDS during a given "contact." With all this gay-play going on why aren't we all getting AIDS instead of only 1279 of us?[21]

Few people took such pseudo-statistics seriously, but there was dissent from some gay political leaders who saw moves against the baths as a general move against gay businesses and bitterly attacked the Harvey Milk Gay Democratic Club, which had led the campaign for "safe sex" awareness. The bitterness of the disagreement among gay politicos was heightened by an article in *California* magazine which claimed that "recognizing this as an issue that threatens the political momentum that could lead to gay control of the board of supervisors within the next decade, gay leaders have made the matter of AIDS transmission into a 'dirty little secret.' "[22]

For a while attention moved away from the baths to a stress on increased public education. Indeed, the attitude toward the baths by many of those involved in the gay movement was rather like that of the nineteenth-century British settlers toward Australia's aborigines: they hoped they'd die out, but they preferred to say nothing that would lead to their being blamed if it happened. Attendance at the baths did appear to drop markedly during 1983; one estimate, by Sal Accardi, owner of a large bathhouse in San Jose, was that it had fallen by 65 percent in San Francisco during the year.[23] Increasing numbers of observers were claiming that there had been major changes in behavior, and, perhaps more telling, bathhouses began to close (at least one, The Hothouse, because its owner said he could not "morally" continue to stay open).[24]

But most owners did not feel such scruples, and clearly numbers of men were still using the baths (though many, one assumes, fairly carefully, a possibility which is often overlooked in the argument). The issue was relaunched in a big way in February 1984 by reports of increased rectal gonorrhea in San Francisco—it appears that the increase was somewhat illusionary—and an article by gay journalist Randy Shilts, who claimed support from both Dr. Jim Curran and gay supervisor Harry Britt for closing the baths.[25]

The following month a veteran gay activist, Larry Littlejohn, announced moves to place a measure to prohibit sexual behavior in the baths on a citywide ballot. (The use of referenda to decide controversial issues is more established in California than in most states.) This initiative immediately created new pressures on Dr. Silverman to act, some of them from gay politicians horrified at the idea of a public campaign that would focus on the regulation of gay sexual behavior. For several weeks the question produced front-page stories in San Francisco's mainstream press, no doubt telling many suburban readers much more than they had ever wanted to know about gay bathhouses. To most people's surprise, Dr. Silverman temporized, and then proposed a ban on sexual activities at baths and sex clubs, a ban to be enforced by the Health Department rather than the police.

This opened up a six-month period of confusion, during which time, after several about-faces by Harry Britt (who as the only gay supervisor was looked to by the Board for guidance), the city supervisors refused to give the Health Department the powers sought by Silverman, the city's four gay political clubs fought bitterly on the issue, everyone agreed on delay (at least until after the Democratic Convention), several more baths and clubs closed and the remaining bathhouse owners planned legal action should they be shut down. Some of the atmosphere of the time is caught in a letter written by the staff and owner of the Sutro Bathhouse, famous as the first "coed" bathhouse, in which they announced its closure :

> Political hysteria and political abuse have grabbed the headlines, distorted the facts and turned our customers and supporters into frightened and confused people willing to give up their civil rights with little or no protest . . . We have felt very strongly about educating our customers and have done more than any other business that we know of to help change the sexual patterns of the gay community . . . We are angered to think how hard we have tried to co-operate and have even gone beyond what was required, and then to have our own politically ambitious self-proclaimed "gay leaders" point their fingers at us and demand our death.[26]

By September the pressures for closure re-emerged, with the mayor, long a proponent of such action, stating she would seek to do so if Silverman didn't. It seemed as if this move might be forestalled by a plan initiated by the new head of the AIDS Foundation, Jim Ferels, and worked out in cooperation with the political clubs, to impose a "safe-sex code" on all gay sex venues that would be enforced through "community pressures," which might even include picketing. (Measures would include the presence of posters, literature, condoms and personal-size lubricants, public-service announcements, access for AIDS information groups and minimum standards of lighting.)[27] In fact, the Foundation was on the verge of officially announcing the plan when Dr. Silverman acted, ordering fourteen establishments to close immediately and claiming that undercover inspections had shown that these places "demonstrate a blatant disregard for the health of their patrons and the community." Silverman spoke very strongly, claiming that the baths were "literally playing Russian roulette" and that they "promote and profit from the spread of AIDS."[28]

The fourteen places concerned all reopened within a matter of hours, forcing the city to go into court. Seven weeks later Judge Roy Wonder of the state superior court ruled that the baths could, in fact, remain open, but under strict requirements, rather similar to those Silverman had sought to impose the previous summer. (The judge instructed baths to no longer provide private rooms and to establish regular monitoring to prevent high-risk behavior, opening up considerable argument about who would define such behavior and employ the monitors.)[29] The issue had been resolved, at least for the time being, by what was an extremely American process; I can imagine no other country in which a Health Department order, based on claims about the transmission of an epidemic disease, could be overruled by a judge following a suit in which both bath owners and patrons were represented. A few of the places affected have since reopened; others continue to fight the imposed conditions in court.

The debate over the baths raises medical, legal, political and ethical questions that go far beyond the specific dispute in San Francisco. The first question is whether closing baths and clubs would, in fact, alter sexual behavior sufficiently to really affect the transmission of AIDS. To some people it seemed obvious that if you remove the opportunities for instant sexual gratification these places offered, risks would decline. Figures showing that people with AIDS had frequented baths more than other homosexuals were thrown around, but such figures were not conclusive, nor were they very meaningful in a later period when people were considerably more aware of the dangers of unrestricted sex. Indeed, there was evidence that the debate itself had led many people to drastically alter their behavior, while still using those places that remained open.[30] Opponents of closure claimed that they were perfect places for "safe sex" education and that men could be reached *in situ* who would otherwise ignore warnings. Certainly the combination of educational material and sex monitors, ordered by Judge Wonder, must have a very powerful impact on those exposed to these measures.

There was also considerable argument over the symbolic effect of closure. To its proponents it was a way of underlining the seriousness of the problem. To opponents it was a move that would be understood by the public at large as anti-gay and would be a green light to puritans across the country. To which one could add two further arguments: first, that closing the baths would signal a false message that it is locale rather than the nature of certain acts that is the problem; second, that if such venues no longer existed many men would continue unsafe practices in environments that were more risky and where there was less possibility of reaching them with information.

Targeting the baths was a way of publicly restressing the connection of AIDS not only with homosexuals but with a certain type of homosexual, the ultra-promiscuous. Not surprisingly, passions ran high and the pages of San Francisco's gay press were full of letters denouncing closure as the work of "traitors" and the first step toward the banning of all gay sex. According to one man, "soon we'll all be celibate or we'll be outlaws."

The larger question is, even if the baths do facilitate the transmission of disease, should the state proscribe consensual adult behavior to reduce it. Again the debate has taken on very American overtones, with arguments about basic civil liberties and the rights of businesses being invoked to protect the baths. Gays are strongly conscious of earlier attempts to control such places, and many argued, in the words of historian Alan Berube, that "bathhouses should be preserved as zones of safety, privacy and peer support as long as gay men are attacked for their sexuality."[31] In particular, there was a widely expressed fear that closure of the baths would inevitably lead to attacks on other venues. As Neil Schram, president of the American Association of Physicians for Human Rights, wrote:

> The closing of businesses to protect people from themselves cannot be accepted. We must try to educate people there as well as elsewhere—and indeed it may be easier in bathhouses—but ultimately each individual is responsible for himself.
>
> The gay community has finally found places where it is safe to meet other gay people without fear of arrest or harassment. We cannot accept what could be the beginning of the end of that major advance. Why could people not argue next that since "gay sex causes AIDS," prevent gay people from meeting each other, so close the bars. And finally outlaw sex in the bedroom again.
>
> There should be no misunderstanding. AAPHR strongly discourages sexual contact with multiple partners. But we cannot and will not support any efforts to enforce that viewpoint.[32]

At one of Dr. Silverman's press conferences, demonstrators, clad only in towels, carried placards saying: "Today the tubs, tomorrow your bedrooms."

I have problems with this position. Governments do, and

should, "protect people from themselves." (The closest parallels are drug and suicide laws, but there are other restrictions, such as the wearing of safety helmets and seat belts.) It is too easy to brand as authoritarian and homophobic any desire to use the powers of the state to protect health. Nathan Fain came close to this position when he argued that "the real issue breaks over whether you believe in telling people how to express themselves, how to *be*, even if they crave endangering their own lives."[33] Only if one believes that there are no conditions under which the state should intervene could one maintain that there is never a case to be made for closing the baths. I would prefer to see the problem as one of balancing two equally legitimate concerns of public policy, the preservation of civil rights and privacy on the one hand, the safeguarding of public health on the other. I would come down against closing the baths because I do not think a persuasive case has been made that links their continued operation to the spread of AIDS, but I recognize there can be genuine disagreement on this question that need not imply one is homophobic, whether one supports closure or opposes it. Unlike Schram and Fain, I do not believe such matters are purely questions of individual choice; there is a social interest in controlling and helping to prevent disease.

This does not necessarily mean that the decision should be left to medical experts, as was argued by some politicians anxious to get themselves off the hook; the issues involved require an expertise that is broader than that (as Judge Wonder recognized in mandating the AIDS Foundation to play a role in defining "safe sex"). Indeed, the way the question was resolved in San Francisco seems to me a model of how to go about establishing policy on such a charged issue, and demonstrates the strengths of that peculiar American reliance on the courts to resolve broad questions of public policy in a way that is not possible in other legal and political systems.

Oddly, the San Francisco debate was only gradually echoed elsewhere. In the summer of 1984 one angry young gay man wrote in New York: "I don't understand why, outside of San Francisco, they aren't demanding the closing of bathhouses and back rooms, where anonymous sex is likeliest to take place. What on earth are they waiting for here? Another couple of hundred deaths? The only call I personally have heard to close the bath-houses and back rooms came from a straight man."[34] The atti-tude of public health officials in other cities seemed to be ex-pressed by Dr. Shirley Fannin, deputy director of Los Angeles County's communicable disease control program, who said: "In some ways it is comparable to past history when cities tried to close down houses of prostitution to control venereal disease. That didn't work, and we don't think closing down the bath-houses will work either. People will just go elsewhere."[35] This view was subsequently upheld by the Los Angeles City Council AIDS Task Force.

Whenever the suggestion for closure has surfaced in New York, gay leaders have scrambled to denounce any such moves. How-ever, in late 1984 the state AIDS Advisory Council agreed to discuss the issue, and established a subcommittee to investigate what position should be adopted. Whatever such a committee might find, there was a fear that events might force the issue, leading the governor to order closure of the baths even against the expressed opposition of his Health Commissioner. At least in early 1985 there was no evidence that such action was imminent, although a group of gay men did meet with some bathhouse owners and attempted, with some success, to persuade them to implement the sorts of changes that had been envisaged in the San Francisco "safe-sex code."[36] In February 1985 police raided two gay bathhouses in Atlanta, and then filed suit against the establishments on the grounds of being public nuisances—and spreading AIDS.[37]

Outside the United States there seems to have been little dis-cussion so far of closing the baths in response to AIDS, although it has been mooted in Germany, and members of the Festival of Light in Sydney picketed one of the city's better-known bath-houses. (In Australia and the Netherlands the gay saunas cooper-ated with local AIDS organizations in organizing forums on "safe sex" within the baths themselves.) Even so, it is likely that San Francisco's lead will be followed elsewhere if the epidemic con-tinues, and the absence of the institutionalized power of the gay community in San Francisco may lead other authorities to act with far less concern for questions of civil rights or personal privacy.

With or without state action, gay men are clearly changing their sexual behavior. "What we're seeing," said Dr. Silverman, before he made his decision, "is the most dramatic change in behavior of any group in society that I have seen in my career in public health."[38] The evidence for such change came from anecdotes, surveys and, above all, rapidly declining venereal disease rates. As early as 1983 reports showed a sharp decline in both numbers of partners and incidence of venereal disease among homosexuals[39] and over the following year similar reports came from a number of American cities. Surveys in Chicago and San Francisco found major reductions in both numbers of partners and high-risk activities.[40] A major study in San Francisco commissioned by the AIDS Foundation in 1984 concluded that gay men were almost all aware of the problem and that two-thirds have changed their behavior so as no longer to be at risk for sexual transmission of AIDS.[41]

Outside San Francisco, however, information on the risks of transmission was far less available. In most other cities it was comparatively difficult to find information on AIDS in most bathhouses, bars or clubs; as late as mid-1984 a number of bathhouses were distributing a handbook which included an article entitled "How to Enjoy a Night at the Baths," in which the only health advice given was to "thoroughly clean your body after contact, and you have little to fear, despite what you've heard."[42] My own observations during the course of writing this book suggested that while quite major shifts in behavior have taken place, surprising numbers of people continue to use the baths in the same way as before the epidemic. Certainly visits to the largest baths in New York (in June 1984) and Paris (November) suggested that most of the patrons either were unaware of the problem or, if aware, were deliberately ignoring the warnings. It is, of course, possible that some men may even have increased high-risk sex as a means of denying the reality of the epidemic. The scene in New York's St. Marks Baths reminded me of stories of people during the Black Death turning to sex as a way of warding off the disease.

Changing Sexual Behavior

The central dilemma that faces gay men as the epidemic spreads is how to develop "safe sex" without feeding the traditional moralism that condemns both homosexuality and sex outside a committed relationship and so easily feeds into the heightened homophobia unleashed by AIDS. The related question, as the baths dispute made clear, is what should be the respective roles of individuals, businesses, community organizations and the state in fostering such changes.

As awareness of the need for behavioral change as the only apparent safeguard against AIDS developed, two sorts of responses emerged, one arguing for fewer partners, and by extension for monogamy, the second stressing, not a reduction in "promiscuity," but rather the creation of a sexuality which might still involve numbers of partners but which was based on "risk-free" sex. The debate was rarely posed this clearly; more often both messages were involved, as in the flyers in Los Angeles which advised men to "play safely" *and* not to "play with strangers," although the latter advice is unnecessary if the former is followed. Implicit in the statements of a number of authorities, both gay and non-gay, was a model of "safe sex" that suggested a slightly revised version of conventional monogamy, thus ignoring the fact that monogamy is of little use if one's partner is infected and the acts involved can transmit the viral agent.

Luckily, much of the information made available by AIDS organizations implicitly accepted that gay men would continue to have multiple partners and urged caution in "exchanging bodily fluids." In fact, disagreement about what constitutes "safe sex" persists; I have sat through heated arguments about whether the provision of condoms should be encouraged or whether the total elimination of anal intercourse should be urged. At the time of writing no one can be certain about what is totally safe; we are all forced to make decisions based on best guesses and hunches, on which even medical experts disagree. No wonder some men ask: "Why should I stop going to the baths when medical authorities disagree about the cause of AIDS?"

In the search to avoid "exchanging bodily fluids" all sorts of alternative forms of sex and sexual adventure were being developed by gay men as the epidemic grew. Classified ads seeking sex partners began to reflect the new caution, such as this one in *The Advocate:*

> Did you reply to "AIDS CONSCIOUS, SO AM I" ad in issue 368? Sorry, but the 157 responses I received are more than one guy can handle. I suggest you place your own ads since there is plenty of interest out there for "health-conscious" action.[13]

Commercial operators were not long in catching up with these developments, with an increasing number of services offering "phone sex," often chargeable to major credit cards. These allowed patrons to call up a fantasy and, presumably, masturbate during the ensuing conversation.[44] In Los Angeles one bathhouse sought to encourage "safe sex" by revamping its facilities:

> The PT1202 has been recognized as a leader in meeting the changing needs of the gay community by offering something for everyone; by providing alternatives to high pressured sex—the Phantasy Phones, for example, where anyone can call PT members at any time and act out their fantasies; the J/O activity area provided on the PT boat; and the Book Nook for "sleaze" reading.

The most interesting example of new forms of sexuality was the expansion of "jerk-off clubs" in large American cities. In fact, the first such club, the New York Jacks, predates AIDS, and was established to cater to men who enjoyed "jerk-off" sex before it became mandated for health reasons. (Five years after its formation the club was under fire for allegedly barring people with AIDS from membership.[45]) The San Francisco Jacks, however, were developed as a deliberate response to AIDS by men who wanted to maintain the possibility of erotic adventure without endangering their health; it proclaims itself as "a meeting of men who wish their primary sexual outlet to be masturbation in the company of other like-minded men."

Partly because of its origin as a communal rather than a commercial venture, the San Francisco Jacks are developing into a club, with a growing number of activities outside the Monday-night "parties." Unlike the San Francisco bathhouses, where monitors are required, the Jacks are self-regulating; peer pressure has proved sufficient to limit activities to what is generally regarded as safe. The thought of several hundred men in an abandoned warehouse, naked except for their sneakers, and in various states of sexual excitement, may seem disgusting to some, comical to others, but many of the men who attend have found in these clubs an important source of both communal support and sexual satisfaction.

Something very profound is going on here, which squeamishness about sex may lead non-gays to overlook, and that is the creation of new forms of sexuality through public discourse and discussion. The jerk-off clubs represent the deliberate eroticization of a practice often referred to as "juvenile" and "unfulfilling"; for many people "safe sex" means "dull sex." To counter this attitude several pornographic videos are being developed to demonstrate the joys of masturbation. Equally, one sees in the gay press a conscious attempt to eroticize the use of condoms, of massage, of non-genital stimulation (e.g., of nipples). Most controversial is whether deep kissing is safe or not; that the HTLV-III virus has been found in saliva has been used by some to argue that it can therefore be transmitted by kissing, to which some gay men retort: this means the end of anything we can meaningfully call sex.

The role of pornography in changing sexual behavior is particularly tricky. The AIDS epidemic seems to have coincided with a boom in gay pornography, the great bulk of which represents sexual acts which are generally considered "high-risk." What is not clear is whether pornography encourages people to be careless or provides a safe outlet for fantasies that most people recognize cannot easily be acted out in real life. On the whole, those involved in "safe sex" education have tended to overlook the enormous potential of pornography, partly because of the difficulty of reaching many of the producers. (At least one gay press has published a collection of erotic stories following "safe sex" guidelines.[46])

Developments like the jerk-off clubs seem to me a more attractive—and potentially successful—means of regulating sexuality than are attempts to instill monogamy or even celibacy. It is not necessary to believe that gay men, qua men, are incapable of monogamy, which is the argument of some sociobiologists,[47] to recognize that monogamy is not a realistic choice for many of us, both gay and straight, whether because we don't find the right partner or because, even if in a committed relationship, we don't find one partner sufficiently fulfilling. People who argue that there would be no problem if all gay men would just be monogamous are ignoring both medical and emotional realities; with an unknown number of people already exposed to "the virus" and an unknown incubation period, such advice is just too restrictive.

There is an increasing tendency for people to use terms like "sexual compulsion" or "obsession" in their eagerness to alter gay men's behavior. Thus one gay paper could claim: "Sexual compulsiveness in the 1980's is very much what alcoholism was in the war years of the 1940's or drugs were in the Woodstock days of the 1960's—a way of life that is closeted and misunderstood."[48] All too often such rhetoric is no more than a way of arguing for conventional moral precepts in the name of health needs. This is a particularly insidious form of argument, since it reinforces the popular belief that AIDS is the direct result of unrestrained promiscuity, and effectively pathologizes behavior that in another time or place would be perfectly harmless. Thus one therapist could quote with apparent approval a 1950s study by the Public Health Service's Venereal Disease Division purporting to "explain" why people become promiscuous, which, it is assumed, is "a problem of interpersonal relations" and "associated with an incapacity to sustain love relationships."[49]

The idea of "sexual addiction" began appearing in the clinical literature from the late 1970s on, and the concept of "sexual compulsion" was first used to control heterosexual behavior in the Bible Belt.[50] AIDS allowed this movement to spread to homosexuals. Under the impetus of the epidemic therapists began to set up groups to work on "compulsive" and "obsessive" sex drives, sometimes modeled on the Alcoholics Anonymous model, despite its heavily moralistic overtones. "Fortunately," wrote one observer, "groups are now springing up across the country—private therapy groups: groups like Sexual Compulsives Anonymous, Excessives Anonymous and Sex Anonymous in New York; Sex and Love Addicts Anonymous in San Francisco, Los Angeles and Boston—designed to help people deal honestly and openly with the problem. Unfortunately the denial involved in sexual compulsion is so strong it can take years, even decades, for its victims to realize they suffer from it."[51] Or, one might suggest, to buy the ideology contained in this formulation.

A new orthodoxy began to emerge, remarkably like the orthodoxy of pre-liberation psychiatry: gay "promiscuity" was a sign of immaturity and self-hate. One therapist, beating up business for his profession, wrote: "What is not obvious is why the gay media deal exhaustively with every aspect of AIDS except *the* cause of the epidemic: people's difficulty in sustaining satisfying long-term relationships because of their sexual problems."[52] Whether intended or not, the implication of such a statement is that monogamy alone is "well adjusted." Another therapist, applying for a grant for AIDS-related research in San Francisco, claimed categorically that "men in relationships are healthier."

Leave aside the exaggeration *(the* cause?): what is interesting is the use of a medical model to promote a certain moral position. Many gay men had developed workable models for committed relationships that were not necessarily monogamous, and even if such models were decreasingly viable because of AIDS this did not mean they were psychologically unhealthy. (Indeed, while some in relationships might have been relieved that outside tricking was now more difficult, some relationships which had thrived while they incorporated a certain amount of outside sex now came under considerable strain as AIDS made this more difficult.)

Nor were monogamous relationships that easily established, particularly in an atmosphere where increasing homophobia and panic create grave doubts among at least some men about the validity of their identity, doubts very easily projected onto any possible partner. What little evidence there is suggests that while more gay men may have sought monogamous relationships, they were not necessarily successful. For many, AIDS has meant an increase in sexual misery and frustration; for others, maybe a decline in sexual feelings altogether. In one survey in San Francisco a quarter of the respondents, classified as gay or bisexual men, agreed that AIDS had made them less interested in sex.[53] We can only speculate on the effects on sexual desire when sex comes to be equated, if only symbolically, with death and disease.

In his survey of American urban gay life in the late 1970s, Edmund White suggested that "the current notion of hot sex in New York [may] be a mere transition, a new recuperation of old oppression, and we would expect this period to be followed by a sweeter, calmer one in which romance and intimacy and sustained partnership between lovers would emerge again."[54] There are those who claim that this has already occurred because of AIDS, and that gay men have been led to develop a new balance between commitment and excitement. This may be too optimistic a view. Rather, I suspect, many men have generally de-emphasized sexual satisfaction, settling for more fantasy and pornography, and in some cases denying the possibility of intimacy altogether.

Public Education

No aspect of AIDS has been more controversial than the development of public education aimed at reducing high-risk sex. Any discussion of this will immediately raise the fear that it must, of necessity, feed homophobia, both by publicizing existing gay sexual mores and by seemingly seeking to invalidate them. Certainly a fear of how the public would react to widespread discussion of gay sexual activities was a major factor influencing attitudes toward education campaigns. Thus early attempts to offer guidelines for less risky sex bent over backwards not to appear either moralistic or judgmental.

Again San Francisco led the way. The Sisters of Perpetual Indulgence, a group of male nuns, albeit one not recognized by the official Catholic Church, had made STD education a priority even before AIDS was named. (Their pamphlet, "Play Fair!," produced in 1982, spoke of "mysterious forms of cancer and pneumonia lurking among us.") The first brochure on "safe sex" specific to AIDS was produced by the KS/AIDS Foundation of Houston in 1982 and was followed by a publication of San Francisco's Harvey Milk Gay Democratic Club in May 1983. Entitled "Can We Talk?" it became a model for similar publications across the country. (Locally its production and distribution were taken over by the Health Department and the AIDS Foundation.) In graphic language it outlined the risks medical opinion associated with certain sexual activities for transmitting AIDS, stressing the possibility of having sex "which is sensuous, satisfying, *and* safe." The Milk Club also took out safe-sex billboards in the city's underground MUNI stations. Both the city Health Department and the AIDS Foundation developed a number of programs aimed at helping men to change their sexual behavior.

Most ambitious was the city's underwriting of an AIDS Health Project, which provided mental health services, both through individual assessment and psychotherapy and through group workshops and training services for "the worried well" to deal with the challenges of AIDS. Many men, however, were unwilling to use professional counseling, and the project was supplemented by an even more ambitious program, which aimed at establishing peer support groups of gay and bisexual men to help in changing sexual behavior and deal with the grief, anger and confusion unleashed by AIDS. Within San Francisco discontent with the efforts of the city and the AIDS Foundation have been frequently expressed. Compared with anywhere else it is striking how much has been done.

San Francisco seemed in part a model, because it appeared to offer an attractive combination of communal activity through the AIDS Foundation and political clubs with city backing. Yet the decision to close the baths by city fiat could be seen as the failure of this policy, and illustrated the enormous difficulty of changing the sexual behavior of a large and varied population including many who were completely isolated from the community in question. Indeed, the stress on the responsibility of the community to undertake education, while usually stemming from the best of motives, has some uncomfortable consequences, above all the reinforcement of the idea that gays are responsible for AIDS. Already in congressional hearings there have been hints that gays should not expect support for research unless "a self-awareness program on the lifestyle of individuals" is mounted.[55] Quite apart from the punitive view involved—would Congress cut back on research into heart disease because "type A" individuals were not taking enough exercise?—the problem is that we do not know how much high-risk behavior is engaged in by people with no sense of belonging to "the gay community."

Insofar as changes in sexual behavior can be seen as the problem of a particular community, a fully effective program to alter sexual behavior will involve communal organizations, sex businesses and governments. The reality is that, except for San Francisco, governments at all levels have shown almost total unwillingness to become involved in education about high-risk sex, and while some individual businessmen have shown concern the overall response of businesses has been spasmodic and half-hearted. Where education goes on at all it is because gay organizations—political, medical and welfare—have taken on the job and pushed businesses and governments for support.

A good example of the complexity of organizing such programs is found in Los Angeles, which has a high number of AIDS cases and a large and diverse homosexual population, and which had a belated governmental response to the epidemic. Before government monies became available, both AIDS Project Los Angeles and the Gay and Lesbian Community Services Center had provided limited educational programs, hampered by limited resources. APLA ran a hot line, distributed large amounts of information in both English and Spanish and provided workshop training for professionals. The Center's clinic has a long history of working with street hustlers and black and Hispanic populations, and through these contacts was able to reach groups not normally touched by forums and articles; for a time an ex-hustler worked for the Center as a street educator. Most interesting was the program run by the Center which provided a health-screening service in most of the county's bathhouses—paid for by the bathhouse owners.

Unlike the arrangements in either San Francisco or New York, the county rather than the city government has central responsibility for health programs, and the sheer size of Los Angeles County, and the fact that only one out of the five county supervisors showed any real concern about the problem, made it very difficult to mount an effective response. In fact, the funds for a public education program known as L.A. Cares, and administered jointly through APLA and the Center, came from state rather than either city or county monies. Launched in 1985, the campaign involved a very public campaign aimed at modifying homosexual behavior, using billboards, bus tailgates and print

and electronic media and built around the slogan "L.A. Cares
. . . Like a Mother." The posters—using a well-known actress as
"mother"—were sufficiently catching to attract national attention.

In New York the city government proved similarly slow and
reluctant to act. From early on in the epidemic GMHC sponsored
a continuing series of public forums at which "safe sex" was a
constant preoccupation. Large numbers of men attended these
events, and they were undoubtedly very significant in affecting
those who were aware of and motivated to attend such forums.
Equally, it was true that by and large attendance, like the membership of GMHC itself, was far more white, middle-class and
middle-aged than the population at risk. (In Boston similar forums have been used as opportunities to organize small group
discussions.)

Broadening public education was a matter of some controversy. More than in either San Francisco or Los Angeles, there
was apparent resistance to any form of pressure on baths or back
rooms in New York. It was not until the summer of 1984 that a
"safe sex" brochure was produced by a coalition of interested
groups, and its graphic language provoked outrage from one
non-gay newspaper and complaints to the mayor about the involvement of the Office of Gay and Lesbian Health Concerns in
preparing the brochure.[56] GMHC accepted responsibility for
printing and distributing the brochure, but supplies were quickly
exhausted and reprinting delayed. Meanwhile the AIDS Institute
began limited public advertising on AIDS through both posters
and radio announcements.

The controversy over the New York City brochure illustrates
one of the problems inherent in public education on "safe sex":
for it to be effective it has to reach an audience greater than the
self-identified gay one, and this inevitably runs the risk of both
titillating and inflaming the general public. (When *The Village
Voice*, which is generally regarded as a mouthpiece of enlight-
ened radicalism, reprinted a safe-sex poster in an article on safe
sex, there were a great many protesting phone calls from people
who seemed more affronted by mention of sex than of death.)
Thanks to the much greater visibility of homosexuals in San Fran-

cisco, AIDS information on buses and subways is more acceptable there than it would be in Dallas, Chicago or Mobile, Alabama.

A somewhat different strategy was attempted by the KS/AIDS Foundation of Houston. There gay businesses were enrolled as participants in a safe-sex campaign that stressed the idea that safe sex could also be good business:

> We want you to continue to influence the community's attitudes, behaviors and choices with messages like "Live to play another day" and "Adapt, enjoy and survive!"—positive messages which enhance the gay patrons' perception of your business as safe and attractive while simultaneously effective in stopping the spread of AIDS.
>
> For example, we hope to make the "checker" design and the "checkered flag" the symbol of "safe sex." It can be utilized in advertising and on novelty items; eventually a checker design and/ or the checkered flag will come to be associated with people into "safe sex"; bars, clubs, baths and businesses which promote "safe sex"; special events and parties which encourage "safe sex" and so on.[57]

The campaign ran into opposition, both from some gay political figures who claimed that it compromised civil rights and from gay businesses, which were slow to respond. However, the program seems to have had a real impact on the gay population of the city; special events, such as "AIDS Play Safe Week" in 1983 and the "Mr. Playsafe Playmate Contest" of 1984, and the use of the checker motif have reinforced the basic message of risk reduction. And, not incidentally, the campaign has provided the Foundation with a way of raising money. Similarly, in Minneapolis the bars have been involved in the Minnesota AIDS Project's "Captain Condom" campaign to encourage use of rubbers.

The Houston campaign has worked because it is so remarkably American. Where else but in America could the idea of safe sex be turned into a commodity and used as a means of strengthening a communal organization? Such a question became increasingly relevant as gay organizations in other countries began addressing the problem of risk education. In late 1984 I attended a discussion on safe-sex education at a conference of the Terrence Higgins Trust in England. Britain has in some ways fewer problems than the United States—unlike almost every other Western country, Britain has virtually no gay saunas—but what was interesting was that neither government nor gay business was looked to with much confidence by the speakers at the conference. Even some of the American safe-sex literature, it was feared, would be seized as obscene in Britain. In the discussions there were suggestions about how the threat of AIDS could be used to stress the need for more gay-related sex education in schools, a theme yet to surface in the United States. In New South Wales the state Health Department withdrew at the last moment from a commitment to fund a campaign entitled "Rubba Me" that was aimed at encouraging safe sex.[58] Only in the Netherlands was there government support for educational programs of the sort offered in San Francisco.

There is a fine line between education and control: the demand to disseminate information leads almost inevitably to demands to enforce certain standards, as the history of the baths controversy in San Francisco illustrates. This dilemma is not confined to sexual behavior. It is very apparent in arguments over cigarette smoking and how far governments have a responsibility to actively discourage smoking. One might note that whatever criticisms can be made of the gay sex industry's response to the problem of AIDS, on the whole it has been far more responsive than the tobacco industry has been to lung cancer. (It is interesting that Dr. Brandt also ran into political opposition within the Administration in pursuing public health measures concerned with smoking.[59]) It is ironic that no support for research has come from the manufacturers of condoms and spermicides, even though they stand to gain from any breakthroughs that would allow safe intercourse. Indeed, approaches from one researcher to the manufacturers of condoms to finance a study of their efficacy in preventing the transmission of HTLV-III were totally unsuccessful, and while there is some evidence that nonoxynol-9, a substance found in many spermicides, kills the virus, chemical companies have been unwilling to acknowledge the importance of this finding.[60]

Governments have long controlled sexual behavior in the interests of what they perceive as morality; one of the basic demands of the gay movement has been to "get government off our fronts." In almost every Western country the state has relinquished the anti-sodomy laws, which in large part were a legacy of the medicalization of sexuality in the nineteenth century. It is a sad irony that in the name of health some gay groups are now being forced to demand renewed state controls. As psychologist William Wedin put it:

> If we continue to pursue the voluntary approach, we must accept the continued spread of the disease among those who cannot be reached through reason and education. Whereas, if we demand that the government intervene to make such people "behave," we must accept the same principle being applied to ourselves—precisely what the New Right wants.[61]

Even where direct controls seem inappropriate, because of the extent of the AIDS threat, and the assumed role of sexual transmission, governments will have new opportunities and motives for extending surveillance and control over gay sexuality.

And perhaps not just *gay* sexuality. By the end of 1984, with increasing reports that AIDS was in all probability also transmitted through heterosexual contacts, the San Francisco Health Department had begun discussing the need for education for risk reduction among heterosexuals. Were this to become perceived as a general need, the impact of AIDS on sexual mores would be potentially as great as was the contraceptive pill some decades earlier. As *Life* magazine put it: "If the virus is as widespread as some fear, sexual mores may change radically; it's happening already among homosexuals. Virginity and abstinence, prolonged courtships and AIDS tests before marriage or pregnancy —all these could make late 20th century America an anxious and altered society."[62]

AIDS and Sexual Liberation

During the past decade, homosexuals have become increasingly associated with a larger social shift toward the acceptance of what is sometimes called "recreational sex"—that is, sex that has no justification other than enjoyment. It is not too fanciful to see gay men as pioneering in some ways new attitudes toward sexuality, as symbolized in the transformation of a New York gay bathhouse, the Continental, into a heterosexual sex palace,

Plato's Retreat. While many gay men did not necessarily live in the sexual "fast lane," gay life did tend to accept the idea that meaningful and enjoyable sex can take place outside relationships and, by extension, that commitment to a relationship need not be measured by sexual monogamy. Indeed, one might argue, perhaps cynically, that cruising, the search for new partners, is the only specific characteristic of "the gay lifestyle."

It is not surprising, therefore, that the impact of AIDS on gay sexual behavior has a symbolic meaning for gays and straights alike. The equation is hard to avoid: gay men carried sexual freedom to its furthest limits; now gay men are paying the price. As the composer Ned Rorem wrote:

> It still seems news that, as Reich and Mailer tell us, sex means life, regeneration, the affirmative orgasm. Yet for some, sex means death. Literally. More and more the daily news is AIDS, and like homosexuality itself, about the "cause" of which even the wisest spin no persuasive facts, theological allusions abound. I am wise, wiser perhaps than even Jerry Falwell, yet cannot help wondering (I who don't believe in God) if some chastisement is at work.[63]

I suspect Rorem is articulating a view that almost everyone who has thought about AIDS has felt, however vigorously we may deny such feelings. It is no longer a question of being seen as evil, sick, corrupt, decadent, maladjusted or immature; while many have suffered enormously from their belief that they were, in fact, these things, such views were, after all, imposed by outside authorities and hence could be dismissed. Even where homosexuality was linked to death, as in novels by Thomas Mann, Mishima and Genet, this remained on the level of metaphor. That homosexual sex might lead literally to fatal disease is upping the ante considerably, and men now coming to terms with their homosexuality need simultaneously to come to terms with real restrictions imposed, it would seem, by a vengeful nature.

To follow the various guidelines for safe sex, unless one has been in a totally monogamous relationship for the past four years, is to adopt sexual restrictions that go far beyond what most people can easily accept. I have heard straight doctors say they would hate to have to abide by the advice they are giving their gay patients. As one letter in *The New York Native* said:

I find myself trying to make affectionate sexual interaction out of mutual masturbation while trying to keep myself cool with the use of video. I find myself feeling envious of times past. I want to cry.

To be able to feel like a strong, robust, sexual and sensitive man in this age has become a nightmare. I rechanneled much of my sexual energy to the dance floor, but I leave alone.[64]

One of the most moving parts of William Hoffman's play *As Is* is the exchange between the two main characters about what they miss in the sexual possibilities, once seen as liberating, that have now become so life-threatening.

One of the problems in talking about sex is to disentangle what people actually do from how they think and talk about it—that is, to separate behavior from ideology. It is not merely that gay men have drastically altered their sexual behavior in response to AIDS; even more important, the epidemic has forced us to think very differently about sex and to question many of the assumptions about the sort of life gay men have been constructing over the past ten years. As Adam Carr put it in the Australian journal *Outrage:*

> This prospect [of a widespread increase in cases] raises deep and difficult questions about the gay urban lifestyle that gay men in Western countries have constructed for ourselves over the past decade. If the network of bars, saunas and back rooms that make up the sexual "circuit" have now become the means of spreading an infectious disease with devastating symptoms and a high mortality rate among the gay men that use it, and if those gay men are then unwittingly spreading it out into wider communities, then the question has to be asked: would we be better off without that network?[65]

What would remain of gay life as we know it were that network, in fact, to disappear? Edmund White, one of the most insightful commentators on gay life, has suggested:

> Perhaps the new sexual abstinence will lead to new forms of gay life. Now time is available—indeed is required—to elaborate the art of courtship. The tension that has been lacking in gay love—the very lack that, according to such writers as C. A. Tripp and Michel Foucault, has led to the formation of antagonistic pleasures such as gay S & M—may now be replaced by the more traditional anxieties and frustrations of courtship.[66]

One frequently hears claims that what White forecast is already true, that gay life has become much calmer, less bound up in a constant round of discos and "hot" sex places, that friendship, dating and intimacy are all playing a greater role in gay male life.

Carr and White don't go beyond these few comments to the deeper questions of whether AIDS has the potential to lead not just to a change in sexual pace but to a wholesale retreat from homosexuality, indeed from sex itself. (Friends have suggested to me that the young post-punk gay generation is far less interested in sex, certainly in sexual adventure, than we were.) It is my hunch that we are living through a shift that could as dramatically change the meaning of being gay as did the political movements of the late 1960s and early 1970s. Just as that period led tens of thousands of women and men to assert a homosexuality that might otherwise never have been expressed, will AIDS have a reverse effect and lead thousands to once again deny their homosexuality?

So far there is no hard evidence to suggest this is happening. Popular discussion seems to assume that homosexuality is a fixed characteristic, and even many psychologists seem to assume one either is or is not homosexual, rather than adopting a model of a fluid and varied potential for sexual response. Yet we must remember that a gay identity is both a comparatively recent one and one not found in most societies.[67] It is certainly conceivable that a continuing association of homosexuality with fatal disease could lead to a rejection of gay identity and of the acting out of homosexual feelings. Undoubtedly one could find examples where this has happened; one could also find examples of AIDS strengthening a sense of gay identity. When I visited Oberlin College in the fall of 1984, I raised the question in a workshop with gay students; the feeling was that AIDS was not leading people to avoid a gay identity, but that it was certainly affecting the way they perceived what this identity meant. I have heard from other men in their early twenties a mixture of frustration at missed opportunities and anger at an older generation as a result of the changes in sexual mores. Yet it is my guess that even if a safe vaccine against AIDS were to be developed most men would not wish to return to a pre-AIDS way of life, and the longer the period before such a vaccine and/or cure is discovered, the more entrenched new mores are likely to become.

If AIDS is leading to changes in gay mores in such a way that gay male sexual behavior comes to resemble more closely traditional sexual norms, does this mean that gays are, once again, in the vanguard of social change? These changes are not, after all, taking place in a social vacuum. In promoting the safe-sex campaign of the Houston KS/AIDS Foundation, one therapist wrote: "Let people realize for themselves that the 'sexual revolution' of the 1960's–1970's is drawing to a rapid close; both gay and straight societies are evolving/changing—from fast-lane sex to intimacy."[68] Like so many other areas of life, sexual life in the 1980s seems to have seen something of a conservative reaction, at least in the United States. The right-wing rhetoric that denounced the sexual freedoms of the 1970s undoubtedly tapped a deep sense of unease many felt at the rapid social changes of the past several decades; many of those who despise the rhetoric of the Moral Majority have nonetheless changed their behavior in a more conservative direction.

Whole series of articles and books have claimed there is a new conservatism in sexual behavior. *Time* magazine even declared in a cover story on sex in the eighties that "the revolution is over": "After the sexual revolution, the voices of Thermidor. From cities, suburbs and small towns alike, there is growing evidence that the national obsession with sex is subsiding."[69] Apparently *Time* doesn't think that "sex" includes homosexuality, which they prefer to discuss in cover stories on disease, even though they invoke pollster Daniel Yankelovich to the effect that "the rise of herpes has revived feelings of guilt and the idea of disease as a form of moral punishment for promiscuity. Beneath the veneer of liberation, he says, 'we have a residual guilt and the idea that promiscuity breeds disease falls on prepared ears.' "[70] The story could only have been strengthened had the writers also mentioned AIDS; even before there was medical evidence to suggest that heterosexual intercourse was a possible route of transmission, one heard people who were exclusively heterosexual talking of AIDS as another reason to slow down sexually. Several years earlier the magazine *Mother Jones* ran a cover with the caption "Fear of Sex / Disease in the Age of Desire," and posed the question: "Is disease shaping a new sexual ethic?" (Nora Gallagher's article suggested a somewhat tentative yes.[71]) One popular Australian women's magazine suggested that "AIDS could herald an almost universal return to monogamy. Even celibacy could enjoy a vogue."[72]

Reasons other than fear are involved in the new retreat from permissiveness. June Reinisch, director of the Kinsey Institute, suggested that the recession had played a part: "Hard times tend to bring people back to their puritanic roots and they become more moralistic about disease."[73] We cannot assume, however, that the alleged end of the recession in 1984 has led to a swing-back in sexual behavior. The *Time* story suggested that "the softening of support for the sexual revolution owes something to the softening of support for liberalism in general,"[74] and there seems to be some commonsense truth to this proposition.

The equation of sex and disease suggested by AIDS can best be compared to sixteenth-century fears of syphilis, and not surprisingly it is having a deep impact on the ways in which we think about sex. The specter of death and disease haunts us even when we are fairly sure that both our partners and our practices are "safe"; even in the privacy of the bedroom, in the intimacy between two lovers, the fears and doubts engendered by AIDS persist. (And if this is true for already established couples, imagine the barriers fear of AIDS presents in the creation of new relationships.) There may be no better example available of the assertion that "the personal is the political."

It is very difficult in view of the restrictions imposed by AIDS to escape the feeling that those of us who argued for liberating sex in the 1960s and 1970s were wrong. For some gay men AIDS seems to negate earlier assumptions about "gay lifestyle"; in what ten years earlier would have undoubtedly been denounced as a homophobic and sexophobic remark, one man wrote: "Sex with multiple partners has always been a classic way for one to avoid intimacy, love, romance, and, most importantly, one's self."[75] But to simply assume that a return to conventional mores is either possible or desirable is a mistake. The attacks on "promiscuity" ignore the effects of old-style repression and the way this frequently led to self-hatred, loneliness, alcoholism and even suicide. The legacy of a decade of sexual debate persists, and there are plenty who would agree with Cindy Patton when she wrote: "Now, at a time when sex and health seem mutually exclusive, it is essential for women and men to reaffirm the vision of lesbian and gay liberation: we were not wrong to attack the anti-sex morality of our society by discussing and exploring our sexuality."[76]

Indeed, the onset of AIDS coincided with a new stage in "the sex debate," one that saw questions of sexuality taken up as a central concern by at least some sections of the American feminist movement. There is a certain irony in the way in which during the eighties lesbians took up many of the arguments about sexual freedom previously associated with gay men, while gay men were forced into a retreat to more conventional mores.[77] In her introduction to a series of essays that grew out of the 1982 Barnard Scholar and the Feminist Conference, Carole Vance wrote: "The tension between sexual danger and sexual pleasure is a powerful one in women's lives. Sexuality is simultaneously a domain of restriction, repression and danger as well as a domain of exploration, pleasure and agency."[78] Although the reasons were somewhat different—oddly, Vance does not include fear of disease among the dangers traditionally associated by women with sexuality—the tensions of which she writes were becoming part of everyday life for gay men, a new and unexpected threat beside which the older dangers of gay sexuality—fear of violence, of the police, of blackmail, of betrayal—seemed preferable.

Even as recently as five years ago, few of us would have guessed that fear of disease would re-emerge as one of the most powerful forces determining sexual morality, or that gay men would find themselves thinking about sex in a way that needed to balance—literally—questions of death and desire. Even if the threat of sexual transmission of AIDS does not spread to the whole population, the disease has already had a major impact on the way in which we think about sex, reintroducing to a generation that believed itself liberated from many of the strictures of the past the idea that there may be real limits beyond human control to our ability to satisfy sexual desire.

CHAPTER EIGHT

A Very American Epidemic?

> An epidemic was never just an epidemic. It was a reflection on
> the health of government.
>
> —Ian Watson, *The Martian Inca*

As AIDS spread to more and more countries—by 1985 it seemed
likely to become universal, although it was still unreported in
most Asian countries—it grew less and less accurate to think of it
as a gay American disease. Yet the popular perception of it remained largely in these terms, in part because the media failed to
convey its extent among other populations. Thus a *Newsweek*
story at the end of 1984 remarked that "even such remote countries as Rwanda and Zaire in Black Africa have reported AIDS
cases," with no acknowledgment of the extent of the disease in
these countries or of the theories that central Africa was the
place where AIDS most likely originated.[1] It is my experience
that otherwise well-informed people have managed to ignore the
reports from Africa that do exist, and that throw severe doubt on
the whole concept of AIDS as a "gay disease."

The perception of AIDS as a gay American disease has real
social and political consequences. From the little evidence available it seems that AIDS in the Soviet Union and Eastern Europe
may be severely underdiagnosed and underreported because of
its association with "Western decadence" and the reluctance of
Communist states to acknowledge a homosexual population.
Cuba also claims very few AIDS cases, which seems on the face of
it surprising, given Cuban links with Africa. AIDS became an

issue internationally because of media reports coming out of the United States, and reports everywhere have drawn on the American experience with AIDS, often as a dire warning for what lies in store. In those countries where the existence of AIDS is recognized, the United States is looked to for information and guidance, although this can go hand in hand with resentment against American medical imperialism, as seems to have been the case in France. In Denmark, the first European country to initiate AIDS research, there is remarkably close cooperation at all levels with American researchers. In Britain officers of the Terrence Higgins Trust have spent time with the Gay Men's Health Crisis in New York seeking to learn from its experience. Australia's and Ontario's Health Ministers have made trips to the United States to examine AIDS research and programs. In most countries the CDC is looked to as a constant source of news and information for the management of the epidemic.

The perception of AIDS as a gay American disease easily feeds into a particular moralistic view that depicts AIDS as a disease of modern decadence, for which both homosexuality and America itself can stand as convenient symbols. The apocalyptic mood is particularly attracted to AIDS, which can very easily be painted as a fulfillment of Nostradamus' prediction of a plague in 1984. In that year Bhagwan Shree Rajneesh, the leader of a sect named after him that has a considerable following worldwide, predicted that two-thirds of the world will die of AIDS, and exhorted his followers to strive for celibacy and, failing that, to use condoms and rubber gloves in sexual activity.[2] And in letters to the Australian press at the same time there were several attacks on "American decadence" as being responsible for AIDS and calls to ban homosexuals from traveling to the United States. To the scapegoats Americans can find for AIDS—homosexuals, drug users, Haitians—others add America itself.

Viruses know neither nationality nor sexuality, and AIDS is American and homosexual only in the sense that the first group in which the disease was discovered was American homosexuals. This is not to deny that the course of the disease will be affected by differing patterns of national and sexual behavior. The very scale of a certain kind of gay life in the United States, a reflection of larger aspects of American society, helped shape the pattern of

AIDS in the United States; one French writer commented rather smugly on the link to "the stress on consumption of American gay life, which always wants more: sex, music, beer, strong sensations."[3] But AIDS is intrinsically no more gay or American than Legionnaires' disease is an illness of ex-soldiers or than rubella ("German measles") is inherently German. In speaking here of "an American epidemic" I am thinking, not of any intrinsic qualities of the syndrome, but rather of the way in which its history to date has reflected certain characteristics of American political culture. Because AIDS has so many social and political overtones it becomes a particularly rich source for examining political culture, and the differences between the United States and other Western societies.

In his book *Un Virus étrange venu d'ailleurs*, Jacques Leibowitch wrote:

> The film of AIDS is an international production . . . But the script is American and it bears the cultural signs of its origins. To speak and research openly, to proclaim the illness and its fatalities, to warn the patient of what will happen, to get his specific consent, to reveal everything, these are the cultural traits of North America. The dramatization which results from this conception of openness —which for us, prudish and withdrawn Latins, sometimes appears to border on obscene voyeurism—is the mark of an American-style AIDS. Including the funeral marches, candles held in the hand, organized by the gays of New York to symbolize and dramatize, in the most human sense, the violence and death which have descended on them. One ought not laugh. This is their culture. Their relation to the law and to death. One has only to see the masks which children wear for Halloween to understand that this culture is not without its own frontiers.[4]

If the reference to Halloween masks seems forced—what is the difference from the very Latin custom of Mardi Gras?—Leibowitch is right in suggesting that there is something very American in the openness and the demands for accountability that surround AIDS in the United States. As another Frenchman, François de Laboulaye, former ambassador to Washington, said in comparing the United States with the Soviet Union: "Here you have to guess, not because you are not shown much, but because you are shown everything."[5] The sort of debate over public policy toward AIDS that the American political system allowed through institutions such as congressional and judicial hearings has no real counterpart in other systems, and, partly as a result, the American medical and research establishment is used to more demands for accountability than is true in other countries. The access of the gay movement and press to researchers at the CDC and NIH seems remarkable to non-Americans (and compares well with the secrecy that surrounds research in private enterprises). Moreover, one of the aspects of American openness is the willingness of the media to ask more awkward questions than is often the case in other countries. Despite the hype and hysteria associated with AIDS coverage, some of the media did raise serious questions about both the disease and the adequacy of the government's response.

Given this openness and the slowness of the Administration to respond to the challenges of the epidemic, it is not surprising that AIDS became politicized in a way that reflected the particular circumstances of American politics at the time. The onset of AIDS occurred in the first year of the Reagan Administration, and its unfolding social and political history reflects this.

It would be as ridiculous to blame President Reagan for AIDS as it would be to ignore his role in the social construction, research and treatment of the disease. In 1976 the Ford Administration decided upon a massive national vaccination campaign against what was feared to be a new and virulent strain of influenza ("swine flu"). The President was publicly committed to this campaign and was himself televised being vaccinated. The expected epidemic never, in fact, eventuated, and the vaccination program was aborted after several widely publicized deaths of people who had been immunized. The point is that a hypothetical epidemic received far greater public attention from President Ford than has this very real epidemic from President Reagan.

It is not merely that a presidential response could have ensured far greater resources and care, important as this would have been. Just as significant, a presidential response could have limited the scapegoating effects of AIDS and brought some sense of support to those suffering from the disease, their families and friends. Maybe a presidential expression of concern and compassion, similar to Mayor Dianne Feinstein's proclamations on AIDS, might have made it that much harder to brand AIDS as a punishment from God, and might have inspired so-called Christians to seek ways to help the sick rather than assail them. What a President chooses to express concern about, even where this has no immediate legislative or budgetary implications, affects the whole national agenda. The failure of the "great communicator" to address what his own authorities called the most serious epidemic disease of the time helped prevent a full-scale national response to AIDS and made it that much easier to see AIDS as the concern of a particular pressure group rather than a health crisis.

Even though the epidemic has attracted precisely the sort of communal and volunteer response that Reaganism extolls—what could be a more appropriate response at a time of supply-side economics than the Houston KS/AIDS Foundation's educational campaign enrolling the business sector?—the Moral Majoritarian constituency has seemingly prevented the recognition that other such groups get from the White House. (A nomination, backed by Senator Moynihan, Representative Green and Governor Cuomo, of the Gay Men's Health Crisis for an Administration award honoring volunteer work was turned down by the White House.[6]) Moreover, one should note that the voluntary response has come almost entirely from within the groups perceived as "high-risk." No major foundation or charity group has made AIDS a priority, and though San Francisco's United Way (an umbrella charity organization) has given some support, it has done so surreptitiously. It may be a reflection of how little gays expect in Reagan's America that this lack of response has been pointed out to me by non-gay observers.

As has already been discussed, Reagan's presidency meant considerable cutbacks in funds available for both medical care and research. Inevitably, then, AIDS advocates would cast the Administration in an adversary role, and winning more resources for AIDS would mean that less was available for other medical needs. Such developments were not confined to the United States in the 1980s: in Great Britain the Thatcher government followed a policy of consistently cutting back on national health expenditure and forcing a greater privatization of the health system, which placed a greater burden for AIDS care on local authorities. But even from the perspective of Thatcherism, the American reliance on a hodgepodge of job-related and private insurance schemes, and an extremely complicated state welfare system to fill in the gaps, must seem both an inequitable and an inefficient way of providing health care. Nowhere are the defects of liberal individualism clearer than in the failure of American politicians to seriously address the uneven delivery of health care in the 1980s, a failure in part explained, if not excused, by the inability of the various disease advocacy groups to seriously raise such issues.

More than the question of who bears the cost is involved in the medical response to AIDS. There is, clearly, a national style to medicine, even among the various Western countries. (The growing interest in Eastern techniques such as yoga and acupuncture has made many Westerners acutely aware of the cultural preconceptions that underlie our myths about medicine as objective science, transcending cultural formations.) The experience of going to a doctor in France is different from a visit in the United States; in France the doctor will usually work out of his home, act as his own secretary and receptionist, be less inclined to use high technology and expensive pathology and, where he does undertake medication, use somewhat different techniques (for example, suppositories). As in Britain, the doctor is far more likely to be a general practitioner than is true in the United States; in Britain, as in most countries outside North America, one sees a specialist only after referral by a general practitioner. Hospitals, too, will vary considerably, and American hospitals perform more surgery and make more use of expensive technology than do their counterparts elsewhere.[7] All these factors are involved in the response to and treatment of AIDS in different countries. One can only imagine the inadequacy of treatment available to the growing number of AIDS cases in African countries, or the indignities to which AIDS patients would be exposed in countries where homophobia is officially encouraged.

Equally, certain aspects of the research on AIDS seem to reflect particular American conditions. Over the past several decades the United States has established itself as the pre-eminent center of medical research, to the point that researchers in Western European countries automatically write and publish in English. (France remains a partial exception.) But it is also true that the sheer amount of resources available for research carries its own burden: "grantsmanship, as much as discovery, has become the art form of American science."[8] AIDS research is hardly unique in the dominance of the field by certain key institutions—above all, in this case, the National Cancer Institute—and the theories that they espouse. The competitiveness, the hierarchy, the star system (reflected in the enormous media attention paid to Dr. Gallo after the announcement of the HTLV-III discovery) and the enormous expense of American science all impact upon AIDS research. The role of private firms, concerned primarily with profits rather than medical discovery, is, of course, more developed in the United States than elsewhere, where governments are less inclined to leave the development of blood tests and vaccines to the vagaries of the marketplace.

The failures, to date, of medicine to find either a cure for or a means of prevention of AIDS may be more galling for Americans to accept than most people. The American belief that any problem can be solved if one throws enough money at it makes it tempting to locate blame for the continuance of the epidemic, and to harbor the suspicion that the government could end it if it wanted. (There is no doubt that the government could do *more*. It is not the case, however, that political will is enough to conquer disease, as the "war on cancer" made clear.) In the attitudes of those concerned with AIDS one finds the coexistence of two apparently opposing American beliefs: faith in "experts" and an equally strong suspicion of authority. Thus the CDC can be simultaneously quoted as the fount of wisdom on the disease and bitterly attacked for somehow colluding in its existence.

To understand the politics of AIDS in the United States requires an understanding of certain unique features in the nature of both American politics and American values. A crucial element is the extreme division of powers, both between the private and the public sector, and then within the public sector itself, where federal, state, county and city governments all have particular responsibilities that in most other political systems are more heavily concentrated at the central level. Even control over blood transfusions depends upon a very complex interaction among the federal government (through the Food and Drug

Administration), local authorities, the Red Cross and private blood banks. In no other country would one be likely to find the extreme differences in response already discussed in the contrast between Miami and San Francisco. This localism, too, is reflected in the media; unlike most countries, the United States has no real national press, although the television news networks tend to play something of that role.

Localism is closely connected with another crucial American trait, the importance of volunteerism. Organizations like the Gay Men's Health Crisis and the AIDS Foundation sprang up all over the country, responding to the emergency by fund-raising and setting up volunteer services. Observers from Tocqueville on have commented on the American facility for volunteer organization rather than relying upon governments, and I have heard admiring comments from those involved in AIDS work in other countries, who look with envy at the willingness of Americans in large numbers to commit time and money to such organizations. (One English writer, bemoaning the sad state of the current British gay movement, wrote: "How, I wonder, can we achieve your American fighting spirit and a relative solidarity? Will you lend us a hand somehow? I believe that it is gay Americans who can urge us into activity—who can encourage us into the first phase of fighting back to end the age of gay apathy."[9]) The other side of volunteerism, it need be noted, is the reality that much of what private groups in the United States do is necessary because in many cases governments fail to provide services taken for granted elsewhere. Those Europeans who bemoan the relative apathy of their own gay movements overlook the fact that what appears to be a lack of volunteer activity may be no more than a different assumption about the role of the state versus private groups.

All modern democracies are faced with the need to balance the benefits and the dangers of a strong state. On balance, Americans are less likely than other Westerners to turn to government and more likely to be suspicious of the benefits of government intervention. The American concern for civil liberties is matched by a greater stress on individual responsibility for basic economic survival than is found in other Western societies. Conservatives would argue there is an inevitable payoff between expanding welfare programs and state interference, and would point to the fact that San Francisco, which has done more for people with AIDS than any other local government, is also the place where government has tried to restrict sexual venues. There are those concerned with AIDS work who would rather support education programs, for example, with exclusively volunteer resources than risk state control by seeking government money. The problem with this formulation is that it ignores the fact that restrictions on personal behavior can occur anyway when the state acts in the name of traditional morality (as in the raids on the Atlanta baths) or even when it does nothing and allows private groups, such as churches and the media, to impose their versions of morality. The awfulness of Reaganism is that it restricts the freedoms of those who are poor, non-white or outside the dominant moral order while simultaneously depriving them of basic economic and social services.

The openness, the localism and the communal basis of the American system all help explain the particular way in which Americans respond to political and social crises. In some ways they tend to defuse passions, despite the strong apocalyptic tendencies in American political life and a fondness for seeing things in black and white. It may well be that panic over AIDS is more easily restrained than would be the case in countries with a more centralized media and state system and where there is both greater expectation of a government response and less willingness to criticize what governments do.

AIDS and Moral Panic

There are those who see in AIDS an overwhelming metaphor for the clash between different sets of values concerning sexuality and "lifestyle." Because AIDS is perceived as an illness intrinsic to homosexuals, it can be interpreted as their just reward for flouting the laws of God, and, by extension, when it afflicts others this can be explained by homosexual perfidy. Even those who think in more secular terms can see AIDS, in the rather odd words of Charles Krauthammer, as a symbol of "the identity between contagion and a kind of desire."[10] There is a paradox here, for it has usually been progressives who have associated disease with environmental and lifestyle factors, as against conservatives who have stressed a narrower medical model. (This is very obvious in disputes over the etiology of cancer.) In the case of AIDS it is the rhetoric of the conservatives that has tended to emphasize lifestyle, whereas most progressives have sought to explain the disease in terms of an infectious organism.

As the epidemic entered its fourth year, with no real signs of either a cure or a vaccine in sight, it is not surprising that one could detect in the United States reactions that suggested what Richard Hofstadter has called "the paranoid style" of American politics. AIDS is not the first disease to be ascribed to the work of malevolent governments; in her short novel about the 1919 flu epidemic, *Pale Horse, Pale Rider,* Katherine Anne Porter wrote of current conspiracy theories:

> "They say it is really caused by germs brought by a German ship to Boston, a camouflaged ship, naturally . . . They think the germs were sprayed over the city—it started in Boston, you know—and somebody reported seeing a strange, thick, greasy-looking cloud float out of Boston Harbor and spread slowly all over that end of town."[11]

In their time such suggestions must have seemed as plausible as the various theories about CIA experiments running amok that were heard in discussions about AIDS in the mid-1980s.

The American tendency to see things in simple terms of good and evil was illustrated in the rhetoric of both Moral Majoritarians, who saw AIDS as stemming from the wrath of God, and gay activists, who saw such language as the first step on the road to concentration camps. Americans are, compared with most people, more prone to extreme passion in their political language; few Englishmen or Frenchmen would feel comfortable with the Old Testament language AIDS brought forth from all sides, whether it was Jerry Falwell decrying sin and sodomy or Larry Kramer denouncing the failures of New York to meet the needs of the epidemic. Right-wing attacks on homosexuals as bearers of the new plague were matched by those in the gay movement who saw such responses as symptomatic of a larger homophobia: "We should be clear on the conflict between our dreams and the dreams of straight people in the suburbs. We dream of a cure for AIDS. They dream of a way to keep our 'bad blood' away from them."[12]

The history of AIDS in the United States illustrates nicely that uneasy balance between attraction to moralistic crusades and respect for civil liberties that underlies much of American life. Certainly AIDS contained all the ingredients to attract a moral crusade, which would single out its victims as targets for both fear and loathing. In fact, some of this occurred. However, four years after the epidemic began, it seemed possible to suggest that this response was less widespread than many had anticipated, and that while AIDS had produced many examples of persecution and discrimination, these did not amount to a national campaign against homosexuals and Haitians. Indeed, the general attitude seemed one of neglect rather than persecution. If the President did not respond to the AIDS epidemic, neither did he use it in his appeals during the 1984 campaign to conservative morality, and even in local races AIDS seemed to be rarely mentioned. On the other hand, the increasing power of the religious right within the Republican Party meant that attacks on homosexuality, along with abortion and pornography, were pressed by Republican candidates in a number of cases, and there were certainly frequent attempts to link Democrats, even those who were not pro-gay (such as Governor Jim Hunt of North Carolina, who was engaged in a bitter, expensive and unsuccessful race with a leading right-wing senator, Jesse Helms), to homosexual issues. There is little doubt that association with AIDS is an often understood if not stated subtext to such attacks, as it has been in attacks on anti-discrimination proposals in Houston and Seattle.[13] The Moral Majority has continued to assail homosexuals as bearers of disease as well as of immorality, but I wonder whether they have found in the epidemic the ammunition for which they might have hoped. I understand the fears of those who see AIDS as opening the way for new pogroms and who compare current right-wing rhetoric with the early stages of the Nazi persecution of the Jews, but I think their fears are somewhat exaggerated.[14]

Nor is the apocalyptic view confined to the United States, though the best examples come from Anglo-Saxon societies, where puritanism and a fear of contamination from outside seems particularly developed. Perhaps the nastiest example so far of an AIDS scare being used to arouse anger and hostility came in Australia at the end of 1984. The death of three babies in the state of Queensland, allegedly from blood transfusions from a donor carrying the HTLV-III virus, unleashed what the Sydney *Morning Herald* described as "a modern-day witch-hunt," in which conservative politicians, led by the premier of Queensland, competed to blame gays and to insinuate that gays were deliberately setting out to contaminate others with "bad blood." The Call to Australia Party, a minor right-wing group, spoke in election advertising of "the satanic spread of the AIDS homosexual 'wrath of God' disease," the Anglican Dean of Sydney said gays have blood on their hands and there were calls to indict homosexuals for manslaughter, if not murder. As one commentator wrote:

> Letters to the *Herald* have proposed shooting homosexuals or castration. A prominent radio personality suggested that venues in Oxford Street—the center of Sydney gay night life—should be boarded up and he didn't care if the people were boarded up with them. A reader proposed that homosexuals should be rounded up and packed off to island isolation where they could be "happy as pigs in mud." And another referred to less enlightened centuries where dissidents found themselves up against walls and shot. "Though this seems a rather drastic measure of eliminating the problem, the thought is there."[15]

The state of Queensland, going further than has any American state to date, proposed to make blood donation by a homosexual a criminal offense, and even mooted the idea of confining blood donations entirely to women. On the other hand, the federal Labor government responded by trying to defuse public anxieties, and in other states there was a willingness both to cooperate with gay organizations and to provide backing for AIDS services and education.

One can suggest several reasons why AIDS seemed to unleash such panic in Australia. The most obvious was the charged event of three babies dying, allegedly of "AIDS blood," especially in a state with an extremely conservative and homophobic government; this in turn gave the media the perfect ingredients for promoting hysteria, which the more liberal papers could then deplore, ignoring their own role. (For all the dangers of such generalization, it seems to me that the media treatment of AIDS has been more irresponsible and sensationalist in Australia and Britain than in the United States or Canada.)

But beyond this, the Australian panic was a perfect illustration of the dangers that flow from seeing AIDS as essentially a homosexual disease. I do not think that homophobia per se is more extreme in Australia than in the United States. From my experience of the four major English-speaking societies—the United States, Great Britain, Canada and Australia—I would find it hard to rate them in terms of greater or lesser homophobia, let alone to compare them with such dissimilar societies as Greece, the Philippines or Mexico. It seems to me that a more useful approach is to recognize that homophobia occurs in all societies, and will be expressed in different ways depending on national cultures, traditions and political structures.

Thus the Australian AIDS panic is not only a product of homophobia but is also tied in to the Australian belief that they can insulate themselves from the rest of the world through rigid immigration and quarantine laws; the other side of Australia's "tyranny of distance" has been its ability to exclude diseases such as rabies and foot-and-mouth. (Visitors to Australia are either amused or shocked when they discover they cannot deplane before the aircraft has been sprayed with insecticide.) Similar attitudes are found in New Zealand. Australians, too, are particularly sensitive to natural disasters; there seemed something essentially Australian in the banner headlines in one Sydney paper proclaiming: "Mozzies (mosquitoes) Could Spread AIDS," which at least removed the onus from homosexuals.[16]

Certainly the AIDS hysteria suggested a less sophisticated understanding and acceptance of homosexuality than exists in the United States. A more accurate way to see this is that the idea of a gay minority, with both political clout and civil rights, is less entrenched in Australia than on the American coasts, where AIDS has been most significant. Yet any of the remarks made by clergy and politicians about gay responsibility for AIDS could easily be matched in the United States; the difference may be that in Australia the mainstream media gave them more credence, that at least one state government was prepared to act on them—and that the gay movement was less able to mobilize countervailing pressures.

Similar threats of draconian legislation have been heard from politicians in West Germany and even, more surprisingly, Sweden, which leads one to feel that the link between AIDS and homosexuality has the potential for unleashing panic and persecution in almost every society. The English theorist and historian Jeffrey Weeks argues that AIDS is another in the history of "moral panics" that arise when societies are in flux:

> The mechanisms of a moral panic are well known: the definition of a threat in a particular event (a youthful "riot," a sexual scandal); the stereotyping of the main characters in the mass media as particular species of monsters (the prostitute as "fallen woman," the paedophile as "child molester"); a spiralling escalation of the perceived threat, leading to the taking up of absolutist positions and the manning of the moral barricades; the emergence of an imaginary solution—in tougher laws, moral isolation, a symbolic court action; followed by the subsidence of the anxiety, with its victims left to endure the new proscriptions, social climate or legal penalties. In sexual matters the effects of such a flurry can be devastating, especially when it touches, as it does in the case of homosexuality, on public fears, and on an unfinished revolution in the gay world itself.[17]

Weeks's description seems particularly appropriate in cases like the Australian hysteria of late 1984. It is undoubtedly true that AIDS has tapped a rich reservoir of fear, panic and homophobia; a number of people have remarked on the cruelty of so many of the "AIDS jokes" heard from otherwise liberal "straights." The disease seems to give a macabre permission to many people to express homophobic reactions they would previously not have uttered, maybe not even thought.

It is evident that AIDS has had a major impact on the way in which homosexuality is expressed and perceived in most Western societies. At the beginning of the eighties most observers would have agreed that homosexuality was becoming increasingly accepted, both as an alternative lifestyle and as the basis of a political identity. In a number of Western countries the gay movement had made major inroads in removing entrenched discrimination and prejudice, and gradually heterosexism was being recognized as undesirable in a free society (although in the Communist world, and much of the Third World—especially where a fundamentalist Islam was influential—there was, if anything, a sharpening of anti-homosexual policies). Not only in the United States but also in most of Western Europe, Canada, Australasia, and the more liberal states of Latin America, the idea that to be homosexual required one to live a double life, hiding one's deepest sexual and emotional feelings, was fast disappearing, and homosexuals, both women and men, were carving out public space for a new form of gay identity.

In some ways AIDS has not changed this. Indeed, in some countries—the United States, Australia, Scandinavia, the Netherlands, less clearly Great Britain and Canada—AIDS has meant a greater recognition by governments of the gay movement and "community," whose representatives are enlisted in policy-making bodies and research projects to deal with the epidemic. What has changed, however, is the idea that being gay is a choice (or a fate: both gay and non-gay ideology are uncertain which is more accurate) without consequences. As long as AIDS remains so closely identified with homosexuality, those who deny the validity of homosexuality have powerful new ammunition at their disposal.

So far AIDS has probably acted to strengthen feelings of homosexual identity, and if it makes us more vulnerable to stigmatization, the response, at least in the United States, has been to fight back. But there are limits to such developments. As Gayle Rubin argued: "The disease will have a significant impact on the choices gay people make. Fewer will migrate to the gay ghettos out of fear of the disease. Those who already reside in the ghettos will avoid situations they fear will expose them. The gay economy, and the political apparatus it supports, may prove to be evanescent."[18] Support for Rubin's fears comes in reports of a falloff in gay business in San Francisco and the enormous money problems that seemed to beset most gay organizations by the beginning of 1985, except, ironically, those which could tap government funds made available for AIDS work.[19]

The risk to say identity seems greater in countries such as Great Britain and the Irish Republic, where the gay movement has less legitimacy and seems less able to withstand a new ideological onslaught, backed by real fears and dangers. In the United States it may be more accurate to see AIDS as leading to a change rather than a weakening in homosexual style, a change prefigured by Neil Alan Marks when he wrote:

> If, during the past half decade, the sexually aestheticized pseudo working-class *hot* look has been the criterion, the impact of the life-and-death fantasies we are projecting on ourselves and on each other will probably result in the naif "I crew for Groton" persona. The subtext of the look is: "I am innocent and therefore *free from disease.*"[20]

Even without AIDS, one would expect gay life to have changed over the past few years. It is tempting to see here a parallel with the rise of the "yuppies" and the much-vaunted conservatism of the eighties, in which the emphasis is less on seeing sex as a form of celebration and community and more on seeing it as a means of finding security and commitment.

The Dangers of Metaphor

In discussing the panic connected with the epidemic we need to separate legitimate fear and ignorance from the willful manipulation of prejudice. Often what is attributed to homophobia is more likely due to incompetence, fear of disease and limited resources. AIDS has been difficult to deal with, not only because of psychological and political factors but also because it presents such unexpected medical problems. Its appearance undermined the optimism of those who claimed that Western society had conquered infectious diseases; in the beginning of his *Natural History of Infectious Diseases*, Sir Macfarlane Burnet wrote: "In many ways one can think of the middle of the twentieth century as the end of one of the most important social revolutions in history, the virtual elimination of infectious disease as a significant factor in social life." (This was an odd claim, because later on he acknowledged the appearance of "apparently genuinely 'new' virus diseases" in this century.)[21]

Not only medical science but the provision of health-care services has been severely challenged by AIDS. The emergence of a spreading infectious disease requiring considerable hospitalization has placed a burden on the health-care systems of those countries affected—to date, most obviously the United States and countries of central Africa, but with others undoubtedly to come. The real test posed by AIDS was expressed by Jesse Jackson in a speech to the Human Rights Campaign Fund dinner in New York in 1983 when he said:

> Gay health issues, such as a cure for AIDS, *are* important. But I suggest to you this night that when you give life you gain life. If there is a commitment to health care for *whatever* the disease, based upon need and not based upon wealth or class—then within health care is encompassed the issue of AIDS. AIDS is not the only disease in the nation tonight. Be concerned about AIDS but also sickle cell. Never let it be said that you are a one-agenda, self-centered, narcissistic movement.[22]

Rodger McFarlane, who as executive director of GMHC operated in one of the largest and most intractable welfare bureaucracies in the Western world, likes to talk of AIDS as a "stunning metaphor" for the problems of New York City's health and welfare systems.

Much of the political debate on AIDS is marked by confusion as to whether it is a health or a gay issue. As Gerald Connor, employed for a time as FARO's lobbyist, put it: "We cast it as a public health issue to give it the broadest appeal. I'm not running away from the fact that this is a gay issue . . . But I have to make connections to the rest of the health lobby in this town."[23] Had there been a clearer perception from the beginning that AIDS was, in fact, a health issue that was too often cast as a gay one, it might have been easier to win adequate government response and prevent at least some scapegoating. Perhaps the voyeuristic scapegoating engaged in by some of the media and the tradition of pressure-group politics in the United States are too strong for this to have been a real possibility. As the gay movement was by and large the only group prepared and able to demand action, avoiding voyeurism and scapegoating would have required that they stress the gay aspects of AIDS to rally their own supporters and at the same time downplay them to emphasize the public health issues. That might be asking the impossible. The central dilemma in thinking about AIDS is that while it is medical non-sense to think of it as a "gay disease," it is the gay experience of AIDS, rather than, say, that of drug users, hemophiliacs or Zair-ians, that has shaped the perceptions and the politics of the epidemic. (When I wrote a piece on AIDS for *The Village Voice* in early 1985, the copy editor queried my comment that over 30 percent of the city's cases were not gay; she had never encoun-tered that figure.)

Perhaps the most disappointing consequence of the homosexu-alization of AIDS was that even as the epidemic pointed up the failings of the nation's health-care system, this rarely surfaced in public discussion. Too often the very real needs for adequate medical insurance and services were ignored in discussions of the more dramatic questions of research and education, yet as the cases mounted so, too, did the strains on city hospitals and medi-cal facilities. Perhaps the inability to make this an issue was the clearest evidence of the impact of Reaganism on the course of the epidemic in the United States. It is impossible to estimate the extent of individual suffering and hardship that the deficiencies of the American health-care system have meant for many with AIDS.

When we look at the development of AIDS in the United States, what appears most American of all is the way in which the discourse and the management of the disease have been fitted into the pluralistic framework of American public life. Once AIDS was identified as "a gay disease," the political response became largely a response to the gay movement, and the prob-lems of AIDS were equated with the needs of "the gay commu-nity." That this meant a greater degree of visibility and strength for the gay community than ever before should not hide the reality that it was a potentially dangerous development (and one that ignored large numbers of other cases). Only when AIDS threatened to cross the boundaries that confined it to "high-risk groups," most obviously in the case of blood transfusions or blood products, was there a widespread response to it as a problem of public health, and then, because of the homosexual label, it was very easy to promote the distinction between the "innocent" (hemophiliacs, babies, receivers of blood transfusions and heterosexual partners of AIDS "carriers") and the presumed guilty (homosexuals, drug users, prostitutes and, though less clearly, Haitians).

In the Third World, where AIDS may reach levels far greater than in the West, it is already clearly linked to heterosexual trans- mission. If this linkage becomes more widespread in the United States and other developed countries, it will no longer be possi- ble to think of AIDS as essentially linked to homosexuality. Such a development, while tragic for the increased numbers who will become sick, will at least make clear that the disease has been laden with too much symbolic baggage, and that thinking about disease as the issue of particular groups rather than as a general problem of health is invidious. A comparison with anti-Semitism comes to mind. After the traumas of the Holocaust most of us would agree that its existence is not merely a Jewish problem, that it poses a challenge to everyone because a society that toler- ates such prejudice is that much less a good and a just society. The same test, I would argue, can be applied to the way in which a society deals with a new and lethal disease, even when—espe- cially when—those it strikes come largely from unpopular and distrusted groups.

In his articles on AIDS for *Rolling Stone*, David Black quoted Henry Miller as saying: "A great scourge never appears unless there is a reason for it."[24] It is a human trait to want to ascribe meaning to events; we find it hard to tolerate the idea that there is no sense or purpose to what happens in our lives. Through human history, epidemics have been viewed as divine judg- ments, somehow merited by those who suffer. It is very easy to see AIDS as a judgment on sexual promiscuity, on "fast-lane" life, as some sort of warning about the "excesses" of modern life. This is particularly effective, as Andrew Britton pointed out, "because we already have a contagion theory of desire: gay men 'recruit' young straight men, and young straight men can be recruited, because homosexuality is itself conceived of as a virus that can be transmitted."[25]

Rightists have found in AIDS a powerful boost to their attacks on homosexuality. Similarly, it is tempting to see AIDS as a meta- phor for the awfulness of so much of social and political life in the eighties, which is how a number of people have interpreted my

comment that AIDS is "a very American disease." As Susan
Sontag pointed out in her powerful indictment of this way of
thinking: "Illnesses have always been used as metaphors to enli-
ven charges that a society was corrupt or unjust."[26] (Sontag's
warning of the dangers of conflating the language of war and
disease is a perfect commentary on the rhetoric of Secretary
Heckler, who in her speech at the International Conference on
AIDS in Atlanta spoke of "the mobilization of an international
war on AIDS" and "training our largest scientific and medical
cannon on the AIDS target."[27])

For those who are afflicted, finding a meaning is more difficult,
although one finds examples of people able to extract something
good from the epidemic. One letter writer to a gay newspaper
claimed:

> I hear over and over again: "I am afraid to live without this
> condition because I have never experienced such love in my life."
> Last night a friend told me, "I would rather live one year more with
> this disease than 50 years of my previous lifestyle. I have never been
> so loved or closer to my purpose in life."
>
> Yes, I believe AIDS means death. Death of an old lifestyle and
> *creation* of a new one. This is the full circle of love. The gay commu-
> nity is the healer of our times, because of your total freedom to be
> creative, your joy in living and the enormous opportunity to love
> yourself and others at this time. This is the healing of our times.[28]

And one gay commentator has spoken of AIDS as "almost like an
enlightenment": "I felt terribly sad for them [people with AIDS]
of course, but I also envied them. And I wondered if ultimately
they weren't far luckier than the gay men whose lives are frit-
tered away hanging out in bars, tricking with new bodies every
night . . ."[29]

There is something very American, perhaps particularly Californian, in this insistence on extracting good from any event,
however horrible. Perhaps the most difficult thing to accept
about AIDS is that it is, in human terms, without meaning: disasters occur for which there is no rational explanation or any meaning beyond the suffering itself. What Sontag called "the trappings
of metaphor"[30] prevent us from seeing AIDS for what it is, a very
nasty disease that all possible medical, political and social re-

sources should be mobilized to conquer. The attempt to find good in a fatal disease is ultimately insulting, for those who "hang out in bars" can choose to do otherwise, but those who are sick have no choice about their condition.

This may be the hardest lesson of all. When young men die in war a whole panoply of ideological justifications exist to make such losses more bearable. (This is why the argument that America's intervention in Vietnam was wrong is so painful for so many people.) But disease is far more difficult to explain away. AIDS, it is clear, touches a whole set of fears and prejudices that go very deep. The link with sexuality and blood makes AIDS particularly susceptible to metaphorical use. Just as important may be the realization that medical science has failed where we believed it triumphant, that we in the richest and most technologically advanced countries in the world face AIDS with essentially no more real chance of saving lives at this point than do the people stricken with the disease in Haiti and Zaire. Curing people, far more than arguments about homosexual decadence, is the real challenge of AIDS.

As the epidemic spreads we face a two-pronged challenge: to find ways to cure and prevent the illness and to overcome the panic associated with it. There seems no realistic end to the mounting case load; in April 1985 Dr. Curran of the CDC was forecasting 20,000 cases in the United States by 1986, and health authorities in countries across the world predicted corresponding increases.[31] In some countries in Africa and in some American cities, experts began to talk of "an AIDS economy," an exaggerated phrase but one that drew attention to the mounting costs of looking after those affected. In the face of such forecasts the temptation to retreat into panic and public relations solutions, such as those imposed by the British and Queensland governments, is understandable. But one can take heart, too, from the scientific and medical advances made in understanding and treating (though not yet curing) the disease. What AIDS requires is political will, public education, and rational thought, not appeals to fear and hatred.

NOTES

CHAPTER ONE

1. Cindy Patton, "Illness as Weapon," *Gay Community News* (Boston), June 30, 1984.
2. Larry Kramer, "1,112 and Counting," *The New York Native*, March 14, 1983.
3. Michael Callen, in a speech to the New York congressional delegation, May 10, 1983, reprinted in F. and M. Siegal, *AIDS: The Medical Mystery* (New York: Grove Press, 1983), pp. 182–83.
4. Quoted in Michael Helquist, "An AIDS Journal: Mark Feldman's Personal Battle," *The Advocate* (Los Angeles), Oct. 27, 1983, p. 29.
5. Richard Goldstein, "Fear and Loving in the Gay Community," *The Village Voice*, June 28, 1983, p. 11.
6. Judith Daniels, "Editor's Note," *Life*, July 1985, p. 6.
7. "AIDS Epidemic Called a Major 'Catastrophe,'" San Francisco *Examiner*, Jan. 27, 1985.

CHAPTER TWO

1. Lesley Doyal, with Imogen Pennell, *The Political Economy of Health Care* (London: Pluto Press, 1979), p. 12.
2. Samuel Butler, *Erehwon* (first published 1872; New York: Random House, 1927), p. 88.
3. Irving Zola, "Medicine as an Institution of Social Control," in John Ehrenreich (ed.), *The Cultural Crisis of Modern Medicine* (New York: Monthly Review Press, 1978), p. 84.
4. A good introduction to immunology for the lay reader is found in the latest edition of the Encyclopaedia Britannica.
5. William McNeil, "The Plague of Plagues," *The New York Review of Books*, July 21, 1983.
6. James Fletcher, "Homosexuality: Kick and Kickback" (editorial), *Southern Medical Journal*, Feb. 1984.

7. Gay Talese, *Thy Neighbor's Wife* (Garden City, N.Y.: Doubleday, 1980).

8. On parasites, see James d'Eramo, "All about Parasites," *The New York Native*, Jan. 16, 1984, and Richard Pearse, "Co-factors and AIDS," *The New York Native*, May 6, 1985.

9. Susan Sontag, *Illness as Metaphor* (New York: Farrar, Straus & Giroux, 1978).

10. Allan Brandt, *No Magic Bullet* (New York: Oxford University Press, 1985), p. 177.

11. See Ted Stroll, "Brazil: Official Concern and Cruising on the Copacabana," *Body Politic* (Toronto), Sept. 1984, p. 21.

12. "Le Fléau qui vient de l'Amérique," *Le Nouvel Observateur* (Paris), June 17, 1983.

13. Oliver Gillie in *The Sunday Times* (London), March 27, 1983.

14. John Wetzl, "Belli Told South African AIDS Problem Heterosexual," *Sentinel USA* (San Francisco), April 25, 1985.

15. Christine Guilfoy, "AIDS Forum: Politics and Science Collide," *Gay Community News*, Feb. 23, 1983.

16. Alan Petrucelli, "Gay Plague," *Us*, Aug. 31, 1982.

17. Michael Daly, "AIDS Anxiety," *New York*, June 20, 1983.

18. *Newsweek*, April 18 and Aug. 8, 1983.

19. On the impact of these reports, see Harry Schwartz, "AIDS in the Media," in *Science in the Streets*, a report of the Twentieth Century Fund (New York: Priority Press, 1984), pp. 92–93.

20. *Newsweek*, April 18, 1983; *Time*, July 4, 1983.

21. Olli Stalstrom, "The AIDS Crisis and the Press in Finland," paper delivered at a European AIDS Conference, Amsterdam, Jan. 1984.

22. See Nathan Fain, "AIDS and the Media," *The Advocate*, Sept. 29, 1983, and Edwin Diamond, "TV News and AIDS," *TV Guide*, Nov. 22, 1983.

23. The *Chronicle* has published a collection of its coverage of AIDS in 1984. See *The Year of the Plague* (San Francisco Chronicle, 1985).

24. Rodger McFarlane, "After 10,000 Cases, Where Are We Now?" (New York: mimeo., 1985).

25. Schwartz, "AIDS in the Media," p. 96.

26. See Julian Meldrum, "Fighting Back," *Capital Gay* (London), Feb. 8, 1985, and Terry Sanderson, "Mediawatch," *Gay Times* (London), Feb. 1985.

27. Kevin Leary, "Bay Woman Dies after Transfusion," San Francisco *Chronicle*, Sept. 6, 1984.

28. See Allan White, "Anatomy of an AIDS Scare," *Bay Area Reporter* (San Francisco), April 17, 1985.

29. Adam Carr, "AIDS: The Coming Crisis," *Outrage* (Melbourne), Nov. 1984, p. 38.

30. Quoted in Richard Labonte, "What Are You Thinking about AIDS?" *Update* (San Diego), March 21, 1984.

31. Aaron Shurin, interviewed by Michael Helquist in "Facing the Gay Health Crisis," *Coming Up!* (San Francisco), Feb. 1983.

32. On the experience of the polio epidemics, see C. Mee, Jr., "The Summer before Salk," *Esquire,* Dec. 1983.

33. Andrew Holleran, *Nights in Aruba* (New York: Morrow, 1983), p. 231.

34. San Francisco: Gay Sunshine Press.

35. See Michael Kearns, "Gay Dramatists Pen New Works Responding to 'Age of AIDS,' " *The Advocate,* Jan. 22, 1985, and Samuel Freedman, "AIDS Deaths Prompt Wave of Plays," New York *Times,* March 28, 1985.

36. Lawrence Altman, "Drug Abusers Try to Cut AIDS Risk," New York *Times,* April 17, 1985.

37. Mark Perigard, "AIDS/Nightmares," *Gay Community News,* Feb. 18, 1984.

38. Quoted in Brandt, *No Magic Bullet,* p. 180.

39. Peter Seitzman, "Guilt and AIDS," *The New York Native,* March 1, 1983.

40. Yvonne Preston, "The AIDS Panic: A Modern-Day Witch-hunt," Sydney *Morning Herald,* Dec. 10, 1984.

41. Michael Lynch, "Living with Kaposi's," *Body Politic,* Nov. 1982, p. 36.

42. Alan Wolfe, "The Rise of Logo America," *The Nation,* May 26, 1984, p. 627.

43. "Le Fléau qui vient de l'Amérique."

44. Bob Cecchi, in a speech to a Candlelight Vigil for AIDS, New York, May 2, 1983.

45. Quoted by David Talbot and Larry Bush, "At Risk," *Mother Jones* (San Francisco), April 1985, p. 30.

Chapter Three

1. New epidemics are a staple of modern science fiction. See, e.g., Geoffrey Simmons, *Pandemic* (New York: Arbor House, 1980).

2. G. Williams, T. B. Stretton and J. C. Leonard, "AIDS in 1959?" *The Lancet,* Nov. 12, 1983.

3. See J. Leibowitch, *Un Virus étrange venu d'ailleurs* (Paris: Grasset,

1983), and letters from Dr. I. C. Bybjerg and Dr. W. Sterry in *The Lancet*, April 23, 1983, pp. 924–25.

4. F. and M. Siegal, *AIDS: The Medical Mystery* (New York: Grove Press, 1983), p. 70.
5. See David Black, "The Plague Years," *Rolling Stone*, March 28, 1985.
6. See Gerald Astor, *The Disease Detectives* (New York: New American Library, 1983), pp. 5–6.
7. On these early stages, see testimony to the House of Representatives subcommittee on Health and the Environment, April 13, 1982, no. 97–125, and, for France, W. Rozenbaum, D. Seux and A. Kouchner, *SIDA: Réalités et Fantasmes* (Paris: POL, 1984), pp. 20–25.
8. Morbidity and Mortality Weekly Report, CDC, Atlanta, June 5, 1981.
9. Ibid., July 3, 1981.
10. Ibid., Aug. 28, 1981.
11. F. and M. Siegal, *AIDS: The Medical Mystery*, p. 110.
12. S. West, "One Step Behind a Killer," *Science*, March 1983, p. 39. See also Ann Fettner and William Check, *The Truth about AIDS* (New York: Holt, Rinehart and Winston, 1984), pp. 67–70.
13. Lawrence Altman, "Rare Cancer Seen in 41 Homosexuals," New York *Times*, July 3, 1981.
14. Michael Marmor et al., "Risk Factors for KS in Homosexual Men," *The Lancet*, May 15, 1982, pp. 1083–86.
15. Charles Krauthammer, "The Politics of a Plague," *The New Republic*, Aug. 1, 1983.
16. Michael Lynch, "Living with Kaposi's," *Body Politic*, Nov. 1982, p. 32.
17. There are several suggestions of this sort in Margot Joan Frommer, *AIDS* (New York: Pinnacle Books, 1983), esp. p. 40.
18. Fettner and Check, *The Truth about AIDS*, p. 58.
19. See Donald Drake, "How Scientists Unraveled the Skein of Illness," Philadelphia *Inquirer*, Dec. 31, 1978.
20. Larry Mass, "The Epidemic Continues," *The New York Native*, March 29, 1982, p. 13.
21. Quoted in "Explaining AIDS," *Gay Community News*, Jan. 29, 1983, p. 3.
22. Leibowitch, *Un Virus étrange*, p. 26.
23. See H. Jaffe, D. Bregman and R. Selik, "AIDS in the U.S.: The First 1,000 Cases," *Journal of Infectious Diseases*, Aug. 1983, p. 345.
24. Morbidity and Mortality Weekly Report, CDC, June 11, 1982.
25. Ibid., Dec. 17, 1982.

26. See "Debate Grows on U.S. Listing of Haitians in AIDS Categories," New York *Times*, July 31, 1983.

27. Quoted in "CDC Changes AIDS Terminology," *The New York Native*, Aug. 29, 1983.

28. One of the first reports came from Lawrence Altman in the New York *Times*, Nov. 29, 1983. See also his "AIDS in Africa," New York *Times*, April 17, 1984.

29. F. Brun-Vezinet et al., "Prevalence of Antibodies to Lymphadenopathy-associated Retrovirus in African Patients with AIDS," *Science*, Oct. 26, 1984, pp. 453–56. See also Ann Fettner, "The African Connection," *The New York Native*, Dec. 3, 1984, p. 10.

30. Andrew Veitch, "The AIDS That Africa Could Do Without," *The Guardian*, Oct. 31, 1984.

31. See "AIDS aumenta il pericolo," *La Repubblica* (Rome), Dec. 21, 1984.

32. Charles Seabrook, "AIDS: No Longer a Limited Disease," Atlanta *Constitution*, April 10, 1985.

33. Randy Shilts, "New Fears about Spread of AIDS," San Francisco *Chronicle*, April 18, 1985.

34. See, e.g., Randy Shilts, "New York's Gamble on Hookers Carrying AIDS," San Francisco *Chronicle*, Feb. 18, 1985.

35. Roger Lancaster, "What AIDS Is Doing to Us," *Christopher Street* (New York), #75, 1983.

36. See John Boswell, *Christianity, Social Tolerance and Homosexuality* (Chicago: University of Chicago Press, 1980).

37. See R. Bayer, *Homosexuality and American Psychiatry* (New York: Basic Books, 1981).

38. Ted Weiss, "The Public Response," in K. Cahill (ed.), *The AIDS Epidemic* (New York: St. Martin's Press, 1983), p. 158.

39. Gina Kolata, "Congress, N.I.H. Open Coffers for AIDS," *Science*, July 29, 1983, p. 436.

40. See interview with Gallo by James d'Eramo, *The New York Native*, Aug. 27, 1984, p. 16.

41. See special issue of *American Psychologist*, Nov. 1984.

42. Gerald Weissman, "AIDS and Heat," New York *Times*, Sept. 28, 1983.

43. Richard Berkowitz, "When the Epidemic Hits Home," *The New York Native*, Dec. 20, 1982, p. 22.

44. See René Dubos, *Man Adapting* (rev. ed.; New Haven: Yale University Press, 1980), Ch. 7.

45. The only publishing information on this leaflet is an address: "Cienfuegos #94, 215-A Second Ave., N.Y."

46. Letter from "Living in the shadow of life," *Coming Up!*, April 1984.

47. "Press Clips," *The Village Voice*, Nov. 29, 1983.

48. "S. F. Supervisor Seeks Probe of AIDS, Fluoride," San Francisco *Chronicle*, Sept. 5, 1984.

49. See G. Thomas and M. Morgan-Witts, *Anatomy of an Epidemic* (Garden City, N.Y.: Doubleday, 1982).

50. Quoted by Robert Harris and Jeremy Paxman, *A Higher Form of Killing* (New York: Hill and Wang, 1982), p. 241.

51. Quoted by Nathan Fain in his "Health" column, *The Advocate*, Oct. 30, 1984.

52. Black, "The Plague Years," p. 120.

53. See Kathleen Fisher, "Stress: The Unseen Killer in AIDS," *A.P.A. Monitor*, July 1983; T. Coates, L. Temoshok and J. Mandel, "Psychosocial Research Is Essential to Understanding and Treating AIDS," *American Psychologist*, Nov. 1984, pp. 1309–14; and Jeffrey Mandel, "Affective Reactions to a Diagnosis of AIDS or ARC in Gay Men," unpublished thesis, Wright Institute, Los Angeles, 1985.

54. Toby Johnson, "AIDS and Moral Issues," *The Advocate*, Oct. 27, 1983.

55. Advertisement in *The Advocate*, March 5, 1985.

56. "Federal Response to AIDS," subcommittee hearings, Aug. 1–2, 1983, no. 26–097.

57. Robin Henig, "AIDS: A New Diseases's Deadly Odyssey," *The New York Times Magazine*, Feb. 6, 1983.

58. Remarks of Tim Westmoreland to the American Association for the Advancement of Science, New York, May 26, 1984.

59. F. and M. Siegal, *AIDS: The Medical Mystery*, p. 164. See also Office of Technology Assessment, Review of the Public Health Service's Response to AIDS, U.S. Congress, 1985, p. 29.

60. See Dorothy Nelkin, "Background Paper," in *Science in the Streets*, a report of the Twentieth Century Fund (New York: Priority Press, 1984), p. 62.

61. Fettner and Check, *The Truth about AIDS*, p. 97.

62. David Talbot and Larry Bush, "At Risk," *Mother Jones*, April 1985, p. 33.

63. Martin Levine, "Bad Blood," *The New York Native*, March 28, 1983, p. 23.

64. "An 'Elegant' Disease: An Interview with Ann Giudici Fettner," *The New York Native*, July 30, 1984, p. 27.

65. "AIDS Has Kept CDC's Medical Detectives in Frenzy," Atlanta *Constitution*, April 23, 1984.

66. These quotes are all from the New York *Times*, April 26, 1984.

67. "Federal Official Says He Believes Cause of AIDS Has Been Found," New York Times, April 22, 1984.

68. "Tracing the Origins of AIDS," Newsweek, May 7, 1984.

69. See Ludwig Fleck, Genesis and Development of a Scientific Fact (first published in German in 1935; Chicago: University of Chicago Press, 1979).

70. See John Beldekas, "Face to Face," The New York Native, Feb. 25, 1985.

71. Office of Technology Assessment, p. 28.

72. Alan Cantwell, AIDS: The Mystery and the Solution (Los Angeles: Aries Rising, 1983).

73. For example, "Antibodies to Arboviruses in Patients with AIDS," presented to the American Society of Tropical Medicine and Hygiene, Baltimore, Dec. 1984.

74. Jane Teas, "Could AIDS Agent Be a New Variant of ASFV?" The Lancet, April 23, 1983, p. 923.

75. Jane Teas, "An AIDS Odyssey, The New York Native, Dec. 17, 1984, p. 15.

76. Charles Shively, "The CIA-CDC-AIDS Political Alliance," Gay Community News, July 9, 1983, p. 5.

77. "Willie Sutton's Retrovirus" (editoral), The New York Native, Oct. 24, 1983. Most issues of the paper in the latter half of 1983 and early 1984 contained some story related to ASFV. In June 1985 the Native began listing "Cases of AIDS or African Swine Fever Virus."

78. Nathan Fain, "Friends in the Enemy Camp," The Advocate, Feb. 21, 1984.

79. See Teas, "An AIDS Odyssey."

80. See ibid. and "New Theories about AIDS," The New York Native, Jan. 28, 1985.

81. Some early problems with reporting were acknowledged by the Department of Health and Human Services in material presented to the House of Representatives subcommittee of the Committee on Government Operations, Aug. 1–2, 1983, no. 26–097, p. 575.

82. "Local Responses to AIDS," U.S. Conference of Mayors, Washington, D.C., Nov. 1984, p. 9.

83. "Public Policy Aspects of AIDS," address to the International Conference on AIDS, Atlanta, April 17, 1985.

84. Talbot and Bush, "At Risk," p. 31.

85. Beldekas, "Face to Face."

86. Jo Sonnabend and Serge Saadoun, "AIDS: A Discussion of Etiological Hypotheses," Journal of AIDS Research, V. 1., no. 2, 1984.

87. See Walter Sullivan, "New Drug Appears to Curb AIDS Virus," New York *Times*, Feb. 9, 1985.

88. See, e.g., Gary Spokes, "A Retro-Virus Lab for New York City?" *The Connection*, June 26, 1985.

89. Office of Technology Assessment, p. 29.

90. See Judith Walkowitz, *Prostitution and Victorian Society* (Cambridge: Cambridge University Press, 1980).

91. See Joan Trauner, "The Chinese as Medical Scapegoats in San Francisco, 1870–1905," *California History*, Spring 1978.

92. S. Landesman et al., "Special Report on the AIDS Epidemic," *New England Journal of Medicine*, Feb. 21, 1985.

CHAPTER FOUR

1. Testimony to House of Representatives subcommittee of the Committee on Government Operations, Aug. 1–2, 1983, no. 26–097, p. 129.

2. Seymour Kleinberg, "Dreadful Night," *Christopher Street*, #76, 1983, p. 45.

3. The classic work on this is E. Simmel (ed.), *Anti-Semitism: A Social Disease* (New York: International Universities Press, 1946).

4. *Newsweek on Campus*, May 1984.

5. New York *Post*, May 24, 25, 1983.

6. See "Confusion over Infant Herpes," *Time*, Jan. 16, 1984; "Experts Try to Allay Fear on Herpes," New York *Times*, Jan. 12, 1985.

7. Peter Ebbsen and Mads Melbye, "Lessons to Be Learned from the AIDS Epidemic," draft paper, Institute of Cancer Research, Aarhus.

8. "Court Officers Wear Masks and Gloves at Trial of a Defendant with AIDS," New York *Times*, Oct. 24, 1984.

9. See Christine Guilfoy, "Delta Backs Down on AIDS Policy," *Gay Community News*, Feb. 23, 1985.

10. "Home Office Backs Ban at AIDS Scare Gaol," *The Guardian*, Feb. 7, 1984.

11. See "Young Victims of AIDS Suffer Its Harsh Stigma," New York *Times*, June 17, 1984, and "AIDS Children Struggle with Tragic Legacy," New York *Times*, July 1, 1985.

12. Memorandum from Secretary Heckler to all SSA employees, July 7, 1983.

13. See "A Move to Evict Physician Fought by State," New York *Times*, Oct. 1, 1983. Lambda has produced an *AIDS Legal Guide* (New York: Lambda Legal Defense and Education Fund, 1984).

14. See Francis Flaherty, "A Legal Emergency Brewing over AIDS," *National Law Journal*, July 9, 1984.

15. George Mendenhall, "Flight Attendants Win Bias Case in U.A. AIDS Firing," *Bay Area Reporter*, Jan. 17, 1985.

16. See Rhonda Levine, "In the Spirit of Stonewall," *Worker's Viewpoint*, April 7, 1984.

17. "City Employees Can't Refuse to Work with People with AIDS," *Bay Area Reporter*, Jan. 17, 1985.

18. "Doctor's World: Making the Rounds among Patients Suffering from AIDS," New York *Times*, Jan. 3, 1984.

19. Dudley Clendinen, "AIDS Spreads Pain and Fear among Ill and Healthy Alike," New York *Times*, June 17, 1983.

20. Robin McKie, "Doctors Who Do Not Care for the Sick," *The Observer* (London), Dec. 2, 1984.

21. Tom Philip, "AIDS: Too Hot to Study," *Alberta Report*, April 6, 1984.

22. David Talbot and Larry Bush, "At Risk," *Mother Jones*, April 1985, p. 36.

23. Sue Hyde, "AIDS Quarantines, the Government and Us," *Gay Community News*, March 24, 1984.

24. Neil Miller, "Public Health and Civil Rights in the Age of AIDS," Boston *Phoenix*, March 26, 1985.

25. "W. Germany Studies Moves to Curb AIDS," *International Herald Tribune*, Nov. 17, 1984; "Jail Urged for AIDS Promiscuity," New York *Times*, Jan. 31, 1985.

26. Jo Thomas, "AIDS Victims Are Targets of New Rules in Britain," New York *Times*, March 23, 1985.

27. Morbidity and Mortality Weekly Report, CDC, Atlanta, Sept. 9, 1983.

28. Fran Smith, "The New Leprosy," San Jose *Mercury-News*, Jan. 20, 1985.

29. Michael Daly, "AIDS Anxiety," *New York*, June 20, 1983.

30. Santa Cruz *Sentinel*, Aug. 8, 1983.

31. Barbara Tuchman, *A Distant Mirror: The Calamitous Fourteenth Century* (New York: Knopf, 1978), pp. 103–4.

32. James Fletcher, "Homosexuality: Kick and Kickback," *Southern Medical Journal*, Feb. 1984, p. 149.

33. See *The New York Native*, Aug. 1, 1983.

34. Letter reprinted in *The New York Native*, July 15, 1985.

35. Quoted by Cindy Patton, "Illness as Weapon," *Gay Community News*, June 30, 1984.

36. See Allen White, "Reno Rodeo Will Go On," *Bay Area Reporter*, July 28, 1983.
37. Allen White, "Fundamentalists Make Hay Out of AIDS Dead and Dying," *Bay Area Reporter*, March 29, 1984.
38. See Bob Nelson, "New York Groups Counter AIDS Hysteria," *Gay Community News*, Dec. 31, 1984.
39. *The Advocate*, March 20, 1984; "Viewpoint," *Bay Area Reporter*, Sept. 20, 1984.
40. *The Star* (Sydney) (editorial), May 31, 1984.
41. Jo Baker, "Houston to Vote on Gay Rights Issues," *The Advocate*, Sept. 4, 1984.
42. See "Houston Voters Reject Gay Rights 4–1," *Update*, Jan. 23, 1985.
43. Nathan Fain, "Yet Another Injured Foot," *The Advocate*, April 17, 1984.
44. Warren Hinckle, "Cop Makes It Safer for Gays," San Francisco *Chronicle*, Oct. 1, 1984.
45. See Peter Freiberg, "Antigay Violence," *The Advocate*, Dec. 22, 1983.
46. Peter Freiberg, "AIDS and Legal Problems," *The Advocate*, April 3, 1984.
47. Congressional hearings, Aug. 1, 1983, p. 55.
48. Ibid., p. 96.
49. Lawrence Altman, "Debate Grows on U.S. Listing of Haitians in AIDS Category," New York *Times*, July 31, 1983.
50. See David Perlman, "The Search for a Cure," San Francisco *Chronicle*, Dec. 15, 1984.
51. See Tom Waddell, "The Simian Connection," *Coming Up!*, April 1984, who bases this suggestion on the observations of novelist Herbert Gold.
52. This is argued strongly in Robert Bazell, "The History of an Epidemic," *The New Republic*, Aug. 1, 1983.
53. Marlise Simons, "For Haiti's Tourism, the Stigma of AIDS Is Fatal," New York *Times*, Nov. 29, 1983. See also Joseph Treaster, "Haiti's Hotels Hit Hard as Tourists Shun Island," New York *Times*, Oct. 11, 1984.
54. J. Leibowitch, *Un Virus étrange venu d'ailleurs* (Paris: Grasset, 1983), p. 126.
55. Letter from Fritz Cineas, *New England Journal of Medicine*, Sept. 15, 1983.
56. Dr. Dowdle, director of the CDC, quoted in "Haitians Removed from AIDS Risk List," New York *Times*, April 10, 1985. See also

Regina Hichl-Szabo, "Haitians Removed from AIDS Risk List by Control Centres," *The Globe and Mail* (Toronto), July 5, 1985.

57. S. Landesman et al., "Special Report: The AIDS Epidemic," *New England Journal of Medicine*, Feb. 21, 1985, p. 522.

58. Seymour Kleinberg, "Gay Health Organizations," *The Advocate*, July 10, 1984.

59. Kathy McCarthy, "Haitians: Taking Us off AIDS List Can't Lift Stigma," Miami *Herald*, April 11, 1985. On Canada, see M. Cooley, "Haiti: The AIDS Stigma," *NACLA Report*, Sept.–Oct. 1983, pp. 47–48.

60. Robin Henig, "AIDS: A New Disease's Deadly Odyssey," *The New York Times Magazine*, Feb. 6, 1983, p. 36.

61. Quoted by C. Krauthammer, "The Politics of a Plague," *The New Republic*, Aug. 1, 1983, p. 20.

62. This view is often associated with Richard Titmus' *The Gift Relationship* (New York: Pantheon, 1971). For an update see A. Drake, S. Finkelstein and H. Sapolsky, *The American Blood Supply* (Cambridge, Mass.: MIT Press, 1982).

63. Ann Fettner and William Check, *The Truth about AIDS* (New York: Holt, Rinehart and Winston, 1984), p. 132.

64. "Study Confirms Fears on Spread of AIDS," *The Guardian*, Aug. 31, 1984.

65. Congressional hearings, Aug. 1, 1983, p. 165.

66. See Lawrence Mass, "Gays and Bad Blood: No Scapegoating—Yet," *The New York Native*, Feb. 14, 1983.

67. Marilyn Chase, "Bad Blood," *The Wall Street Journal*, March 12, 1984.

68. See Fettner and Check, *The Truth about AIDS*, p. 137.

69. Ronald Bayer, "Gays and the Stigma of Bad Blood," *Hastings Center Report*, April 1983.

70. Charles Petit, "Bay Area's Blood Banks Make Plea for Donors," San Francisco *Chronicle*, July 20, 1984.

71. Michael Winerip, "Groups Setting Up Own Blood Banks," New York *Times*, June 26, 1983.

72. Robin McKie and Olivia Timbs, "Anatomy of a Panic," *The Observer*, Feb. 24, 1984.

73. Robert Pear, "AIDS Blood Test to Be Available in 2 to 6 Weeks," New York *Times*, March 3, 1985.

74. One exception was Bruce Voeller. See his "Take the Test!" *The Advocate*, April 30, 1985.

75. "Furor over Army's AIDS Testing Order"—San Francisco *Chroni-*

cle, April 18, 1985; "Pentagon Orders an AIDS Test for All Military Recruits"—Washington *Post*, Sept. 1, 1985.

76. Letter from Dr. Stuart Shapiro to Secretary Heckler, Philadelphia, March 6, 1985.

77. "Proposed Government AIDS List Draws Fire," *The Advocate*, Oct. 2, 1984.

78. Chris Collins et al., "Who Knows What About Us?" *The New York Native*, June 20, 1983.

79. See Christopher Collins, "Confidentiality," in *AIDS Legal Guide*.

80. Cindy Patton, "The Ethics of AIDS Research," *Gay Community News*, March 9, 1985.

CHAPTER FIVE

1. Seymour Kleinberg, "Gay Health Organizations," *The Advocate*, July 10, 1984.

2. Michael Helquist, "AIDS: Will San Francisco Meet Its Challenge?" *Bay Guardian*, June 2, 1983.

3. Quoted in a letter by Alan Selby, *Bay Area Reporter*, July 26, 1984.

4. See my *The Homosexualization of America* (Boston: Beacon Press, 1983), esp. Chs. 4 and 5.

5. See GMHC *Newsletter*, #2, Jan. 1983.

6. Maureen Dowd, "For Victims of AIDS Support in a Lonely Siege," New York *Times*, Dec. 5, 1983. See also Peg Byron, "AIDS and the Gay Men's Health Crisis of New York," *Gay Community News*, July 30, 1983.

7. William Carroll, quoted in Dowd, "For Victims of AIDS . . ."

8. "GMHC News," *The New York Native*, Oct. 8, 1984.

9. Marvie Howe, "Housing Is Hard to Find for People with AIDS," New York *Times*, June 25, 1984.

10. David Harris, "Re-thinking Priorities: Where Should the Money Go?" AID Atlanta *Newsletter*, Sept.–Oct. 1983.

11. See Judy Klemesrud, "Dr. Mathilde Krim: Focusing Attention on AIDS Research," New York *Times*, Jan. 3, 1985.

12. "Commitment Remains through Changes," Report to the Community from the SF AIDS Foundation, San Francisco, Dec. 1984, p. 4.

13. See Mike Hippler, "Facing Life, Facing Death," *Bay Area Reporter*, Sept. 13 and 20, 1984.

14. See Peg Byron, *"No Aid for AIDS,"* *The Village Voice*, June 12, 1984.

15. See William Franklin, "Urban Heroes," *The LA Reader*, June 15, 1984.

16. "KC Bar Raises AIDS Money," *Gay News-Telegraph* (St. Louis), Oct. 1984.

17. Testimony to House of Representatives subcommittee of the Committee on Government Operations, Aug. 1–2, 1983, no. 26–097, p. 192.

18. Letter from Jean (no surname), *Le Gai Pied*, Nov. 1984.

19. See Roland Surzur, "SIDA: La Peur Allemande," *Le Gai Pied*, Dec. 22, 1984, p. 9.

20. See Steven Burn, "Intensive Care," *Capital Gay*, May 24, 1985.

21. Testimony of Virginia Apuzzo to congressional hearings, Aug. 1–2, 1983, p. 18.

22. On the women's health-care movement, see Sheryl Burt Ruzek, *The Women's Health Movement* (New York: Praeger, 1979), and Helen Rodriguez-Trias, "The Women's Health Movement: Women Take Power," in V. and R. Sidel, *Reforming Medicine* (New York: Pantheon, 1984).

23. Karen Peteros, "Organizing for Health," *Coming Up!*, Aug. 1983.

24. Marilyn Lamkay, quoted in "Homosexuals Struggle with Changes in Living," New York *Times*, June 16, 1984.

25. Michael Helquist, "Taking Care of Our Own," *Coming Up!*, June 1983.

26. Michael Callan, "People With AIDS—New York: A History" (New York: mimeo., March 19, 1984).

27. See Allen White, "Candles and Tears on Castro: 1,000 Mourn Bobbi Campbell," *Bay Area Reporter*, Aug. 23, 1984.

28. Quoted in Barbara Ehrenreich and Deidre English, *For Her Own Good* (Garden City, N.Y.: Anchor Press/Doubleday, 1979), p. 102.

29. Glen McGahee, "Personal Advocacy for People with AIDS and AIDS-related Complex" (AID Atlanta, 1984), p. 8.

30. On the growth of a gay identity, see my *The Homosexualization of America* op. cit.; Jeffrey Weeks, *Coming Out* (London: Quartet, 1977); Jonathan Katz, *Gay/Lesbian Almanac* (New York: Harper & Row, 1983).

31. Quoted in William Franklin, "Urban Heroes: Behind the Scenes at AIDS/Project LA," *The LA Reader*, June 15, 1984.

32. Chuck Ortleb, "An Elegant Disease" (interview with Ann Giudici Fettner), *The New York Native*, July 30, 1984, p. 29.

33. See Jacky Armstrong, "AIDS Victims Watch as the Parade Passes By," Sydney *Morning Herald*, Feb. 28, 1985, and the retractions of much of that story in the *Herald* the following day.

34. For a somewhat sensationalistic account, see Peter Collier and David Horowitz, "Whitewash," *California*, July 1983.
35. "Gay America: Sex, Politics and the Impact of AIDS," *Newsweek*, Aug. 8, 1983.
36. John Rechy, "AIDS Mysteries and Hidden Dangers," *The Advocate*, Dec. 22, 1983, p. 35.
37. "Apuzzo Assesses Taskforce and Community," *Gay Community News*, March 9, 1985.
38. Richard Gottlieb, "Why Cuomo Accepted the AIDS Bill," *The New York Native*, July 18, 1983.
39. "Black Caucus Gets AIDS Rep," *Bay Area Reporter*, June 14, 1984.
40. See his "Opening Space," *The Advocate*, July 10, 1984.
41. Nathan Fain, "Europe Convenes First AIDS Conference," *The Advocate*, March 6, 1984.

CHAPTER SIX

1. See, e.g., an editorial calling for more research funds in the New York *Times*, June 25, 1983.
2. Quoted by Randy Shilts, "The Establishment Lurches into Action," San Francisco *Chronicle*, Jan. 15, 1984, p. 15.
3. On swine flu, see Arthur Silverstein, *Pure Politics and Impure Science* (Baltimore: Johns Hopkins University Press, 1981).
4. Remarks of Tim Westmoreland to the American Association for the Advancement of Science, New York, May 26, 1984.
5. "Kaposi's Sarcoma and Related Opportunistic Infections," hearings before House of Representatives subcommittee on health and the environment, April 13, 1982, p. 2.
6. Quoted by Larry Bush, "Bipartisan Congress Busts AIDS Budget Ceiling," *The New York Native*, June 6, 1983, p. 14.
7. See Office of Technology Assessment, Review of the Public Health Service's Response to AIDS, U.S. Congress, 1985, p. 40.
8. See Randy Shilts, "The Establishment Lurches into Action," cited above, and "Memos Show Administration Falsified AIDS Funding Needs," *The New York Native*, Dec. 19, 1983.
9. For a report on the hearings unsympathetic to these criticisms, see Anna Mayo, "Grandstanding on AIDS," *The Village Voice*, Nov. 1, 1983, and the response by Richard Goldstein, *The Village Voice*, Nov. 8, 1983.
10. David Talbot and Larry Bush, "At Risk," *Mother Jones*, April 1985, p. 35.

11. See Peg Byron, "House Approves More AIDS Funding," *The New York Native,* Aug. 13, 1984.

12. Office of Technology Assessment, p. 7.

13. See Linda Demkovich, "Margaret Heckler Shows Fighting Style, Proving She Came to Stay at HHS," *National Journal,* May 19, 1984, esp. p. 978.

14. See "Heckler to Boost Funding Request," *The New York Native,* Aug. 29, 1983.

15. American Life Lobby, press release, Washington, D.C., May 1, 1984.

16. See "Reagan Official Cancels Appearance," *The Advocate,* June 12, 1984.

17. Talbot and Bush, "At Risk," p. 35.

18. Nathan Fain, "Health Watch," *The Advocate,* Sept. 4, 1984.

19. Ann Hardy et al., "Economic Impact of AIDS in the United States," paper presented to International Conference on AIDS, Atlanta, April 17, 1985.

20. See T. Marmor and J. Christianson, *Health Care Policy* (Beverly Hills, Calif.: Sage Publications, 1982).

21. Paul Starr, *The Social Transformation of American Medicine* (New York: Basic Books, 1984), p. 437.

22. See Judith Fedar et al., "Health," in J. Palmer and I. Sawhill, *The Reagan Experiment* (Washington, D.C.: Urban Institute Press, 1982), p. 273.

23. E. Richard Brown, "Medicare and Medicaid," in V. and R. Sidel, *Reforming Medicine* (New York: Pantheon, 1984), p. 71.

24. Robert Pear, "Many States Limit Medicaid Program," New York *Times,* Dec. 17, 1984. See also John Holahan, "Paying for Physician Services in State Medical Programs," *Health Care Financing Review,* Spring 1984.

25. See Tony Bale, "Pain and Plenty," *Health/PAC Bulletin,* Sept.–Oct. 1984.

26. See "Four Wasted Years" (editorial), *Capital Gay,* Feb. 22, 1985.

27. "Local Man with AIDS Makes Plea to House," Washington *Blade,* April 27, 1984.

28. See ". . . Into the Courts," newsletter of the Gay Rights National Advocates (San Francisco), Spring 1984.

29. Sandra Panem, "AIDS, Public Policy and Biomedical Research," *CHEST 85,* March 1984, p. 419.

30. Reported by Loretta McLaughlin in the Boston *Globe,* quoted in "AIDS Treatment Costs Staggering," *The New York Native,* Oct. 22, 1984.

31. Dr. Stephen Caiazza, "Will New York Become Plague City?" *The New York Native*, Feb. 11, 1985.

32. Talk by Peter Arno at the International Conference on AIDS, Atlanta, April 17, 1985.

33. "New AIDS Ward at S.F. General," San Francisco *Sunday Examiner & Chronicle*, July 24, 1983.

34. See "Mayor Furious over Dumping of AIDS Victim," San Francisco *Chronicle*, Oct. 8, 1983, and "Another Very Sick AIDS Patient 'Dumped' on San Francisco," San Francisco *Chronicle*, Aug. 9, 1984.

35. Philip Lee, "Public Health Policy Aspects of AIDS," paper delivered at the Division of Infectious Diseases, UCSF, Nov. 4, 1983.

36. "Local Responses to AIDS," U.S. Conference of Mayors, Washington, D.C., Nov. 1984.

37. Ibid., pp. 16, 19, 18.

38. On Los Angeles, see several articles in *The Advocate*, Oct. 30, 1984.

39. See David France, "The Challenging of E.O. 50," *The New York Native*, Dec. 31, 1984.

40. San Francisco *Sentinel*, July 5, 1984.

41. On the Office, see the interview with Roger Enlow, "Informational Lightning Rod," *The New York Native*, Nov. 2, 1983.

42. Quoted in "Should David Sencer Be Declared an Emergency?" *The New York Native*, June 6, 1983.

43. Larry Kramer, "2,339 and Counting," *The Village Voice*, Oct. 4, 1983, p. 11.

44. See my "Malign Neglect," *The Village Voice*, April 2, 1985.

45. Quoted by Randy Shilts, "AIDS Crisis Hits an Unprepared New York," San Francisco *Chronicle*, Feb. 14, 1985.

46. "City Expanding Its Plans to Help Victims of AIDS," New York *Times*, March 30, 1985.

47. "Disease and the State," *The New York Native*, July 4, 1983.

48. See Richard Gottlieb, "State Funds AIDS Programs over Cuomo's Rejection," *The New York Native*, April 23, 1984, and the exchange with Governor Cuomo, *The New York Native*, July 9, 1984.

49. See John Nordheimer, "Poverty-scarred Town Now Stricken by AIDS," New York *Times*, May 2, 1985.

50. R. Rettig, *Cancer Crusade* (Princeton, N.J.: Princeton University Press, 1977), p. 8.

51. NIH Data Book (Washington, D.C., 1984).

52. "Blind Men Describing an Elephant: An Interview with the Head of the AIDS Institute," *The New York Native*, Nov. 7, 1983.

53. See Barbara Culliton, "AIDS Amendment Angers Cancer Institute," *Science*, Nov. 30, 1984, p. 1056.

54. Congressional hearings, House of Representatives subcommittee of the Committee on Government Operations, Aug. 1, 1983, no. 26–097, p. 277.

55. "The Federal Response to AIDS," 29th Report of the Committee on Government Operations, H. of R. 98–582, Nov. 30, 1983, p. 33.

56. See Rettig, *Cancer Crusade*, esp. p. 79.

57. Office of Technology Assessment, esp. p. 28.

58. Letter by Bernard Fitzgerald *The Star* (Sydney), Sept. 27, 1984. Note also the letter by Don Baxter in the same issue.

59. Dan William, "If AIDS Is an Infectious Disease . . . ," *The New York Native*, Aug. 16, 1982.

60. Michael Lynch, "Living with Kaposi's," *Body Politic*, Nov. 1982, p. 31.

61. See Brian Jones, "MDs Plot 'Behavior Modification' for Tricking Gays," *Bay Area Reporter*, May 10, 1984, and Michael Helquist, "Media Drive for 'Safe Sex' Complicated by Politics," *Gay News* (Philadelphia), May 24, 1984.

62. Philip Fotheringham, "AIDS in Europe," *The New York Native*, Feb. 13, 1984.

63. See Dave Walter, "Antibody Test Debate Rages in Atlanta," *The Advocate*, May 14, 1985.

64. See "Racing to Sell an AIDS Test to Blood Banks," *Business Week*, Feb. 18, 1985.

65. David Perlman, "Promising Advance in AIDS Research," San Francisco *Chronicle*, Sept. 10, 1984.

66. See Office of Technology Assessment, p. 30.

67. "The Race to Develop Vaccine against AIDS Mobilizes Researchers," *The Wall Street Journal*, Sept. 4, 1984.

68. D. Koshland, Jr., "Benefits, Risks, Vaccines and the Courts," *Science*, March 15, 1985, p. 1289.

69. *New Vaccine Development: Establishing Priorities*, Vol. I (Washington, D.C.: Institute of Medicine, National Academy Press, 1985), p. 125.

70. Ibid.

CHAPTER SEVEN

1. Theodore Rosebury, *Microbes and Morals* (New York: Viking, 1971), p. 31.

2. Ibid., p. 132.

3. S. Andreski, "The Syphilitic Shock," *Encounter*, Oct. 1980.

4. Dr. John Stokes, quoted in Allan Brandt, *No Magic Bullet* (New York: Oxford University Press, 1985), p. 170.

5. Lois Draegin, "Sex Makes You Sick," *SoHo Weekly News*, Nov. 24, 1981.

6. Quoted in A. Wilentz, "Fanning the Herpes Scare," *The Nation*, Nov. 2, 1984, p. 299.

7. Ibid., p. 300.

8. *Frontiers* (Los Angeles), Oct. 17, 1984.

9. The best continuing source on the Fairy movement is *RFD Magazine*, a quarterly published in Bakersville, N.C.

10. "Sex: The New Frontline for Gay Politics," *Socialist Review* (Berkeley), Sept.–Oct. 1982, pp. 77, 81.

11. "AIDS: The Saliva Scare," *Newsweek*, Oct. 22, 1984. See also Nathan Fain, "A Kiss Is Still a Kiss?" *The Village Voice*, Oct. 9, 1984.

12. Randy Shilts, "Traitors or Heroes?" *The New York Native*, July 16, 1984.

13. Neil Alan Marks, "Sexual Manners," *The New York Native*, June 21, 1982.

14. See stories in *The New York Native*, Aug. 16 and Sept. 13, 1982.

15. Michael Callen and Richard Berkowitz, "We Know Who We Are," *The New York Native*, Nov. 8, 1982, p. 29.

16. For example, see Tom Waddell, "AIDS: Examining the New Phase," *Coming Up!*, Aug. 1983.

17. Larry Kramer, "1,112 and Counting," *The New York Native*, March 14, 1983.

18. For example, see Ann Japenga, "Gays Trying to Deal with Fears of Cancer," Los Angeles *Times*, Sept. 28, 1982.

19. Randy Shilts, "Gay Freedom Day Raises AIDS Worries," San Francisco *Chronicle*, May 27, 1983.

20. See Randy Shilts, "Gay Bars to Co-operate with Health Department," San Francisco *Chronicle*, June 3, 1983.

21. *Bay Area Reporter*, June 30, 1983.

22. Peter Collier and David Horowitz, "Whitewash," *California*, July 1983, p. 52.

23. "Bathhouses: Scapegoat for AIDS Fears or Real Health Threat?" *The Advocate*, March 29, 1984.

24. Randy Shilts, "A Gay Bathhouse Closes Its Doors in San Francisco," San Francisco *Chronicle*, July 11, 1983.

25. "AIDS Expert Says Bathhouses Should Close," San Francisco *Chronicle*, Feb. 3, 1984.

26. "Other Voices," *California Voice* (San Francisco), May 3–9, 1984.

27. Brian Jones, "Community Plan to Regulate Baths," *Bay Area Reporter*, Sept. 27, 1984.

28. Carl Nolte and Randy Shilts, "Gay Bathhouses Told to Close," San Francisco *Chronicle*, Oct. 10, 1984.

29. See Michael Helquist, "Court Allows Bathhouses to Reopen," *Coming Up!*, Dec. 1984, p. 7, and "Bathhouse Decision Fuels Controversy," *Coming Up!*, Jan. 1985, p. 13.

30. See Michael Helquist and Rick Osmon, "Sex and the Baths," *Coming Up!*, July 1984, pp. 75–84.

31. Alan Berube, "The History of Gay Bathhouses," *Coming Up!*, Dec. 1984, p. 19.

32. Letters, *Bay Area Reporter*, April 19, 1984.

33. Nathan Fain, "All Steamed Up," *The Village Voice*, March 27, 1984.

34. Ronald Iacovelli, "Young and Worried in New York," *The New York Native*, July 30, 1984.

35. Los Angeles *Times*, Oct. 18, 1984.

36. See Larry Bush, "Will New York Close the Baths?" *The Village Voice*, Dec. 18, 1984; Peter Freiberg, "Should the Bathhouses Be Closed?" *The Advocate*, March 5, 1984.

37. Dave Walter, "Police Raid Atlanta Baths," *The Advocate*, March 19, 1985.

38. San Francisco *Chronicle*, July 18, 1984.

39. See F. N. Judson, "Fear of AIDS and Gonorrhea Rates in Homosexual Men," *The Lancet*, 1983.

40. See "Gay Males Altering Sexual Behavior, Researchers Report," *American Medical News*, July 7, 1984, and L. McKusick, W. Horstman and T. Coates, "AIDS and Sexual Behavior Reported by Men in San Francisco," *American Journal of Public Health*, May 1985.

41. "Results from the First Probability Sample of an Urban Gay Male Community" (San Francisco: Research & Decisions Corp., 1984).

42. "Handbook of Member Facilities," distributed by the Independent Gay Health Clubs.

43. *The Advocate*, Aug. 11, 1983.

44. See Richard Laermer, "Operators on the Line: The Business of Phone Sex," *The New York Native*, Oct. 24, 1983.

45. "AIDS Discrimination Alleged at J.O. Club," *The New York Native*, Dec. 17, 1984.

46. John Preston (ed.), *Hot Living* (Boston: Alyson, 1985).

47. See, e.g., Donald Symons, *The Evolution of Human Sexuality* (New York: Oxford University Press, 1979).

48. "AIDS Update," *This Week in Texas* (Houston), Oct. 5, 1984.

49. Michael Quadland, "Overcoming Sexual Compulsivity," *The New York Native*, Nov. 7, 1983.
50. See R. William Wedin, "The Sexual Compulsion Movement," *Christopher Street*, #88, 1984.
51. George Whitmore, "Sexual Compulsion," *The Advocate*, Aug. 21, 1984.
52. R. William Wedin, "Sexual Healing," *The New York Native*, July 30, 1984.
53. "Men's Health Study" (San Francisco: Research & Decisions Corp., Aug. 1984).
54. Edmund White, *States of Desire* (New York: Dutton, 1980), p. 279.
55. Remarks by Rep. Al McCandless, congressional hearings, House of Representatives subcommittee of the Committee on Government Operations, Aug. 1, 1983, no. 26–097, p. 72.
56. Nathan Fain, "Health," *The Advocate*, Sept. 18, 1984.
57. "Safe Sex Promotion Kit for Gay-oriented Businesses," KS/AIDS Foundation of Houston, 1983.
58. "Don't Rub It In," *The Star* (Sydney), Feb. 7, 1985.
59. See Peter Taylor, *The Smoke Ring* (New York: Pantheon, 1984), esp. p. 240.
60. Nathan Fain, "Doctor Voeller's Magic Lube," *The Village Voice*, Feb. 19, 1984.
61. R. William Wedin, "AIDS and Fascism," *The New York Native*, Nov. 5, 1984.
62. E. Barnes and A. Hollister, "The New Victims" *Life*, July 1985, p. 19.
63. Ned Rorem, "Paragraphs Before a Birthday," *The Advocate*, Sept. 29, 1983.
64. Signed "Ripped off in the Pines," *The New York Native*, Oct. 22, 1984.
65. Adam Carr, "The AIDS Epidemic," *Outrage*, July 1984, p. 16.
66. Edmund White, "Re: States of Desire," *Christopher Street*, #75, 1983, p. 36.
67. See my *The Homosexualization of America* (Boston: Beacon Press, 1983) and works cited, esp. by McIntosh, Weeks and Foucault.
68. Michael Wilson, "Educational Recommendations," in the KS/AIDS Foundation's "Safe Sex Promotion Kit for Gay-oriented Businesses."
69. "The Revolution Is Over," *Time*, April 9, 1984, p. 74.
70. Ibid., p. 77.
71. Nora Gallagher, "Fever All Through the Night," *Mother Jones*, Nov. 1982.
72. Joan Mooney, "AIDS: A Special Community Report," *Woman's Day* (Sydney), Dec. 17, 1984.

73. Richard Lyons, "Sex in America: Conservative Attitudes Prevail," New York *Times*, Oct. 4, 1984.
74. "The Revolution Is Over," p. 76.
75. Michael Randall, "Sex and AIDS: A Personal View," *The New York Native*, Oct. 22, 1984.
76. Cindy Patton, "Systemic Illness, Lesbians and AIDS," *The New York Native*, Jan. 16, 1984.
77. For an indication of the sorts of arguments involved, see Ann Snitow, Christine Stansell and Sharon Thompson (eds.), *Powers of Desire* (New York: Monthly Review Press, 1982), and Carole Vance (ed.), *Pleasure and Danger* (Boston: Routledge and Kegan Paul, 1984).
78. Carole Vance, "Pleasure and Danger: Toward a Politics of Sexuality," in Vance (ed.), *Pleasure and Danger*, p. 1.

CHAPTER EIGHT

1. "The AIDS Panic Spreads," *Newsweek*, Dec. 10, 1984.
2. "Fear of AIDS Cools Off Sect," San Francisco *Examiner*, July 1, 1984.
3. Frank Arnal, editorial comment in *Le Gai Pied*, Aug. 25, 1984.
4. J. Leibowitch, *Un Virus étrange venu d'ailleurs* (Paris: Grasset, 1983), pp. 142–43 (my translation).
5. Barbara Gamarekian, "To the Capital's Naysayers: Touché," New York *Times*, Dec. 26, 1984.
6. Larry Bush, "D.C. Desk," *The New York Native*, March 26, 1984.
7. See Rosemary Stevens, "Medical Practice," in *The Oxford Companion to Medicine* (New York: Oxford University Press, 1984).
8. June Goodfield, *An Imagined World* (New York: Penguin, 1982), p. 105.
9. Nicholas de Jongh, "God Save the Queens," *The Advocate*, Dec. 11, 1984, p. 42.
10. Charles Krauthammer, "The Politics of a Plague," *The New Republic*, Aug. 1, 1984.
11. Katherine Anne Porter, *Pale Horse, Pale Rider* (New York: Harcourt, Brace, 1939), p. 206.
12. Brian Jones, "Bad Blood," *Bay Area Reporter*, Sept. 13, 1984.
13. See, e.g., Stephanie Poggi, "Backlash Prompts Tabling of Seattle Law," *Gay Community News*, March 30, 1985.
14. For a representative sample of this sort of comparison, see M. Bronski, *Culture Clash* (Boston: South End, 1984), p. 212, and the inter-

view with Larry Kramer by Patrick Merla in *The New York Native*, April 8, 1985.

15. See "States Move on AIDS Peril," Sydney *Morning Herald*, Nov. 17, 1984, and Yvonne Preston, "The AIDS Panic: a Modern-Day Witch-hunt," Sydney *Morning Herald*, Dec. 10, 1984.

16. Sydney *Daily Mirror*, Dec. 21, 1984.

17. Jeffrey Weeks, *Sexuality and Its Discontents* (London: Routledge and Kegan Paul, 1985), p. 45.

18. Gayle Rubin, "Thinking Sex," in Carole Vance (ed.), *Pleasure and Danger* (Boston: Routledge and Kegan Paul, 1984), p. 299.

19. See Isadore Barmash, "Store Sales Lagging on Castro St.," New York *Times*, Dec. 29, 1984.

20. Neil Alan Marks, "Sexual Manners," *The New York Native*, June 21, 1982.

21. Macfarlane Burnet, *The Natural History of Infectious Diseases* (Cambridge: Cambridge University Press, 1962), pp. 3, 84.

22. "Guess Who Came to Dinner," *The Village Voice*, Oct. 11, 1983.

23. David Shribman, "Seeking Research Funds for AIDS," New York *Times*, Dec. 27, 1983.

24. From *The Air-Conditioned Nightmare*, quoted by David Black, "The Plague Years," *Rolling Stone*, April 25, 1985, p. 41.

25. Andrew Britton, "AIDS—Apocalyptic Metaphor" *New Statesman*, March 15, 1985.

26. Susan Sontag, *Illness as Metaphor* (New York: Farrar, Straus & Giroux, 1978), p. 71.

27. Remarks of Secretary Heckler, International Conference on AIDS, Atlanta, April 15, 1985.

28. Letter from Irene Smith, *Bay Area Reporter*, Sept. 13, 1984.

29. Edwin Clark (Toby) Johnson, "AIDS as Myth, AIDS as Blessing," *Gay News* (Philadelphia), Jan. 19, 1984.

30. Sontag, *Illness as Metaphor*, p. 5.

31. Randy Shilts, "AIDS Experts Discuss New Research," San Francisco *Chronicle*, April 16, 1985.

INDEX